MW01289575

ISBN-13: 978-1484133958

ISBN-10: 1484133951

For all correspondence:

Warlock Asylum
51 MacDougal Street #348
New York, N.Y. 10012

# FORWARD

Within the writings of the Atlantean Necronomicon you
will find a work of divine love, inspiration, truth, and the
answers to questions that burn deep inside all of us.
When I was child I asked God: "What is wrong with me?
Why am I not sad when others mourn the dead?" I did
not feel alone. I looked to the stars with longing, while
having dreamed of another life. Growing up, I was
taught about Jehovah and his strict organizational
standards. This gave me the impression that all of my
questions about the meaning of life would be answered,
but my actions to please "his ministers" were greater
than my true sentiment. Deep down inside, I was fooling
myself. I was taking my *Self* hostage. I was suffocating
my spiritual being, due to fear that I might be destroyed
if I didn't find favor with "Jehovah's organization." I
chose to be a fool and just nod my head and smile in
agreement with whatever doctrine was being delivered
from the platform. "Where the hell is the woman's role in
all of this? It's easier to be complacent, but my true
nature would have nothing to do with this sort of
thinking. I cried out from depression, and mustered up
the strength to release myself from spiritual bondage
with the courage to search and discriminate the
information that I had been taught as a child.

The Chaldean Covenant, as described in the Simon
Necronomicon is real. It is your lineage, pure as a dove
and innocent like a baby. You become familiar with the
caress of your mother and the vibration of your father's
voice. The rites described in the *Atlantean Necronomicon*
trigger deep memories that connect us to our divine
family and spiritual birthright. When we are able to
resurrect ourselves from the dead, we become Queens

and Kings, Gods and Goddesses, as we walk and work in this *perfection rite*. We create the proper vessel to fulfill our destiny. In the Necronomicon Tradition, nothing is done for you, but you will have the backing and guidance of divine forces that we simply call The Family. How grateful we should be!

Through constant application of the information contained herein, you will begin to feel planetary shifts within your being. You will be able to hear the stars and nature speak in one voice, and teach us the *ancient secrets of creation*. There is a mingling of science and magic within the beauty of obscurity and calculative technology. We share these experiences as Gate-Walkers, which is the confirmation of this journey and a sign from the world that is to come. After being initiated into the Necronomicon Current, Jehovah has become real to me like never before, never forsaken and never ashamed, always thirsty for the life-water from the Queen Mother Goddess.

Sincerely,

*Fenex*

(R.M. & Acupuncture-TCM Practitioner)

# INTRODUCTION

I was initiated into the Necronomicon Tradition several years ago and my awareness of the Qliphotic Mysteries has grown tremendously sincethis time. I have met with many people from different walks of life who share this same path. It is indeed a great source of encouragement.

The Path of Asaru (Gate-Walking) is not an easy one to follow. The Necronomicon Tradition is a solitaire path, for the most part and it is highly criticized by individuals who stand outside our Tradition. The social tools used to control the masses often insinuate that a spiritual path must have a large following for it to be legitimate, but this opinion does not make a magical work genuine in itself. History reveals that advancement in the way of the occult, philosophical thinking, religion, science, and spirituality, have all come from unpopular occult practices that were often condemned at the time of their inception. Evidence of this can be seen amongst the history of groups like the Assassins, Knights Templar, Freemasons, Ninja Warriors, and etc. People like to honor these traditions only after the persecution has ceased and the miraculous keys that these groups once possessed are no longer in circulation. This shows us that human beings are more inclined to imitate a tradition than actually being a part of one. Practitioners of the Necronomicon Tradition have received this same sort of disfavor from the public. The longing desire to be a part of something, after the *"true work"* has occurred, is an act of cowardice.

The Necronomicon Tradition is a source of tremendous power and has become an object of resentment for this very same reason. I have personally witnessed people from other "occult societies" working with the Simon Necronomicon. These same individuals are members of occult groups and societies that call the Simon Necronomicon a hoax, or a work of fiction. Of course, leaders of occult organizations will deny the Simon Necronomicon's authenticity, since the Initiate can obtain true initiation outside the teachings that these occult groups promote. This is why the Simon Necronomicon is a threat to many occult organizations today. The "new age" movement, even in its darker aspects, is nothing more than a recreation of the Christian doctrine using pagan imagery. Simon makes an interesting comment on page 220 in his occult classic *Gates of the Necronomicon:*

**"Let's face it; there is no intrinsic danger to society in the visions of an individual who claims to have spoken with the angels. The danger comes when that individual then believes he or she has a mandate from God. In that case, of course, our cherished social institutions are threatened. In the Catholic Church, only the hierarchy can determine whether someone has spoken with God. They are often the people least capable of making that determination."**

Simon's observation applies not only to religious leaders, but authorities in the occult community as well. Many of these "new age" organizations are led by individuals who have no authentic initiation and rely solely on the "logical" interpretation of the ancient mysteries found in the writings of anthropologists and other forms of scholarship. The results are seen in "new age" groups that care more about membership numbers than the spiritual progress of each member. The members are left with the satisfaction of being part of an association with others who express their reformed sense of *"Christianity"* using pagan archetypes. Eventually, the novice becomes aware of the fact that membership in an occult organization is nothing more than a machine of people who are searching for companionship and self-esteem.

In ancient times the knowledge and initiations of the Qliphotic Mysteries were passed down from the *"spirits"* to the Initiate. The Adept passed the deeper secrets of these mysteries only to those Initiates who would work on behalf of the advancement of the said tradition. True initiation requires work. The candidate must search through the depths of his/her mental and emotional being until they are able to open the gate that leads to the dormant part of their psyche, also called the chthonic mind in the Qliphotic Mysteries.

Elements of the Necronomicon Tradition revealed itself to H.P. Lovecraft almost a century ago. The magickal aspects of these mysteries came later in the form of the Simon Necronomicon. Simon makes this point very clear on page 34 in *Gates of the Necronomicon*:

**"In the *Necronomicon* system, success is measured in other ways. One is not given the passwords to the various levels or Gates: one must discover them on one's own. And one must begin the operations at a specific time and no other. No one can initiate someone else into the *Necronomicon* system: it initiates you. There is no room for demagoguery, fascist leadership, and spiritual dictators. ...For this reason, the author believes that as a system of magic it is quite the perfect tool."**

The Necronomicon was revealed to Lovecraft through dreams. This is the same way it revealed itself to the Mad Arab. Today, we begin another chapter in the *Ancient Arcane Faith* with the release of the Atlantean Necronomicon.

The Atlantean Necronomicon is a tome of mystical practices and essays about the Qliphotic Mysteries that are found in the Urilia Text. This work is useful to those who are currently going through the process of self-initiation. Many of the essays that are written in the text come directly from the deities in the Necronomicon Tradition.

The Necronomicon Current is growing and initiating all those who are the progeny of *Jinn-Human* relations. A Practitioner could write volumes of information concerning the rites and rituals contained in the Simon Necronomicon. Writing a *"Necronomicon"* can only be done by those who are authorized and initiated into the Qliphotic Mysteries. This same rule applies to translations of the Christian Bible. Biblical translations must adhere to the guidelines created by Christian mystics. An example of this can be seen in Genesis 5:2, where every authorized translation of the Bible must state *the plurality of Adam,* regardless of the beliefs of those translating the text. The same rules apply to the Necronomicon Tradition. Different than popular opinion, a "Necronomicon" must be authorized by the society of Jinn that exist alongside the race of mankind. I wish you success in all your spiritual endeavors.

Happy Hunting!

*Messiah-El Bey a.k.a. Warlock Asylum*

# THE FALL OF CHRISTIANITY

Throughout this writing, various references will be made to the *Necronomicon Tradition*. The meaning of this term, and the responsibilities that it places upon the Initiate, is an extremely important part of the work. According to H.P. Lovecraft, the term *Necronomicon,* is derived from the Greek term *nekros* (corpse), *nomos* (law), *eikon* (image): *"An image of the law of the dead."* This definition could simply be applied to the work of necromancy, but we will soon discover that this term encompasses so much more.

Lovecraft wrote that the Necronomicon was originally called *Al Azif,* an Arabic word that he defined as "that nocturnal sound (made by insects) which supposed to be the howling of demons." In pre-Islamic Arabia, the term *azif* signified the ominous whistling of the Jinn. Parker Ryan supports this conclusion in his essay *The Necronomicon Mythos According to HPL:*

**"Next let's look at Alhazred's title. HPL wrote that Alhazred's title was *"Mad Poet."* "Mad" is usually written "majnun" in Arabic. *Majnun* means "mad" today. However, in the eighth century (Alhazred's time) it meant *"Possessed by Jinn."* To be called *Mad* or *Possessed by Demons* would be highly insulting to orthodox Muslims. The Sufis and Muqarribun regard Majnun as *complimentary title.* They even go so far as to call certain Sufi heroes Majnun.."**

This is a clear indication that the Necronomicon is a book inspired by the Jinn. The Simon Necronomicon also supports Ryan's observation. In the Magan Text we read the following concerning Tiamat:

*"Those from Without*
*Have builded up charnel houses*
*To nourish the fiends of TIAMAT*
*And the Blood of the weakest here*
*Is libation unto TIAMAT*
*Queen of the Ghouls"*

The term *ghoul,* is a derivative of the Arabic *ghul,* meaning *jinn.* In the works of both Lovecraft and Simon, the Necronomicon is a book that is inspired by the Jinn.

In Arabian and Muslim folklore the Jinn are ugly and evil demons having supernatural powers which they can bestow on persons having powers to call them up. In the Western world they are called *"genies."* The term *Jinn* means concealed, or hidden. This is the same definition that we find for the term *"occult."* In Islamic theology, the Jinn are said to be made from a "smokeless fire," while humans were created out of the Earth. Some accounts report that the Jinn were created before Adam from the "hot wind." It is said that the Jinn live in a parallel world next to mankind, though they are undetected by humans. The Jinn are able to marry and have children, and have domesticated pets similar to mankind. Parker Ryan states the following concerning the Jinn:

**"Jinn were powerful creatures of Arab myth. The Jinn,**
**according to legend, came down from heaven (the sky)**
**in the time before Adam. Therefore, they pre-exist**
**mankind and thus called "Preadamites." "Infidel**
**pagans" worship these incredibly powerful beings. The**
**Jinn can "beget young on mankind." The Jinn are**
**usually invisible to normal men. They apparently want**
**great influence on Earth. Much of the magick used in**

Arab countries concerns the Jinn (protection spells against, or spells to call them up). The Jinn are thus virtually identical with *Lovecraft's Old Ones*."

Ryan points out that the Jinn can *"beget young on mankind."* There are many tales throughout the Arab world of human beings having intimate relations with the Jinn. *A Dictionary of Islam* by Thomas Patrick Hughes, B.D., M.R.A.S., states the following concerning the Jinn:

**"The Jinn, it has been already shown, *are peaceable*. They also eat and drink, and propagate their species, *sometimes in conjunction with human beings*; in which latter case, the offspring partakes of the nature of both parents."**

The subject of Jinn-human progeny is highly debated amongst Muslim scholars. However, there is a great deal of evidence supporting the fact that Jinn and humans are able to produce offspring together. The religion of Islam dictates that Allah created both the Jinn and mankind, but the ancient texts of the pre-Islamic era say something different. Hughes continues on page 134:

**"It is said that God created the Jann (or Jinn) two thousand years before Adam (according to some writers, much earlier) and that they are believers and infidels and every sect among them, as among men....It is commonly believed that the preadamite Jinn were governed by forty (according to some seventy-two) kings, to each of whom the Arab writers give the name Sulaiman (Solomon); and that they derive their appellation from the last of these, who was called Jann Ibn-Jann, and who, some say, built the Pyramids of Egypt."**

The Simon Necronomicon describes Tiamat as the Queen of the Ghouls, which in light of our discussion, would also make her the Mother of the Jinn. Parker Ryan, in his essay about the Cthulhu Mythos, also asserts that 'Lovecraft's *Old Ones* are identical to the Jinn of Arab legend. This would indicate that the Elder Gods and the Ancient Ones, which appear in the Simon Necronomicon, are various classes of Jinn who were responsible for creating human beings, as presented in the Enuma Elish and other ancient mythologies. According to Arabic legend, the Jinn were Earth's first inhabitants and will survive the race of mankind. The Magan Text states:

**"For what is new
Came from that which is old
And what is old
Shall replace that which is new
And once again the Ancient Ones
Shall rule upon the face of the Earth!
And this is too the Covenant!"**

The Christian Bible also mentions a race similar to the Jinn:

**"Now the serpent was more subtile than any beast of the field which the LORD God had made. And he said unto the woman, Yea, hath God said, Ye shall not eat of every tree of the garden?"**

The "serpent" described in the Third Chapter of Genesis must have been one of the Jinn that descended to Earth at an earlier time, as recorded for us in Genesis Chapter One:

**"And God said, Let us make man in our image, after our likeness: and let them have dominion over the fish of the sea, and over the fowl of the air, and over the**

cattle, and over all the earth, and over every creeping thing that creepeth upon the earth.... 28And God blessed them, and God said unto them, Be fruitful, and multiply, and *replenish the earth,* and subdue it: and have dominion over the fish of the sea, and over the fowl of the air, and over every living thing that moveth upon the earth."

This is quite different than what is written concerning the creation of mankind in Genesis Chapter Two:

"And every plant of the field before it was in the earth, and every herb of the field before it grew: for the LORD God had not caused it to rain upon the earth, and there was not a man to till the ground. ...6But there went up a mist from the earth, and watered the whole face of the ground.... And the LORD God formed man of the dust of the ground, and breathed into his nostrils the breath of life; and man became a living soul."

We see some differences between the creation story in Genesis Chapter One and that which is found in Genesis Chapter Two. In the first Chapter of Genesis, *"man"* is not created from the ground and the creation of vegetation preceded him. In the second Chapter of Genesis, the *"human"* is created from the Earth before *'every herb of the field grew in the earth.'* Evidently these two accounts describe two different events, one pertaining to the Jinn and the other to human beings.

Interestingly, some Judaic Traditions hold the belief that *"Cain"* was not the son of Adam and Eve, but the son of Eve and the Serpent. *Tree of Souls: The Mythology of Judaism* by Howard Schwartz, states the following of page 447:

"When Cain was born, Adam knew at once that he was not of his seed, for he was not after his likeness, nor after his image. Instead, Cain's appearance was that of a heavenly being. And when Eve saw that his appearance was not of this world, she said, *I have gained a male child with the help of Yahweh.* (Gen. 4:1)"

The perspective given by Schwartz seems to explain why Cain's life was spared after killing his brother Abel.

"And Cain said unto the LORD, My punishment is greater than I can bear...Behold, thou hast driven me out this day from the face of the earth; and from thy face shall I be hid; and I shall be a fugitive and a vagabond in the earth; and it shall come to pass, that every one that findeth me shall slay me...And the LORD said unto him, Therefore whosoever slayeth Cain, vengeance shall be taken on him sevenfold. And the LORD set a mark upon Cain, lest any finding him should kill him."

There is another aspect of this account that has been overlooked by both occultists and scholars alike, and that is the location of where Cain was taken to after the murder of his half-brother:

"And Cain went out from the presence of the LORD, and dwelt in the land of Nod, on the *east of Eden*....And Cain knew his wife; and she conceived, and bare Enoch: and he builded a city, and called the name of the city, after the name of his son, Enoch."

Cain settled in the *"east of Eden."* This indicates that Cain was indeed a progeny of a supernatural being because in Genesis Chapter 2:8, we read the following:

"And the LORD God planted a garden *eastward in Eden;* and there he put the man whom he had formed."

Cain was removed from the presence of the Adamites and was placed in the vicinity of the Garden of Eden. He also had a son named Enoch and built a city and named it after his son. If we analyze what is recorded in the creation account of Genesis, we come to the conclusion that the Enochian language and the famous Book of Enoch describe events and occurrences that took place in the city that Cain built. The city that Cain built is what the Arabs call "Irem Zhat al Imad." Parker Ryan makes the following observation:

"Irem Zhat al Imad" (Irem of the Pillars) is the cities name in Arabic. It is popularly believed by the Arabs that Irem was built by the Jinn under the direction of Shaddad, Lord of the tribe of Ad. The tribe of Ad, according to legend, was a race roughly equivalent to the Hebrew "Nephlim" (giants). In some version of this myth Shaddad and the Jinn built Irem before the time of Adam. The Muqarribun (Arab magicians) have important beliefs about Irem and it's significance....The Muqarribun, whose traditions predate Islam, believe that Irem is a locale on another level of reality, rather than a physical city like NY or Tokyo. (Why Irem is important to the Muqarribun and how they use it will be more fully explained shortly.) The "Pillars" in "Irem of the Pillars" has a hidden meaning. Among Arab mystics pillar is a code name for "elder" or "old one." Thus "Irem of the Pillars" is really "Irem of the Old Ones."

Kenneth Grant asserts, in his work *The Nightside of Eden,* that the City of Irem is the Garden of Eden. Regardless of where these *"mysterious cities"* are said to exist, such as

Enoch, Irem, and etc, we can definitely say that there is a world that exists alongside the world of mankind. There is something else we need to take into consideration first. Genesis 3:15 states:

**"And I will put enmity between thee and the woman, and between thy seed and her seed; it shall bruise thy head, and thou shalt bruise his heel."**

The Biblical text suggests that the Jinn are cursed and will eventually be annihilated. However, this assertion seems to be a calculated response by the ancient monotheistic religions to plunder the Jinn and their progeny. L.A. Waddell mentions this in the *British Edda:*

**"Indeed, the selfsame confusion occurs also in the Egyptian myth, wherein the Semitic priests of the Nile Valley degraded the original pure Sun-worship of Asar or "Osiris" (the Sumerian Asari title of King Dur or Tur) by deliberately introducing into it the Serpent and animal sacrificial cult of their own debased aboriginal Egyptian Mother-Son creed, which was essentially similar to the pre-Adamite Chaldean."**

Although Waddell's observations are somewhat bigoted, he does verify the existence of the *"pre-Adamite Chaldean."* The customs and rites of the "aboriginal Chaldeans" were demonized by the monotheistic religions. Waddell also asserts that the Mother-Son creed existed before the creation of Adam. Therefore, the enmity between the woman's seed and the serpent mentioned in Genesis concerns itself with the battle between the Jinn and mankind. Waddell continues on page 73:

**"Before the advent of Adam Thor and his Sun-cult, the chief religion in the old world appears to have been**

**devil worship of the Serpent and Wolf cult, with its headship in the matriarch priestess Eldi..."**

Waddell later confirms that his matriarch priestess Eldi was also known as the goddess El. It is no coincidence that many angelic names end with *"el,"* as they are of the race of Jinn and keepers of the Moon-Serpent Cult. Waddell also defines *"El"* as a powerful witch, a dark magician that is *"naturally gifted with occult powers."* Those who are naturally gifted with occult powers are those who partake in the *natures of both parents,* jinn and human, as cited earlier in the Dictionary of Islam.

We can also see resistance to the Moon-Serpent cult's teachings in the Biblical history of Jesus. Jesus was conceived of Jinn-human relations and taught a rite that was Sumerian in origin. Evidence of this is found in his parable of the Good Samaritan. According to 2 Kings Chapter 17, Samaritans were worshippers of the god Nergal.

When one carefully observes Biblical lore, it seems that there were other religious rites that existed in Israel, which were not recorded in the Bible. For example, shortly after leaving Egypt the Israelites were said to have made a *golden calf* while Moses was receiving the Law. Centuries later, it is recorded in Ezekiel that the Prophet witnessed women weeping for the Babylonian god Tammuz who was the consort of the goddess depicted as the golden calf during the days of Moses. Evidently, the Israelites weren't constantly turning to the worship of false gods, as claimed throughout the Biblical text, since there has never been a record of any indigenous people who abandoned the worship that their ancestors laid down so frequently. It seems more probable that the Bible writers excluded the full history of the religious rites that existed in ancient Israel in an effort to make a specific "priesthood" and its god appear to be superior.

The customs and traditions of the Jinn and their progeny have been demonized by the monotheistic religions of the world today. Waddell continues in the British Edda on page 175:

**"The Matriarch El and her son Abel of The Garden of Eden...feverishly mustered all their swarms and allied hordes...for an overwhelming attack upon King Adam and his Goths...This epochmaking battle was the greatest of all battles in the world, as judged by its far-reaching effects; for it led to the political supremacy of Adam's Higher Civilization, and its free propagation over the world –to its immediate extension to Carchemish or Eden, and thence down Mesopotamia to the Persian Gulf within a very short period.."**

Waddell describes a battle that occurred between the "aboriginal Chaldeans, who are described as "serpent worshippers," and the invading Sun cult. It seems that these "aboriginal Chaldeans," led by the matriarch EL, were keepers of the traditions that the Jinn had worked so hard to establish and some of these may have been Jinn themselves. Waddell mentions in other writings that the invading Sun cults captured a "stone-bowl," in their war with the "aboriginal Chaldeans." This stone-bowl was the central fetish of the magical rites in relationship to the pre-Adamic race. This bowl was the formulae that opened up a gate, whereby the sorcerer could communicate with the elders of the parallel world and benefit from the wisdom contained therein. However, there is another element that prevented the "aboriginal Chaldeans" from opening up this window and communicating with their ancestors, Christianity.

Christians are involved in a spiritual war, whether they realize it or not. Christianity, as we know it today, was developed by the Council of Nicea in 325 A.D. and continued the tradition mentioned by Waddell in their persecution of the aboriginal Chaldeans. *Egyptian Belief and Modern Thought* by James Bonwick page 182:

**"Constatine, a sun-worshipper, who had, as other heathens, kept the Sun-day, publicly ordered this to supplant the Jewish Sabbath. To make matters worse, the Church, at an early date, selected the heathen festivals of sun-worship for its own...."**

The Christian Church was founded upon the principle structure of ancient Sun worship. Regardless of what domination that exists today, all Christian religions are guilty of honoring the Sun as a symbol of the Christ. The Christian doctrine and the epistles of the Apostle Paul are not inspired scripture, but essays concerning the worship of the Sun. The ignorant are unaware of this fact and regardless of how many holidays, or perspectives these varying dominations of Christianity insist upon, its makes no difference at all. The only way that Christianity can separate itself from its heathen origins is by rewriting the New Testament.

There is a much deeper aspect involved in the customs and rituals of Christianity that are an apparent attack against the world of the Jinn and their progeny. The Christian Bible contains over four-hundred references to the word "wicked." Throughout its seemingly righteous damnation of the *"wicked,"* through prayers, scriptural texts, and etc, the naïve Christian is unaware, along with most monotheistic disciples, that the term *"wicked"* originates from the word *wizard,* or *sorcerer.* This means that on any given day, there are hundreds of millions of Christians pronouncing judgments against sorcerers and witches by their use of certain prayers and recitations from various scriptural texts. This is how the ancient Adamites were able to keep the doors of reality shut in regards to the Jinn and their prgenty. These practices were later adapted by the early leaders of the Christian Church. It is for this very same reason that we find many areas of the world, where the ancient shamanistic rites so dear to the "pre-Adamite" tradition flourish, are also the same areas where extreme poverty and natural disasters occur. However, the doctrine of Christianity with all its hypocritical dogma, followers and leaders, is soon to end. *The Overlan Monthly* printed an article in 1910 A.D. entitled God's Chosen People; states the following on page 543:

**"These beasts are to rule the world until the end of Gentile times of world domination, October, 1914, which will also be the end of the Jewish times of Divine disfavor...The Prophet pictures the end of Gentile times and the manifestation of the Ancient of Days, whose throne was like a fiery flame.."**

Regardless of the use of ancient divination to keep the door to the world of the Jinn closed, it will serve them no good. The Jinn, in the Arab world and the Necronomicon Tradition, are called "those of fire." We find in Christian doctrine that the "Ancient of Days' is described as seated on a *"fiery throne."*

The year 1914 was a significant year not only to Christian cultists, but human society in general with the inception of World War 1. The events that followed align perfectly with Lovecraft's description of Cthulhu rising:

"That cult would never die till the stars came right again, and the secret priests would take great Cthulhu from His tomb to revive His subjects and resume His rule of earth. The time would be easy to know, for then mankind would have become as the Great Old Ones; free and wild and beyond good and evil, with laws and morals thrown aside and all men shouting and killing and revelling in joy. Then the liberated Old Ones would teach them new ways to shout and kill and revel and enjoy themselves, and all the earth would flame with a holocaust of ecstasy and freedom. Meanwhile the cult, by appropriate rites, must keep alive the memory of those ancient ways and shadow forth the prophecy of their return."

The Simon Necronomicon properly aligns the powers of the Ancient Ones, also known as the Jinn, with Tiamat. It is here that we see the reality and meaning of the events that occurred in 1914. Tiamat is the primordial aspect of the goddess Inanna/Ishtar, whose sacred number has been "15" from times memorable. *The Mystery of Numbers* by Annemarie Schimmel, makes the following observation on pages 213, 215:

"Fifteen represents the zenith of lunar power...Fifteen was a sacred number to Ishtar, perhaps derived from the more important Ishtar-number, 5, perhaps also because it forms 1/4 of the 60, the number of the highest god in Babylonia. Ancient Niniveh, the city devoted to Ishtar, had 15 gates,...The Old Testament counts the generations of Israel between Abraham and Solomon as 15, and from Solomon to Zedekiah again as 15. .Fifteen plays an important role in one of the most common magical squares, which built around, the sacred 5, always offers 15 as a sum. Although legend attributes a Chinese origin to this square, it was known in Babylonia where it was connected with Ishtar.

**Combined with the star of Ishtar, with its 8 beams, the diagonals always add up to 15."**

When we look at the year 1914, we see that it is the year of TIAMAT's rising and so it is marked appropriately as the year of Ishtar's return. $1 + 9 + 1 + 4 = 15$. The Gate of Communion has been opened once again and the matriarch EL is seeking to find her children. We have seen a decline in Christianity since the year 1914 and an increase amongst those practicing the occult arts.

In a very short time, those who are of Jinn-human progeny, as well as others initiated into the "pre-Adamic" ways of the Jinn, will enjoy a return to full goodness and power and sit on thrones amongst the kingdoms of men.

The Necronomicon Tradition, as found in the works of Lovecraft and the Simon Necronomicon, are stellar systems that were established before the race of Adam, or the "sons of Marduk" and are thereby known as the *Atlantean Mysteries*. These workings are called Qliphotic by many occultists, but we find this system to be a cosmological treaty pertaining to the world of the Jinn. Simon states the following in the Necronomicon:

**"The method of the NECRONOMICON concerns deep, primeval forces that seem to pre-exist the normal archetypal images of the tarot trumps and the Golden Dawn telesmatic figures. These are forces that developed outside the Judeo-Christian mainstream, and were worshipped and summoned long before the creation of the Qabala as we know it today. Hence, the ineffectiveness of the Golden Dawn banishing procedures against them. They are not necessarily demonic or qliphotic in the sense that these terms are commonly understood in the West, they just simply**

**represent power sources largely untapped and thus far ignored by twentieth-century, mainstream consciousness."**

The Necronomicon Tradition has been veiled in secrecy before the race of Adam was created and still many of us who are of Jinn-human progeny cannot reveal our dual heritage publicly. It is not so strange to our ears to know that one of our parents were possessed during the time of conception, or we may have entered the shell of the embryo from the world that lies beyond time and space, as we attempt to recollect the meaning of our heritage. It is not an easy path to follow. If you want to be effective in this work, then maximize the system to its fullest capabilities. I have seen people jump from one thing to the next, but the mastery comes in the perfection of a craft, not in the paranormal effects that a working can create. This system is one that reveals our heritage, but it is also one that initiates us into the workings of the chthonic mind. Know thyself!

# Initiation Into Self

There is an transformational process that occurs when the candidate walks through the seven gates of initiation, via the Necronomicon Tradition. Some people may feel an increase in psychic abilities. Things such as lucid dreaming become a part of everyday life. Others may sense the thoughts and feelings of others more easily. One thing is certain, if the candidate does not understand the process that occurs during initiation, they will never be able to fully manifest their will in the material world. During my initiation, I relied heavily upon the First Testimony of the Mad Arab. I was instructed by one of my spirit guides, by way of epiphany, to keep reading this section of the Simon Necronomicon over and over again. Shortly after, I realized that it explained accurately the steps that are to be taken when becoming an Initiate of the Necronomicon Tradition. Let us now take a look at a few excerpts from the Mad Arab's Testimony and compare these with the initiatory rites of the Necronomicon Tradition itself.

*"When I was only a youth, travelling alone in the mountains to the East, called MASSHU by the people who live there..."*

One of the most intriguing aspects of the Simon Necronomicon is the poetic language contained in the text. In the passage cited above the Mad Arab gives us the location of his initiation, which is historically known in ancient Mesopotamian literature as Mt. Mashu. Jason Breshears, in his book; *The Lost Scriptures of Giza*, gives us a wonderful definition of Mt. Mashu. On pages 47-49 we read:

"Sumerian writings tell of a mysterious mountain somewhere on earth that was called Mashu. This is intriguing since there are no mountains in Sumer (southern Iraq). Concerning Mashu these texts read, "On high, to the celestial band it is connected; Below, to the lower world it is bound." This alludes that Mashu connected heaven and the underworld to earth. The celestial band refers to the band of 12 constellations called the Zodiac that were long ago believed to harbor great secrets in the images of animals and deities. Even individual stars within the constellations contributed to these mysteries by the meanings of their names but those not initiated into the stellar mysteries saw these star patterns as merely attached to legend and lore....The celestial band was also of prophetic significance, the constellations representing future things. Mashu was also bound to the lower world, or underworld....Perhaps it is this very mountain that is referred to in this Sumerian Temple Hymn: "Enduring place, light hued mountain which in artful fashion was founded. Its dark hidden chamber is an awe-inspiring place; in a field of supervision it lies. Awesome, its ways no one can fathom." This is as adequate a description of the Great pyramid as any given today. Those Sumerian scribes that wrote this were descendants of those who had survived the cataclysm and were aware of its existence....This mountain of the Sumerians is no different in function than their Tree of Life."

Breshears illustrates the antiquity and meaning of Mt. Mashu. Many schools of esoteric thought simulated the initiation process that took place in ancient Egypt before the present age and Sumeria was among these. Mt. Mashu symbolized a place of initiation. We can see further evidence of this by examining the Mad Arab's words that follow:

*"I came upon a grey rock carved with three strange symbols. It stood as high as a man, and as wide around as a bull. It was firmly in the ground, and I could not move it. Thinking no more of the carvings, save that they might be the work of a king to mark some ancient victory over an enemy,"*

The Mad Arab noted that in the *"midst"* of these mountains was some sort of *"stone"* that was firmly planted in the ground. It is said that this stone was the height of a man and as wide as a bull. We find a deeper meaning to all of this in the Mad Arab's statement that it *"might be the work of a king to mark some ancient victory over an enemy."* This event is mentioned in the book, *The Makers of Civilization in Race & History* by L.A. Waddell:

*"This famous magical Stone-Bowl of King Dar or Dur or Sagg or Sakh, the large fragment of which was inscribed by his great-grandson Udu of Kish with the genealogy of the latter back to that first king and deposited by him beneath the central tower of the oldest Sun-Temple in Mesopotamia at Nippur, is frequently referred to in early Sumerian sacred literature as one of the most celebrated war-trophies captured by that first king. And significantly it is specially associated therein with the first Sumerian king under his Sakh title (earlier Sagg) as written on this Bowl, that is the Sig title of Thor in the Nordic Eddas....Thus the first Sumerian king under his Sakh title in the Bilingual Sumerian and Babylonian glossaries (wherein Sakh is shown to be an equivalent of Sagg or Sa-ga-ga and of Adar of the later Babylonians) [Adar we shall find is a Babylonian form of In-dar; but it is also found as a form of one of Thor's titles in the Nordic Eddas. (Waddell footnote)] is called 'The Lord (or King) Sakh, UGU the king of the Precious Stone, the*

*Hidden Vessel of Kish Land, the King of that Hidden (or Disappeared) Vessel."*

One thing that must be understood from Waddell's observations, though bigoted, is that the workings of the Simon Necronomicon are not a work of *"black magic,"* as some have categorized. Another thing that becomes evident to the Initiate is that this "stone" is connected with the deity Adar. In the book *Chaldean Magic* by Francois Lenormant, pages 174-175:

**"The master of the lower abyss had begotten, besides Namtar, one of the warrior gods whose special mission it was to combat demons, monsters, and plagues, like a true Hercules. This was Nindara, who called also Uras, and was afterwards assimilated to the Chaldaio-Babylonian deity Adar,"**

The observations made by Lenormant and Waddell indicate that the *"grey rock,"* which the Mad Arab discovered, was a useful tool for warding off negative energies. We are told in the text that this stone vessel *"stood as high as a man, and as wide around as a bull."* This is clearly a reference to the direction that we invoke the Dingir and the Watcher, which is Northeast. He writes that the grey rock was as tall as a *man* and wide as a *bull*. Later in the Urilia Text we read the following:

*"And the First comes from the North, and is called USTUR, and has a Human Shape. And He is the,Most Ancient of the Four, and a Great Lord of the World. And the Second comes from the East, and is called SED and has the Shape of a Bull, but with a human face, and is very mighty."*

Based on the description given to us in the Urilia Text, we can determine that *man* represents direction North and the *bull* is symbolic of the East. Therefore, the grey rock was situated in the *Northeast*. In the Simon Necronomicon's section entitled *Conjuration of the Watcher*, we read:

*"When the time has come to summon the Watcher the first time, the place of thy calling must be clean, and a double circle of flour drawn about thee. And there should be no altar, but only the new Bowl with the three carven signs on it. And the Conjuration of the Fire should be made, and the sacrifices heaped thereupon, into the burning bowl. And the Bowl is now called AGA MASS SSARATU, and to be used for no other purpose, save to invoke the Watcher... And the bowl must be lain between the Circles, facing the Northeast."*

The grey rock mentioned in the First Testimony of the Mad Arab is actually the AGA MASS SSARATU, which should be placed in the *Northeast* direction of the Temple. It is important for us to investigate what historical value this may have. The infamous Albert Pike in his work *Magnum Opus,* page 19, stated:

**"Abulfaragius says that the seven great primitive nations, from whom all others descended, the Persians, Chaldeans, Greeks, Egyptians, Turks, Indians and Chinese, all originally were Sabeists, and worshipped the stars. They all, he says, like the Chaldeans, prayed, turning towards the North pole, three times a day, at Sunrise, Noon and Sunset, bowing themselves three times before the Sun. They invoked the Stars and the Intelligences which inhabited them, offered them sacrifices, and called the fixed stars and planets Gods."**

Pike noted that praying to the North was an essential part of worship of many indigenous peoples during the ancient era. We have further evidence of this, in the previously cited work, *Chaldean Magic*. Lenormant states the following on page 363:

**"Therefore, the mountains which were still inhabited at the classical epoch by a people whose name resembled very closely that of the Chaldeans, proved to be the very ones from which the people of Babylon and Chaldea the post-diluvial founders of humanity to have descended, and which the Accadians remembered as the home of their ancestors...By these means I shall reach at length that mountain of the north-east, which played so large a part in the Chaldean traditions under the double title of "Cradle of the human race," and "Place of the assembly of god,"**

Reverence for the North as a sacred place of prayers was primarily due to the fact that the Northeast was thought of as the home of the gods and the origin of the human race. It seems that this mountain in the North direction may have been a symbol of a heavenly constellation. Lenormant makes another reference to direction North on page 169 of the previously cited work:

**"..for the Accadians the east was *mer kurra*, "the cardinal point of the mountains," ...the north *mer sidi*, "the point of prosperity, the propitious point,"**

In the Hindu science of Vastu Shastra, which is similar to Feng Shui, the North corresponds to the Hindu deity Kubera (Lord of Wealth) and the Northeast to the Hindu deity Vayu (Lord of the Winds). In the *Yoga Journal of March-April 1986*, which featured an article written by

Kenneth Cohen, entitled *An Inside Look At Little Known Taoist Healing Practices*, it states:

**"And finally, the stars of the Big Dipper are the abodes of gods who also record our deeds and control human destiny."**

The Big Dipper, when viewed from Earth, revolves around the North Pole Star and was considered by many ancient cultures to be the "abode of the gods." This was the case also with the Nation of Israel. C.M. Houck in the work *Celestial Scriptures* writes the following on page 142:

**"Inscriptions from ancient Sumer speak of a great peak in the north as "the mountain of the world," which was the home of the gods and which was the supporting pillar of heaven. The temple mountains of Sumer and Babylon (ziggurats), the pyramids of Egypt, the pyramid temples of Central America, and the cosmic mountain temples of India, to mention a few, all have intimate connection to the Pole Star...The Hebrew god could not be allowed to have less, and so the same was claimed for him. The matter-obsessed believers always regarded the loftiest mountain within their locality to be the symbol of Gods Abode. Thus, the "sacred mountain," Mount Zion, of Hebrew myth corresponds to the North Pole Star."**

We are advised by the Mad Arab to perform our rituals of initiation in the North direction, as found in the traditions and customs held sacred by ancient people in the times of antiquity. There is something, however, that concerns many who are initiated into the Necronomicon Tradition, and that is whether the rites and rituals mentioned in the Simon Necronomicon are benevolent in nature? Some of this may stem from a passage found in the First Testimony of the Mad Arab:

*"Know, then, that I have trod all the Zones of the Gods, and also the places of the Azonei, and have descended unto the foul places of Death and Eternal Thirst, which may be reached through the Gate of GANZIR, which was built in UR, in the days before Babylon was... Know, too, that I have spoken with all manner of spirit and daemon, whose names are no longer known in the societies of Man,"*

The Mad Arab, in the passage cited above, mentions that he invoked the Zonei (the planets) and the places of the Azonei (constellations, fixed stars, zodiac), but he also says that he traveled into Ganzir, or the Land of the Dead. While we have already reviewed information in our present discussion illustrating the benevolence of revering the planets and stars, many still wonder; what place does necromancy have in such a benevolent tradition?

## The Cult of the Dead

With the pages of the Simon Necronomicon the Mad Arab writes about a peculiar "cult" that existed in ancient times. An example of this can be seen in the opening words of the Magan Text:

*"The verses here following come from the secret text of some of the priests of a cult which is all that is left of the Old Path that existed before Babylon was built..,"*

The Mad Arab speaks about a "cult" that existed before Babylon was built on another occasion, which is the Cult of the Dead. His verifies this in the Urilia Text:

*"Bread of the Cult of the Dead in its Place I eat.."*

There is not a lot of information available in print about the Cult of the Dead. Most scholars agree that it is the oldest religion of man. I must also state that without an understanding of the history of the Cult of the Dead, no Initiate can ever gain a true understanding of the Greater Mysteries. In the book *Spiritism and the Cult of the Dead in Antiquity* by Lewis Bayles Paton, we find the following observation on page 18:

**"..,it appears that the cult of the dead is one of the most ancient and most widely-spread forms of human worship....a number of ancient writers formulated the theory that ancestor-worship was the origin of all human religion."**

Paton described the Cult of the Dead's spiritual philosophy as the foundation of all human religion. If this is the case, then we should see aspects of this in human religions that followed this ancient "cult." Paton continues on page 208:

**"The rites of mourning among the Semites were similar to those among other primitive peoples and bear witness to a similar cult of the dead."**

Before we continue to further illustrate the Cult of the Dead's influence on modern religious thought, it is useful to first consider how the dead came to be feared. Paton explains:

**"The great gods whom men loved and adored were gods of the upper world and of the living; their sway did not extend into the dark abodes of the dead...When death came it was a sign that their favor was withdrawn, or that they were unable to help against the powers of darkness. The disembodied spirit passed out of their jurisdiction into that of divinities with whom in life it had established no friendly relations."**

It is important for the Initiate to establish a relationship with the forces of darkness for reasons cited above. This was the case with one of the most legendary kings in history. Paton continues on page 261:

**"The dark holy of holies of Solomon's temple, with its anteroom, in which a lamp was kept burning and bread and incense were offered, was the counterpart of an ancient Canaanite tomb...Sacrifice is a rite that has meaning only in the cult of the dead. The blood, in which the life of the animal resides, is poured out in order that the shades may drink of it and renew their vigour. Offerings of food and drink are not needed by celestial deities, but are needed by spirits of the dead, and have been offered to them from the earliest**

times...and were afterward extended to other divinities..."

Here we can see a clear example of how the Cult of the Dead, while remaining hidden, was influential in the religious rites of ancient Israel. This same "cult" influenced the culture, politics, and religion of the ancient world. Paton continues on page 20:

**"We are told of Confucius that "he sacrificed to the spirits as though the spirits were present," and he consciously enjoined the cult of the dead upon his disciples."**

Paton continues in his introductory notes, and from them we can see some of the bigoted views of his generation, though in some respects, he praises the "savage people," as keepers of this ancient tradition:

**"In the Neolithic caves of Palestine, that were inhabited by a pre-Semitic race, offerings of food and drink were deposited with the dead and their bones were used as amulets. Anthropologists agreed that no savage race exits which does not believe in some sort of immortality and practise some rites in honour of the dead."**

Earlier in Paton's writing, he identifies this "savage race" as Africans, Native Americans, East Indians, and Asian peoples. He reveals the Cult of the Dead was influence in Europe. In an online article from the *Encyclopedia Britannica,* entitled Death Rite, we find the following:

**"The Christian cult of the dead found early expression in the catacombs....."**

The Cult of the Dead is the same organization that the Mad Arab described as *"existing before Babylon was built."* It is this same "cult" that Simon referred to in the Simon Necronomicon's Introduction, under the section entitled, *WORSHIP OF THE ANCIENT ONES IN HISTORY,* we read:

**"In the West, the conjuration, cultivation, or worship of this Power was strenuously opposed with the advent of the Solar Monotheistic religions and those who clung to the Old Ways were effectively extinguished."**

The Cult of the Dead existed before the Babylonian religion. After the "deluge" the cult's power was weakened by the advent of solar religions. It was kept alive by Initiates who performed the work in secret. It is evident that this "cult" was in existence before the Babylonian civilization emerged because the esthetics of the "cult," although pre-historic, were thought to be evil by the groups that followed them, which is a clear indication that they did not understand these ancient rites. Paton continues on page 211:

**"Unlike China, where ancestors were believed to bless their descendants,...in Babylonia and Assyria the activity of spirits of the dead was entirely maleficent."**

The "cult" that the Mad Arab mentioned in the beginning of the Magan Text must have existed before Babylon. The Babylonians regarded wind-spirits as evil, since the wind represented the soul, spirit, or breathe of a deceased person. They also believed that the spirit of the deceased still had some connection to the dead body and this physical body was its chief seat of activity. In some of the early Babylonian incantations we see that these "evil spirits" are described as having no wife, could not stand, or sit, and etc. We can now understand why Pazuzu was considered evil, since he was a "wind spirit." It was an ancient Mesopotamian belief that while the celestial gods showed favor upon man from time to time, they could not do anything to prevent the forces of darkness from taking a soul into the womb of death, since the victim never established a relationship with these said forces. This is what the Mad Arab is talking about in the beginning of his Second Testimony:

*The Lords of the Wind rush about me and are angered..,"*

It is a beautiful opportunity that awaits us today. We have the opportunity to undergo the rites of the dead by our work with the Simon Necronomicon, and it all begins with the process of Gate-Walking.

# Initiation of the Gates

*"The Gates refer to the process of self-initiation contained in the NECRONOMICON. This is a useful Spiritual Guide for those involved in any form of occult self-initiation"* (excerpt from the Necronomicon Spellbook)

Critics of the Simon Necronomicon claim that the Gate-Walking System of Initiation was invented in the 1970's. Others say that these rituals are based on western ceremonial magical practices. Many people who use the Simon Necronomicon may work with some sections of the book, but find the Gate-Walking Process of Initiation a little too difficult to understand. Let us delve a little deeper into the history of the Greater Mysteries and compare these findings with the system of self-initiation that is presented in the Simon Necronomicon. We will begin our search by looking into the meaning and origin of the term *'initiation.'*

The English word, initiation, derives from the Latin, *initium*: *entrance,* or *beginning,* literally *"a going in."* The term initiation refers to moving from one condition to the next, or an entrance, 'a going in.' History about the term initiation, is given by Dennis Chomenky, in his writings on Freemasonry entitled; *Initiation, Mystery, and Salvation: The Way of Rebirth,* he states:

**"The term "initiation" comes from the Latin word initiare, which is a late Hellenistic translation of the Greek verb myein. The main Greek term for initiation, myesis, is also derived from the verb myein, which means "to close." It refers to the closing of the eyes**

which was possibly symbolic of entering into darkness prior to reemerging and receiving light and to the closing the lips which was possibly a reference to the vow of silence taken by all initiates. Another Greek term for initiation was telete. In his Immortality of the Soul Plutarch writes that "the soul at the moment of death, goes through the same experiences as those who are initiated into the great mysteries. The word and the act are similar: we say telentai (to die) and telestai (to be initiated)." The fact that myein means "to close" and its translation, initiare, is derived from the earlier inire, which means to "to go in" or "to begin," further suggests that a notion of endings and beginnings was inherent to the ancient understanding of these terms."

Chomenky gives reference to Plutarch's work, *Immortality of the Soul*, where it states; '*the soul at the moment of death goes through the same experiences as those who are initiated into the Great Mysteries.*' This shows us that the ancients were of the opinion that in order for an individual to be initiated, they must walk through the valley of the dead while alive and through this experience a 'transformation' occurs.

The Spheres described in the *Book of Entrance* written by the Mad Arab are part of the Qliphothic Tree.This can be determined from a passage written by the Mad Arab on page five of the Simon Necronomicon:

**"For this is the *Book of the Dead*, the *Book of the Black Earth*, that I have writ down at the peril of my life, exactly as I received it, on the planes of the IGIGI, the cruel celestial spirits from beyond the Wanderers of the Wastes."**

This shows us that the Mad Arab received his instructions from the 'cruel' celestial spirits, or those that are Qliphothic in nature. On page six of the Simon Necronomicon, the Mad Arab mentions that he 'traveled beneath the Seas, in search for "the Palace of Our Master.' The Mad Arab's journey *beneath the Seas* is a reference to the farthest reaches of the Land of the Dead. The Initiate takes the same path that the soul does when a person has died in order to destroy the false self, which is acquired by inappropriate attachments to the phenomenal world. The false self must be destroyed in order for true initiation to occur. The ancient teachings of initiation and transformation used the 'negative' force to destroy the false self. The Simon Necronomicon is an excellent path for the serious student who seeks initiation into the Greater Mysteries. Leonid Lar mentions the following in an article about the Nenets' Shamans:

**"At the time of initiation a young shaman experiences the "physical destruction" of his body, which the spirits take apart. For a few days he lies "dead", until the spirits put all the parts of his body back together. The encounter with death is a key moment of the shaman's initiation. Next the initiate receives a "new body" and is reborn to a new quality. During the initiation ritual a young shaman receives new supernatural qualities, which allow him to move fast in the space and time and allow for transformation from one state to another. According to the stories told by shamans Yaptik and Mandakov they "were dead" for three days, did not eat or drink anything."**

The Nenets people are spoken of in the Simon Necronomicon on page 7:

*"I have raised armies against the Lands of the East, by summoning the hordes of fiends I have made subject unto me, and so doing found the NGAA, the God of the*

*heathens, who breathes flame and roars like a thousand thunders."*

The Mad Arab speaks about the god NGAA, which is derived from NGA. NGA is the god of death. *Wikipedia* offers us this brief history concerning NGA:

**"Among the Nenets people of Siberia, Nga was the god of death, as well as one of two demiurges, or supreme gods...According to one story, the world threatened to collapse on itself. To try and halt this cataclysm a shaman sought the advice of the other demiurge, Num. The shaman was advised to travel below the earth, to Nga's domain and call upon him. The shaman did as told and was wed with Nga's daughter. After that point he began to support the world in his hand and became known as "The Old Man of the Earth." In another myth, Num and Nga created the world, collaborating and also competing with each other — the myth is an example of dualistic cosmology."**

The Initiate had to walk through the world of the dead in order to be reborn as an Immortal being. The Simon Necronomicon keeps this tradition alive. Those ignorant in the history of the arcane faith have foolishly stated that the Gate-Walking Process was not a part of any ancient system from Mesopotamia, but a western ceremonial magickal working. In Chaldean astronomical lore, Cancer was called the *'Gate of Men,'* the entrance point for souls seeking incarnation into human bodies. Capricorn was called *'the Gate of the Gods'* by which souls passed into heaven. The entrance point, the Gate of Men, is another name for the constellation of Cancer, and this constellation is ruled by Nanna (the Moon). This is the first sphere mentioned in the Gate-Walking Process of Self-Initiation. The constellation of Capricorn is called the *Gate of the Gods*. The ruler of Capricorn is Ninib, which is

the final Gate mentioned in the initiation rites of the
Simon Necronomicon. This shows us that the initiatory
rites in the Simon Necronomicon are perfectly aligned
with the initiatory rites of the ancient world Albert Pike
explains this astrological "initiation" in *Morals & Dogma*
on page 438:

**"The Galaxy, Macrobius says, crosses the Zodiac in two
opposite points, Cancer and Capricorn, the tropical
points in the sun's course, ordinarily called the Gates of
the Sun. These two tropics, before his time [Aries],
corresponded with those constellations, but in his day
[Pisces] with Gemini and Sagittarius, in consequence of
the precession of the equinoxes; but the signs of the
Zodiac remained unchanged; and the Milky Way
crossed at the signs Cancer and Capricorn, though not
at those constellation..Through these gates souls were
supposed to descend to earth and re-ascend to Heaven.
One, Macrobius says, in his dream of Scipio, was styled
the Gate of Men; and the other, the Gate of the Gods.
Cancer was the former, because souls descended by it
to the earth; and Capricorn the latter, because by it they
re-ascended to their seats of immortality, and became
Gods." (155:437-8)**

These are just a few points to illustrate the authenticity of
the Gate-Walking rites of initiation. It is an intense
journey, but for the serious occultist the journey is the
reward.

# The Qliphotic Tree of Transformation

The term Qliphoth, kliffoth, or klippot, is derived from the Hebrew term *qelippot,* meaning "peels", "shells" or matter. The *qliphoth* in Kabbalistic studies, are described as opposites to the sephiroth (singular *sephirah*). The ten *sephiroth* are thought to be ten divine "enumerations" or "emanations" of God in the universe. It is thought that the *qliphoth* are the ten (or eleven) manifestations of darkness, into which God's divine light cannot reach. The *qliphoth* are the personifications of an *anti-God* condition A Hasidic view states that in the process of creation ten sephiroth were created, each encapsuled by a qliphoth. The ten *sephiroth* are thought to be ten divine "enumerations" or "emanations" of God into the universe. The first set of ten qliphoth proved too weak to hold the emanating force, and the lower seven of them broke. They were replaced, but the broken former set, animated by a residue of the creative power of God, remained and conflicts with those aspects of the world corresponding to the lower seven sephiroth. Throughout my research on the Qliphoth, I began to discover that it is always said to pre-date the Judaic-Christian Kabbalistc system. This aroused my curiosity and I decided to look a little further into the origins of the Kabbalah. *The Kabbalah* by Alexander S. Holub, Ph.D he states on page 1:

**"The first mention of the Tree of Life in the Scriptures is in Genesis 3:22 (Masoretic Text). The date of the writing of this text by the Jahwist Priests was sometime around 750-700 BCE. That gives plenty of time to incorporate and include the Tree of Life idea into their religious system and its writings. If you will look at the Semitic tribes, they all had this concept playing quite prominently in their religious beliefs. The Sumerians**

were the first to depict a Sacred Tree, a Tree of Life. Babylon took it from the Sumerians when they overthrew their empire. Assyria then took it from the Babylonians when they conquered the Babylonian empire."

The information cited above indicates that the Tree of Life is Sumerian in origin. I soon realized that it is quite possible that the Judaic-Christian Kabbalists may have demonized the original Tree of Life in an effort to make their culture appear to be superior. According to two authoritative sources, H.P. Blavatsky and the Jewish Encyclopedia, the Jews also acquired from the Chaldeans their doctrine of Eastern Mysticism. These were later developed into a written compendium of esoteric literature known as the Jewish Qabbalah or Kabalah, and in the Middle Ages, as the Latin Cabala.

**"Kabalah (Heb.) The hidden wisdom of the Hebrew Rabbis of the middle ages derived from the older secret doctrines concerning divine things and cosmogony, which were combined into a theology after the time of the captivity of the Jews in Babylon. All the works that fall under the esoteric category are termed Kabalistic."** (Blavatsky, Theosophical Glossary, p. 168)

The following is taken from the JewishEncyclopedia.Com

**"The Pythagorean idea of the creative powers of numbers and letters, upon which the 'Sefer Yetzirah' is founded, and which was known in tannaitic times...is here proved to be an old cabalistic conception. In fact, the belief in the magic power of the letters of the Tetragrammaton and other names of the Deity...seems to have originated in Chaldea (see Lenormant, 'Chaldean Magic,' pp. 29, 43). Whatever, then, the theurgic Cabala was ..., the very fact that Abraham, and**

not a Talmudical hero like Akiba, is introduced in the 'Sefer Yetzirah,' at the close, as possessor of the Wisdom of the Alphabet, indicates an old tradition, if not the antiquity of the book itself...The whole dualistic system of good and of evil powers, which goes back to Zoroastrianism and ultimately to old Chaldea, can be traced through Gnosticism; having influenced the cosmology of the ancient Cabala before it reached the medieval one...The gradual condensation of a primal substance into visible matter, a fundamental doctrine of the Cabala, ... is the ancient Semitic conception of the 'primal ocean,' known to the Babylonians as 'Apsu' (compare Jastrow, 'Religion of Babylonia'), and called by the Gnostics (Anz, 'Die Frage nach dem Ursprung des Gnostizismus,' p. 98)."

History shows us that the Kabbalah is derived from ancient Mesopotamian sources. This would also indicate that the Qliphoth, which predates the Judaic Kabbalistic system, was the original Kabbalistic Rite. In an article hosted by an online Jewish Magazine, entitled MileChai.com, which can be found at this link:

http://www.milechai.com/judaism/kabbalah.html

It states the following:

"In the medieval era, old ideas from Babylon gained new strength. The Qliphoth, or Kelippot (the primeval "husks" of impurity), was blamed for all the evil in the world. Qliphoth are the evil twin of the Sephiroth. The tree of Qliphoth is usually called the kabbalistic Tree of Death, and sometimes the Qliphoth are called the Deathangels, or Angels of Death. The Qliphoth are found in the old Babylonian incantations, a fact used as evidence in favor of the antiquity of most of the cabalistic material."

The above passage informs us that the Kabbalah did indeed derive from Ancient Mesopotamian sources and was later demonized, since *"foreign deities"* could not fit into the Jewish pantheon. Another interesting perspective that we must also consider is that the term Qliphoth, *meaning shell,* was not a term to describe something "negative" in its inception. A "shell" was symbolic of a pregnant woman in ancient Mesopotamia. *Birth in Babylonia and in the Bible: Its Mediterranean Setting* by Marten Stol, on page 52 states:

**"The combination sign for "shell" is identical: a body with water in it. The Sumerian word is iskilla; Akkadian isqillatu. The Babylonians saw this shell as a symbol of the pregnant woman...The Greeks and Romans had similar associations; the cowrie shell was named "Cyprian" after the goddess Venus of Cyprus,...Clearly this shell reminded ancient man of the womb."**

Stol informs us that the "shell" was a symbol of a pregnant woman. The earliest religions of man revered the mother-goddess archetype. In Egypt, the Mother and the Child were worshipped under the names Isis and Osiris [called most frequently Horus]...in Pagan Rome, as Fortuna and Jupiter...the boy; in Greece, as Ceres the Great Mother, with the babe at her breast...and even in Thibet [Tibet], China, and Japan, the Jesuit missionaries were astonished to find the counterpart of Madonna and her child as devoutly worshipped as in Papal Rome itself. Therefore, the Qliphoth may have been viewed as an "evil" tree in comparison to the Judaic Kabbalistc correspondences, because it honored foreign deities. It is also interesting to note that the Kabbalistic tree, which consists of ten Sephiroth, the ten "emanations" of God, consists of three pillars. *The left side of the tree, the female side, is considered to be more destructive than the right side.* Maybe the female side of the Tree was demonized in Judaic-Christian correspondences because it reminded Christian and Jewish scholars of the ancient matriarchic rites that ultimately derived from Sumeria.

*"The method of the NECRONOMICON concerns deep, primeval forces that seem to pre-exist the normal archetypal images of the tarot trumps and the Golden Dawn telesmatic figures. These are forces that developed outside the Judeo-Christian mainstream, and were worshipped and summoned long before the creation of the Qabala as we know it today. Hence, the ineffectiveness of the Golden Dawn banishing procedures against them. They are not necessarily demonic or qliphotic in the sense that these terms are commonly understood in the West, they just simply represent power sources largely untapped and thus far ignored by twentieth-century, mainstream consciousness."*

## Conjuration of the Fire God

Little is written in the Simon Necronomicon concerning the God of Fire, also known by his Sumerian name *Gibil,* and sometimes called by the Akkadian *Girra.* However, the importance of the Fire God can be seen in many of the rituals that appear in the Simon Necronomicon, which require his presence. In the Book of Entrance, for example, we find the following passage:

*"Second, on the Night of the Walking, which must be the thirteenth night of the moon, having begun on the previous thirteenth night, thou must approach the Gate with awe and respect. Thy Temple is exorcised. Thou must light the Fire and conjure it, but the invocation of the God of Fire, and pour incense thereon. Thou must make offering to the Deities on the altar."*

From the above passage, we can see the importance of knowing how to work with the Fire God, for it is one of the first steps that must be undertaken in the Gate-Walking Ceremony. Later, in the Book of Entrance, we are given the following instructions:

*"When the First Gate has been entered and the Name received, thou wilt fall back to Earth amid thine Temple. That which has been moving about thy Gate on the ground will have gone. Recite thine thanksgiving to the Gods upon thine altar, strike the Sword of the Watcher that It may depart, and give the incantation of INANNA which say how she conquered the realm of the Underworld and vanquisheth KUTULU. All Idimmu will vanish thereby and thou wilt be thus free to depart the Gate and extinguish the Fire."*

According to the instructions listed above, we are told to "extinguish the Fire," which is the last action of the Gate-Walking Ceremony as well as other rituals in the Simon Necronomicon. Therefore, it is important that we first understand who and what the Fire God really is.

The people of Ancient Mesopotamia greatly revered the Fire God. We are told the following in *Freethinker, Volume 20, Part 2*, edited by George William Foote, page 796 we read:

**"In the Babylonian religion, therefore, we have a triad of divinities, of whom the first two-Ea and Merodach (Marduk)-stand to one another in relation of Father and Son; while the third, the Fire-God, carries out the commands of both, and acts as the intermediary between heaven and earth, and the purifier of mankind from devilry and witchcraft. In the New Testament, likewise, the Third**
**Person of the Trinity stands in close relation to fire. "I, indeed baptize you with water," says John the Baptist; but he that cometh after me, he shall baptize you *with the Holy Ghost and with fire.*" (Matthew iii, 11)**

Here we see that the effectiveness of the rituals in the Simon Necronomicon are due to the fact that they are identical to the rites of the Ancient Chaldeans and are in effect a form of divination that gave birth to the Christian Mythos. There is no difference between the baptism of the Holy Ghost with fire, and the conjuration of the Fire God and the Watcher. In this instance we can determine that the Holy Ghost is the Watcher, but we will discuss this more at length later in this writing.

*"Spirit of the Fire, Remember!...GIBIL, Spirit of the Fire, Remember!...GIRRA, Spirit of the Flames, Remember!"*

The Fire God was extremely important in the sacred religious rites of the Sumerians and those civilizations that followed them. We can be certain of this since Gibil is the name of the Sumerian Fire-God, whereas Girra is the Akkadian term for Gibil. In some versions of the Enuma Elish, Gibil is said to maintain the sharp point of weapons, have broad wisdom, and that his mind is "so vast that all the gods, all of them, cannot fathom it."

*"O God of Fire, Mighty Son of ANU, Most terrifying among Thy Brothers, Rise!"*

Gibil was considered, in Ancient Mesopotamian Mythology, to be the son of An and Ki, other texts describe him as the progeny of An and Shala. Francois Lenormant makes an interesting observation, concerning Gibil, in his classic work, *Chaldean Magic*, where he states:

**"He was worshipped principally in the flame of sacrifice, and therefore he was called "the supreme pontiff upon the face of the earth." But this god was also recognized in the flame which burnt on the domestic hearth, and protected the house against evil influences and demons...This god, who resided in the flame of sacrifice and in that of the hearth, was also the cosmic fire, distributed throughout nature, which was necessary to her existence, and which shone in the stars. Regarded in this light, he was adored as the son of Ana..."**

Lenormant's observations illustrate the vital role that Gibil played in the sacred rites of Ancient Mesopotamia, and helps us to appreciate the antiquity of the Sacred Necronomicon Tradition in its present form. Gibil was considered a very powerful deity due to the many aspects, which were attributed to him.

*"O God of the Furnace, God of Destruction, Remember!*
*Rise Up, O God of Fire, GIBIL in Thy Majesty, and*
*devour my enemies!...Rise up, O God of Fire, GIRRA in*
*Thy Power, and burn the sorcerers who persecute me!"*

Gibil is conjured to dispel negative influences around the
home and also to vanquish influences that may bring
harm to ones' own personal being. This is also suggested
by the Mad Arab in his First Testimony:

*"Remember, always, in every empty moment, to call*
*upon the Gods not to forget thee, for they are forgetful*
*and very far away. Light thy fires high in the hills, and*
*on the tops of temples and pyramids, that they may see*
*and remember."*

From the Mad Arab's words above we get a clear
indication that fire in itself was a symbol of the Ancient
Race of Gods and Demons that are described in the
Simon Necronomicon and served as a vehicle to
communicate with them. Later, in his Second Testimony,
he states:

*"Remember the ARRA, especially when dealing with*
*Them of Fire, for They respect it, and no other."*

The *Sumer Aryan Dictionary* by L.A. Waddell, it defines
the term *AGGA* on page 7 as "Fiery spirits of the deep." It
also gives us the Akkadian use of the term *AGGA* as
pertaining to "water spirits." However, it describes the
term ARA, as in the Simon Necronomicon's ARRA, as
the "Lofty Ones." It seems however, that these two
distinct groups were still contacted by the use of fire.
These "fiery spirits" are known in modern times as the
Jinn. This is further indicated by another passage that is
found in the Book of Calling:

*"Know, fourthly, that it is become the obligation of the Priests of the Flame and the Sword, and of all Magick, to bring their Power to the Underworld and keep it chained thereby, for the Underworld is surely the Gate Forgotten, by which the Ancient Ones ever seek Entrance to the Land of the Living, And the Ministers of ABSU are clearly walking the Earth, riding on the Air, and upon the Earth, and sailing silently through the Water, and roaring in the Fire, and all these Spirits must be brought to subjection to the Person of the Priest of Magick, before any else."*

One might find it interesting to compare the "Priests of Flame and Sword" to the flaming sword in the Book of Genesis that guarded the path to the Tree of Life. In 1880, Archibald Henry Sayce writes the following in *The Chaldean Account of Genesis*, page 86:

**"The flaming sword, which according to Genesis guarded the approach to the tree of life is paralleled by the flaming sword of Merodach, which is explained to be the lightening. It was with this sword....that Merodach overthrew the dragon and the powers of darkness."**

Sayce's statement relates directly to what we find in the Simon Necronomicon's Fire God Conjuration:

*"Rise up, Offspring of the Golden Weapon of MARDUK!"*

There is also another reference to Anu given in this Conjuration:

*"Rise up, Son of the Flaming Disk of ANU!"*

The passage above, and other sutras that appear in the Simon Necronomicon describe Gibil, not only as a sacrificial flame, but also as a specific star. Gavin White makes mention of this in *Babylonian Star-lore*:

**"So far the Fire Star has only been found in early star-lists and as yet no omens have come to light. Gibil is mentioned in the Menologies in the description of month 3, the hottest and driest month of the year, when mud bricks are manufactured and are left to bake under the scorching sun. Here his star is regarded as equivalent to the Bull's Jaw and the Crown of Anu, which indicates that his star is located among the stars that constitute the face of the Bull of Heaven (*Taurus*). To be more specific, I believe that the Fire Star refers to an individual star rather than a large scale constellation, in which case the bright red star *Aldebaran,* located at the eye of the Bull, would be the most suitable candidate."**

So far we have provided the reader with a enough information in regards to the antiquity of the Fire God Ritual, as it appears in the Simon Necronomicon. I encourage all who walk this path to validate and explore other resources concerning these rites. Now we will discuss how the Conjuration of the Fire God is performed.

Instructions, concerning the Conjuration of the Fire God, are given to us in the Book of Entrance:

*"Second, on the Night of the Walking, which must be the thirteenth night of the moon, having begun on the previous thirteenth night, thou must approach the Gate with awe and respect. Thy Temple is exorcised. Thou must light the Fire and conjure it, by the invocation of*

*the God of Fire, and pour incense thereon. Thou must make offering to the Deities on the altar."*

We are instructed to "exorcise" the Temple first. What does this mean? The Book of Calling gives us very clear instructions on how to "exorcise" the Temple:

*"The Place of Calling shall be high in the Mountains, most preferably; or near the Sea; or in some secluded area far from the thoughts of Man; or in the desert; or atop an ancient temple. And it shall be clean, and free from the unwanted. Thus, the Place, once chosen, shall be purified by supplications to thine particular God and Goddess, and by burning offerings of pine and cedar. And a round loaf shall be brought, and salt. And, having offered it to the personal deities, the Priest shall pronounce, solemnly, the following exorcism that the Place of Calling be cleansed and all Evil that the Place of Calling be cleansed and all Evil banished thereby; and the Priest shall not change one word or letter of this exorcism, but recite it faithfully as it is put down:*

*ENU SHUB*
*AM GIG ABSU*
*KISH EGIGGA*
*GAR SHAG DA SISIE AMARDA YA*
*DINGIR UD KALAMA SINIKU*
*DINGIR NINAB GUYU NEXRRANIKU*
*GA YA SHU SHAGMUKU TU!*

*And they Bread burned in the bronze brazier of Calling: and the Salt scattered about the room, sixty times."*

The first step in preparation of this great work is purification of the ritual space. This is done by setting up an altar, or work area for the ritual that follows. Regardless if we are performing these rites indoors,or outdoors, we should be facing direction *North*. The following appears in the Book of Entrance:

*"Thou must needs prepare an altar to face the North, having upon it the statues of thine deities, or some such suitable Images, an offering bowl, and a brazier."*

We are to prepare our altar, preferably with three white candles for the Three Great Watchers, incense burner and the Aga Mass Ssaratu (*a non-flammable bowl with the Three Seals of MASSHU written upon its outer edges. This will be discussed at length in our examination of the Conjuration of the Watcher.*) Also our ritual tools, such as the Sword of the Watcher, Copper Dagger of Inanna, and the knife of the Fire God, should be within close proximity.

After having prepared our altar, we should recite prayers to *"thine particular God and Goddess."* The God and Goddess mentioned in the Simon Necronomicon is a reference to the several entities found in the tome itself. These deities are listed in the Book of Calling's CONJURATION OF ALL THE POWERS. Some have assumed that the God and Goddess referred to here is Anu and Tiamat, and this has been useful for some. However, with a close examination of ancient history we can get a clear idea about who is the "thine God and Goddess" referred to in the Simon Necronomicon. Nathaniel Altman writes the following in his book *Sacred Trees*:

**"The** *black pine* **of Eridu was the** *Tree* **of Life among the** *Chaldeans,* **and its cone was considered a sign of fertility. This** *tree* **was also the symbol of worship for the earth god Ea, who was later supplanted by Ishtar, the mother goddess. ."**

We can see from the above quote that the "God and Goddess" referred to so often in the pages of the Simon Necronomicon is Ishtar and Marduk. The Mad Arab mentions this in First Testimony:

*"I have summoned the ghosts of my ancestors to real and visible appearance on the tops of temples built to reach the stars, and built to touch the nethermost cavities of HADES. I have wrestled with the Black Magician, AZAG-THOTH, in vain, and fled to the Earth by calling upon INANNA and her brother MARDUK, Lord of the double-headed AXE."*

Interestingly, the Simon Necronomicon gives us the following description of Ishtar in the tome's Introduction:

*"Interestingly enough, the myth has many parallels with the Christian concept of Christ's death and resurrection, among which the Crucifixion (INANNA was impaled on a stake as a corpse), the three days in the Sumerian Hades, and the eventual Resurrection are outstanding examples of how Sumerian mythology previewed the Christian religion by perhaps as many as three thousand years – a fact that beautifully illustrates the cosmic and eternal nature of this myth....Therefore, the Goddess of the Witches has two distinct forms: the Ancient One, Goddess of the Dragon-like telluric Power which is raised in Magickal rituals, and the Elder Goddess, Defeater of Death, who brings the promise of Resurrection and Rejuvenation to her followers those who must reside for a time after death and between incarnations in what is called the "Summerland"."*

The Simon Necronomicon clearly identifies Ishtar as the Goddess of witches, as well as, her primordial aspect, that being Tiamat. We are also told the following in her Purification Invocation:

*"Proud One among the Gods, whose command is
supreme
Mistress of Heaven and of Earth, who rules in all places
ISHTAR, at your Name all heads are bowed down"*

The uniqueness of Ishtar's ability is can be found in the
Urilia Text:

*"But the Dead may be always summoned, and many
times are willing to rise; but some are stubborn and
desire to remain Where they are, and do not rise, save for
the efforts of the Priest, who has power, as ISHTAR,
both in this Place and in the Other."*

Another passage in the Book of Calling likens the Initiate
to Ishtar:

*"Which thou shalt wear at all times, as the sign of the
Power of the Magick of ENKI. And I have told thee all
this before, but I tell thee again, for the Priest, being
furnished with every kind of Armor, and armed, he is
similar to the Goddess."*

Before we continue on in our discussion, I must state that
during my research for this work, I discovered quite an
amazing "find" that I think would be useful to share with
all those reading this book. It seems that the ancient
peoples of Ancient Mesopotamia viewed the *"Tree of Life"*
as that of a cedar or pine tree. I came across many
references that support this. It seems that this was indeed
the origin of the Biblical account concerning the "tree" as
it appears in the Bible, but also that the idea of a *"Tree of
knowledge of Good and Bad"* was tacked on by those who
had a negative view toward magical rituals. Surprisingly,
the following quote comes from a medical journal,
written in 1906, entitled Medical Brief, page 831:

"The fact that the two Babylonian figures are clothed, naturally prevented me, also, from regarding the tree as the tree 'of knowledge of good and evil.' It seems to me at least probable that there may be traced in the biblical narrative in Gen, chap. 11 sq., another and older form which recognized but one tree in the middle of the garden-the Tree of Life....In regard to the tree, and that alone, I agree with the late C.P. Tiele when he sees in the Babylonian representation "a God with his male and female worshippers partaking of the fruit of the tree of life, "a picture of the hope of immortality," as also with Hommel, who observes (p. 23): "The most important point is that it is quite evident that the tree was originally thought of as a conifer—a pine or cedar—whose fruit increased the power of life, and of procreation; there is accordingly an unmistakable allusion to the holy cedar of Eridu, the typical tree of Paradise in the Chaldean and Babylonian legends."

I encourage the reader to explore more on this subject in their own personal research of the Necronomicon Tradition, but for the time being, we will continue to focus on the subject at hand.

After prayers are offered up to 'thine own God and Goddess,' and pine and cedar is offered up to them in great respect, we are to then recite the exorcism mentioned in the Book of Calling:

*"ENU SHUB*
*AM GIG ABSU*
*KISH EGIGGA*
*GAR SHAG DA SISIE AMARDA YA*
*DINGIR UD KALAMA SINIKU*
*DINGIR NINAB GUYU NEXRRANIKU*
*GA YA SHU SHAGMUKU TU!"*

Next, we are instructed to sprinkle "salt water," or "holy water," around the area of our Temple, sixty times. The number sixty refers to Anu. Practitioners can determine that they are to sprinkle "salt water" and not just salt in itself based on the previous cited passage that is taken from the Book of Calling:

*"So, therefore, the Priest who governeth the works of Fire, and of the God of Fire, GISHBAR called GIBIL, must firstly sprinkle with the Water of the Seas of ENKI,"*

Further indication of this is revealed to us in the Mad Arab's words as they appear in his Second Testimony:

*"Remember to carve the signs exactly as I have told thee, changing not one mark lest the amulet prove a curse against thee that wear it. Know that salt absorbs the evil effluvia of the larvae, and is useful to cleanse the tools with."*

The next step in Conjuring the Fire God would be to light the fire first, and then recite the Conjuration of the Fire God exactly as it appears in the Simon Necronomicon. Before this step is taken, I must inform the reader that he/she should have prepared a bowl, non-flammable, with the Three Seals of Masshu written on its outer edges. Many Initiates of the Necronomicon Tradition use a ceramic bowl, preferably white, and write the seals of Masshu upon it with a magic-marker, or paint them on in black paint. Additionally, these Initiates will insert a sterno, often used to heat food in aluminum trays, inside the bowl, and ignite it as the source of fire. Before lighting the fire and reading the appropriate conjuration, it is important that the candidate consider the following, as it appears in the Simon Necronomicon:

*"They must be engraved upon the bowl with a fine stylus, or painted thereon with dark ink. The sacrifice must be new bread, pine resin, and the grass Olieribos. These must be burned in the new bowl, and the Sword of the Watcher, with his Sigil engraved thereupon, at hand, for he will inhabit such at the time of the Calling of the Watcher and will depart when he is given license to depart."*

The prayer to the Fire God must be performed with empty hands or with the Dagger of Ishtar. Evidence of this can be determined from the words that appear in the Urilia Text:

*"..and build the Fire therein, calling GBL when thou dost, after his manner and form... When the Fire is built and conjured, then mayest thou raise thine Dagger,"*

The antiquity of the Fire God ritual is very profound. I wish all Initiates of the Necronomicon Tradition the best in their work and it is my hope that this writing has been a source of great encouragement and serves to further your understanding of the Necronomicon Tradition.

# Alchemy of Initiation

Now that we've covered some of the historical aspects of the Necronomicon Tradition, it is useful for us to look a little deeper into the meaning of the philosophy behind the system and the forces behind the workings. The Mad Arab includes four different aspects, which are the foundation of the Necronomicon Tradition, in his First Testimony he states:

*"On occasion, I was able to convince some learned man that I was a sincere scholar, and was thereby permitted to read the ancient records in which the details of necromancy, sorcery, magick and alchemy are given."*

From the passage above we can determine that the foundation of the Necronomicon Tradition is based on four distinct mystical sciences, which are necromancy, sorcery, magick and alchemy. I thought it might be useful to discuss these one at a time. We will begin with alchemy.

Due to the dark imagery of the Simon Necronomicon, some are surprised to hear that this tome is based on alchemy. However, when we look at the etymology of the word alchemy, we can see how this science has heavily influenced rites of the Simon Necronomicon.

The word alchemy derives from the Old French *alquimie*, which is from the Medieval Latin *alchimia*, and which is in turn from the Arabic *al-kimia* ( الكيمياء ). This term itself is derived from the Ancient Greek *chemeia* (χημεία) with the addition of the Arabic definite article *al-* (( ال ) It used to be thought that the ancient Greek word was originally derived in its turn from "Chemia" (Χημία), a version of the Egyptian name for Egypt, which was itself based on the Ancient Egyptian word *kēme* hieroglyphic Khmi, meaning *black earth*, literally *land of black earth*. Ultimately, the word alchemy originated from the Egyptian word Khemi, or Khem (the native name of Egypt), meaning land of black earth. This compares greatly to what is mentioned by the Mad Arab in his First Testimony:

*"For this is the Book of the Dead, the Book of the Black Earth, that I have writ down at the peril of my life, exactly as I received it, on the planes of the IGIGI, the cruel celestial spirits from beyond the Wanderers of the Wastes."*

The Mad Arab's words are a reference to alchemy, or the science of the black earth. Wikipedia offers this in regards to understanding just what alchemy consists of:

**"The best-known goals of the alchemists were the transmutation of common metals into gold (called chrysopoeia) or silver (less well known is plant alchemy, or "spagyric"); the creation of a "panacea", or the elixir of life, a remedy that, it was supposed, would cure all diseases and prolong life indefinitely; and the discovery of a universal solvent. Although these were not the only uses for the discipline, they were the ones most documented and well-known. Certain Hermetic schools argue that the transmutation of lead into gold is analogical for the transmutation of the physical body (Saturn or lead) into (Gold) with the goal of attaining immortality."**

Alchemy concerns itself primarily with the transmutation of base metals, such as turning lead into gold. Many people have viewed this science as a metaphoric way to obtain immortality. The idea of taking what is "dead" and bringing it back to life, or turning lead into gold,

Saturn into the Sun, is the reason why Leonardo Da Vinci stated that 'neromancy is the sister of alchemy.' In order for one to take what is dead (lead-Saturnian) and transform it into gold (gold-Solar) they must have knowledge of the dead.

The alchemy of the Necronomicon Tradition is based upon taking what is dead in us and transmuting it into something beautiful and immortal. Although this idea is very charming to many reading this work, it is quite a difficult task. When we begin to rise from the dead and observe our inner self it can sometimes be depressing. We begin to realize our errors, the ugliness of our thoughts, and our despairing emotional states. For the first time in our lives we begin to see the truth of God by observing the error of our own ways. This is not an easy thing for people to do. Most people like being asleep. They like to be told by some religious figure that they are doing good, when they are following religious instruction and this is the very thing that keeps them asleep. Throughout the Simon Necronomicon are passages that mention *"may the dead rise and smell the incense."* Passages such as these concern themselves primarily with the alchemy of inner refinement. This is a strong theme in the Necronomicon Mysteries. Let us take, for example, a passage that appears in the Book of Calling, which is originally found in the *Chaldean Oracles of Zoroaster* (we will be using the translation of Thomas Stanley and commentary), note how we see this theme hidden in the ancient mysteries. First, let us look at what is written by the Mad Arab:

*"Know, seventhly, of the Things thou art to expect in the commission of this Most sacred Magick. Study the symbols well, and do not be afraid of any awful spectre that shall invade thine operation, or haunt thine habitat by day or by night. Only charge them with them the*

*words of the Covenant and they will do as you ask, of thou be strong. And if thou performest these operations often, thou shalt see things becoming dark; and the Wanderers in their Spheres shall no more be seen by thee; and the Stars in their places will lose their Light, and the Moon, NANNA, by whom thou also workest, shall become black and extinguished,.... AND ARATAGAR SHALL BE NO MORE, AND THE EARTH SHALL ABIDE NOT."*

The above words speak about the light of the Moon and Stars fading and growing dim. It is evidently relating an alchemical process in symbolic language. The Initiate must get into the habit of studying and exploring all possibilities of what is written in the Simon Necronomicon. In any event, these words have much to do with the refinement of the soul. Notice what is written in the Chaldean Oracles of Zoroaster with the accompanying commentary:

**"If thou speak often to me, thou shalt see absolutely that which is spoken...For there neither appears the cælestial concave bulk...Nor do the Stars shine: the light of the Moon is covered..The Earth stands not still, but all things appear Thunder." (The Oracle speaks as from God to an initiated Person,** *If thou often speak to me* **or call me,** *thou shalt see that which thou speakest,* **viz. Me whom thou callest every where: for then thou shalt perceive nothing but** *Thunder* **all about fire gliding up and down all over the World.) "**

Here we see that the Mad Arab's words, when compared with Thomas Stanley's translation of the Chaldean Oracles of Zoroaster, reveal that the Initiate is soon to gain a relationship with god by performing these rites regularly and that they will come to know the true force that is behind the stars and planets, as if these celestial bodies were to no longer exist and all that can be known is god. The Mad Arab continues in the Book of Calling:

*"And around thee shall appear the Flame, like Lightning flashing in all directions, and all things will appear amid thunders, and from the Cavities of the Earth will leap forth the ANNUNNAKI, Dog-Faced, and thou shalt bring them down."*

We also find this same theme in the Chaldean Oracles of Zoroaster:

**"Certainly out of the cavities of the Earth spring terrestrial Dogs..Which show no true signe to mortal Man." (Sometimes to many initiated Persons there appear, whilst they are sacrificing, some Apparitions in the shape of *Doggs* and several other figures. Now the Oracle saith, that these *issue out of the Receptacles of the Earth,* that is, out of the terresrial and mortal Body, and the irrational Passions planted in it which are not yet sufficiently adorned with Reason, these are Apparitions of the passions of the Soul in performing divine Rites; meer appearances having no substance, and therefore *not signifying any thing true.*)"**

During our process of initiation, and for some time afterwards, we purge our souls of useless passions, thoughts, and etc. Amazingly, these emotional energies have a mind of their own, and to some may appear as outer demons, but they are in fact negative aspects of our psyche that we can now see and feel them for what they are due to the intensity of the initiation. Now let us look at one more example by observing what is written in the Magan Text:

*"Stoop not down, therefore,*

*For an Abyss lies beneath the World*
*Reached by a descending Ladder*
*That hath Seven Steps*
*Reached by a descending Pathway*
*That hath Seven Gates*
*And therein is established*
*The Throne*
*Of an Evil and Fatal Force."*

Now let us look at what is written in the Chaldean
Oracles of Zoroaster:

**"Stoop not down, for a præcipice lies below on the
Earth,**
**Drawing through the Ladder which hath seven steps;**
**beneath which Is the Throne of Necessity."** (He calls the
**Descention into wickednesse, and misery, a Precipice;**
**the**
**Terrestrial and Mortasl Body, the Earth: for by the Earth**
**he understands mortal Nature, as by the fire frequently**
**the Divine; by the place with seven Wayes, he means**
**Fate dependant on the Planets, beneath which there is**
**seated a certain dire and unalterable Necessity: The**
**Oracle therefore adviseth, that thou stoop not down**
**towards the mortal Body, which being Subject only to**
**the Fate, which proceeds from the Planets, may be**
**reckon'd amongst those things which are at our**
**Arbitrement: for thou wilt be unhappy if thou stoop**
**down wholly to the Body, and unfortunate and**
**continually failing of thy Desires, in regard of the**
**Necessity which is annex'd to the Body.)"**

The words of both, the Chaldean Oracles and the Mad
Arab reveal that the mortal body is subject to the fate of
the planets. It is due to such that the ancient Chaldeans
saw it necessary to live through the astral body and used
their physical vehicles to strengthen such.

The Simon Necronomicon is heavily based on the refinement of the soul and immortality. An Initiate must always keep this in mind so that they do not become sidetracked by the appearance that many so-called "enlightened" institutions have established. One must always remember that there is a big difference in serving god and being one. Since the Necronomicon Tradition is based on developing ones' godhood and immortality, as opposed to serving god, many modern-day organizations will label these practices, due to their own ignorance, as an act of black magic.

Initiations into the Necronomicon Tradition are a rare gift indeed. Others may join organizations simply for the association and community. Regardless of the reason for joining such organizations, the Initiate must remember that the primary focus of these organization deal with servants of gods and not the obtainment of godhood itself. An Initiate must prevent their being from becoming intoxicated with the appearance of such groups and teachings and know how to discriminate the information that is being taught in these so-called spiritual organizations.

It is important for the Initiate to understand the meaning of necromancy and its true history. There isn't a lot of information on this subject and most information that is available is by academic researchers, due to their religious ties, deem this science as "demonic." It is for this reason that necromancy is almost a lost art. Originally, necromancy was closely associated with astrology and this association began, as we will see, with the ancient Sumerians. Haig A, Bosmajian in the book entitled, *Burning Books* makes the following observation:

**The fourteenth century inquisitor Nicolas Eymerich tells us, writes Lea, "that if a man was suspected of necromancy and was found to be an astrologer it went far to prove him a necromancer, for the two were almost always conjoined."**

This shows us clearly that astrology and necromancy, along with astronomy, were considered to be one science in the remote past. Earlier in this writing, we discussed the meaning of initiation and how the candidate travels through the zodiac, which is the same path as the spirit of a departed person. It stands to reason that when necromancy was revered as a benevolent science in ancient times, the necromancer understood the condition of a deceased spirit and how they were affected, as it traveled through different signs of the zodiac. The spiritual teachings of ancient Sumeria confirm this for us.

When the Initiate puts aside his/her superstitious belief, which is so prevalent in so-called scholarly works, they can begin to realize that the ancient Adepts were not superstitious, as some moderns would like for us to believe, but used symbolic imagery to explain scientific phenomena. We see a clear example of this in the Simon Necronomicon term *nar mattaru*.

The term *nar marratu* derives from the Akkadian *nar mattaru*, which has many meaning s, but is usually defined as an underworld ocean, or bitter waters. We also find a similar definition in the Simon Necronomicon's Introduction under Chart of Comparisons:

(showing some relationships to be found between the mythos of Lovecraft, the magick of Crowley, and the faith of Sumer.)

| Lovecraft | Crowley | Sumer |
|---|---|---|
| Cthulhu | The Great Beast as represented in "CTHDH 666" | Ctha-lu, Kutulu |
| The Ancient Ones | Satan; Teitan | Tiamat |
| Azathoth | Aiwass (?) | Azag-thoth |
| The Dunwich Horror | Choronzon | Pazuzu |
| Shub Niggurath | Pan | Sub Ishniggarab (?) |
| **Out of Space** | **The Abyss** | **Absu; Nar Mattaru** |
| IA! | IO! IAO! | IA (JAH; EA; Lord of Waters) |
| The Five-pointed grey Star carven | The Pentagram | The AR, or UB (Plough Sign; the original pentagram and the sign of the Aryan Race) |
| Vermis Mysteriis | The Serpent | Erim (the Enemy; and the Sea as Chaos; Gothic; Orm, or Worm, great Serpent) |

In the chart above we can see that *nar mattaru* corresponds to the *abyss*, and *out of space*. This comparison does fall in line with works written by authors outside of the Necronomicon Tradition. E.A.Wallis Budge's book *Amulets and Superstitions*. Budge states the following on page 115-116:

**"The female devil in the boat is LAMASHTU, whose home in the infernal regions whence she comes when she arrives on the earth to carry out her campaign of slaughter and death. The only way to stop her from carrying out her baneful plans is to get her back again in the Underworld, and it is necessary to coax her to leave earth by promising to give her gifts....She must then make her way over the mountains which block the road to hell, and when this is done she must cross the river of hell, which is none other than the great World-Ocean, Nar Marratu."**

Budge identifies *nar marratu* with the Underworld, or great World Ocean. The ancient people of Mesopotamia likened the atmosphere and space to the *sea*. Similar to the appearance of fresh water reflecting the sunlight with its blue appearance, so too is the sky during daylight hours with the abundance of fresh air to breathe. It is this imagery that the ancient Adepts used to describe the portion of the universe that is instrumental in supporting life, the solar system. The deeper region of outer space was likened to the ocean with its salty waters, which does contain life. It is also instrumental in supporting daily life, but its contribution is not directly seen. These *"salty waters"* were likened to the depths of outer space where the Sun's light is not found and was very indifferent to life on Earth, in some cases, it could be said that it was hostile to Earth. This was considered also to be the Land of the Dead since it did not support physical life as we know it, on Earth, but it can be explored, like a deceased person, with ones' astral body. When the Initiate understands this then he/she can understand that what some may call necromancy is actually the ability to communicate with entities that dwell in outer space. We find this in the Simon Necronomicon's Normal Invocation of the Watcher:

*"May He of the Name Unspeakable, the Number Unknowable,*
*Whom no man hath seen at any time,*
*Whom no geometer measureth,*
*Whom no wizard hath ever called*
*CALL THEE HERE NOW!*
*Rise up, by ANU I summon Thee!*
*Rise up, by ENLIL I summon Thee!*
*Rise up, by ENKI I summon Thee!*
*Cease to be the Sleeper of EGURRA.*
*Cease to lie unwaking beneath the Mountains of KUR.*
*Rise up, from the pits of ancient holocausts!*
*Rise up, from the old Abyss of NARR MARRATU"*

The Watcher plays a vital role in many of the rituals that are contained within the Necronomicon Tradition, and from its invocation, we can clearly see that the Watcher comes from outer space. There are other passages in the Simon Necronomicon that use the term nar marratu. In the Magan Text we read:

*"And TIAMAT has promised us nevermore to attack*
*With water and with wind.*
*But the Gods are forgetful.*
*Beneath the Seas of NAR MATTARU*
*Beneath the Seas of the Earth, NAR MATTARU*
*Beneath the World lays sleeping*
*The God of Anger, Dead but Dreaming*

*The God of CUTHALU, Dead but Dreaming!*
*The Lord of KUR, calm but thunderous!*
*The One-Eyes Sword, cold but burning"*

While we can see that the term *nar marratu* applies to the abyss, or outer space, there are also forces beyond these realms, such as a black hole. The Urilia Text states:

*"I AM before ABSU.*
*I AM before NAR MARRATU.*
*I AM before ANU.*
*I AM before KIA."*

In view of all the information that has been covered so far, we can definitely say that necromancy plays a vital part in even our own awakening. We know understand that *nar marratu* refers to outer space, but as seen in the passage cited above, Tiamat's existence predates even the Absu (*nar marratu*). This would seem to have relevance to what some occultists describe as Universe B, a dimension outside of this experience. I find it no coincidence that the term *nar marratu* relates heavily to the Chaldean Goddess of antiquity known as Marratu. Shoni Labowitz, in the work entitled; *God, Sex and Women of the Bible*, mentions the following on page 165:

**"Miriam's names reflected her own ageless enthusiasm. Her most popular name, Miriam, is associated with the ancient goddess Mari, the "Fruitful Mother," who dominated the Holy Land; the Chaldean goddess Marratu; the Persian goddess Mariham and the Christian Mother Mary."**

From this observationTiamat is the supreme god in a manner similar to Mother Mary, who was also known as the "mother of god." The Mad Arab tells us the following in the Simon Necronomicon:

*"Of the three carved symbols, the first is the sign of our Race from beyond the Stars, and is called ARRA in the tongue of the Scribe who taught it to me, an emissary of the Elder Ones. In the tongue of the eldest city of Babylon, it was UR. It is the Sigil of the Covenant of the Elder Gods, and when they see it, they who gave it to us, they will not forget us. They have sworn!"*

The ARRA Sign is symbolic of the *'Race from beyond the Stars.'* This is also mentioned in the Magan Text:

*"WE ARE THE LOST ONES*
*From a Time before Time*
*From a Land beyond the Stars*
*From the Age when ANU walked the earth*
*In company of Bright Angels.*
*We have survived the first War*
*Between the Powers of the Gods*
*And have seen the wrath of the Ancient Ones*
*Dark Angels*
*Vent upon the Earth*
*WE ARE FROM A RACE BEYOND THE WANDERERS*
*OF NIGHT.*
*We have survived the Age when ABSU ruled the Earth*
*And the Power destroyed out generations.*
*We have survived on tops of mountains*
*And beneath the feet of mountains*
*And have spoken with the Scorpions*
*In allegiance and were betrayed.*
*And TIAMAT has promised us nevermore to attack*
*With water and with wind.*
*But the Gods are forgetful.*
*Beneath the Seas of NAR MATTARU*
*Beneath the Seas of the Earth, NAR MATTARU"*

In the passage above reference is made about 'the Race
from beyond the Stars.' Since Nar Marratu represents the
Absu, or the realms of outer space, then this Race that
exists from Beyond the Stars represents Tiamat. It is
known that much of the mythology that appears in the
Bible is borrowed from ancient Mesopotamian sources, as
Abraham originated from Ur of the Chaldees. Christian
mythology tells us that "god" is resting, or has taken rest
away from the phenomenal world on the seventh day. In
any event, these stories, as recorded in the Biblical book
of Genesis, allude to a secret mystery, one that was
revealed in the Atlantean Necronomicon's Fall of
Christianity article.

# The Fall Of Christianity

Throughout this writing, various references will be made about the *Necronomicon Tradition*. The meaning of this term and the responsibility that it places upon the Initiate is an extremely important part of the work. According to H.P. Lovecraft, the term *Necronomicon,* is derived from the Greek term *nekros* (corpse), *nomos* (law), *eikon* (image): *"An image of the law of the dead."* This definition could simply be applied to the work of necromancy, but we will soon see that this term encompasses so much more.

Lovecraft also mentioned in his writings that the Necronomicon was originally called, *Al Azif,* an Arabic word, which he defined as "that nocturnal sound (made by insects) which supposed to be the howling of demons." In pre-Islamic Arabia, the term *azif* signified the ominous whistling of the Jinn. Parker Ryan supports this conclusion in his essay *The Necronomicon Mythos According to HPL*:

**"Next let's look at Alhazred's title. HPL wrote that Alhazred's title was *"Mad Poet."* "Mad" is usually written "majnun" in Arabic. *Majnun* means "mad" today. However, in the eighth century (Alhazred's time) it meant *"Possessed by Jinn."* To be called *Mad* or *Possessed by Demons* would be highly insulting to orthodox Muslims. The Sufis and Muqarribun regard Majnun as *complimentary title*. They even go so far as to call certain Sufi heroes Majnun.."**

This is a clear indication that the Necronomicon is a book inspired by the Jinn. The Simon Necronomicon also supports Ryan's observation. In the MAGAN Text we read the following concerning TIAMAT:

*"Those from Without*
*Have builded up charnel houses*
*To nourish the fiends of TIAMAT*
*And the Blood of the weakest here*
*Is libation unto TIAMAT*
*Queen of the Ghouls"*

The term *ghoul,* is a derivative of the Arabic *ghul,* meaning *jinn.* In the works of both Lovecraft and Simon, the Necronomicon is a book that is inspired by the Jinn.

In Arabian and Muslim folklore the Jinn are ugly and evil demons having supernatural powers which they can bestow on persons having powers to call them up. In the Western world they are called *"genies."* The term *Jinn* means *concealed, or hidden.* This is the same definition that we find for the term *"occult."* In Islamic theology, the Jinn are said to be made from a "smokeless fire," while humans were created out of the Earth. Some accounts report that the Jinn were created before Adam from the "hot wind." It is said that the Jinn live in a parallel world next to mankind, though they are undetected by humans. The Jinn are able to marry and have children, and have domesticated pets similar to mankind. Parker Ryan states the following concerning the Jinn:

**"Jinn were powerful creatures of Arab myth. The Jinn, according to legend, came down from heaven (the sky) in the time before Adam. Therefore, they pre-exist mankind and thus called *"Preadamites."* "Infidel pagans" worship these incredibly powerful beings. The Jinn can "beget young on mankind." The Jinn are usually invisible to normal men. They apparently want great influence on Earth. Much of the magick used in Arab countries concerns the Jinn (protection spells**

against, or spells to call them up). The Jinn are thus virtually identical with *Lovecraft's Old Ones*."

Ryan points out that the Jinn can *"beget young on mankind."* There are many tales throughout the Arab world of humans having intimate relations with the Jinn. *A Dictionary of Islam* by Thomas Patrick Hughes, B.D., M.R.A.S., states the following concerning the Jinn:

**"The Jinn, it has been already shown, *are peaceable*. They also eat and drink, and propagate their species, *sometimes in conjunction with human beings*; in which latter case, the offspring partakes of the nature of both parents."**

The subject of Jinn-human progeny is highly debated amongst Muslim scholars. However, there is a great deal of evidence supporting the fact that Jinn and humans are able to produce offspring together. The religion of Islam dictates that Allah created both the Jinn and mankind, but the ancient texts of the pre-Islamic era say something different. Hughes continues on page 134:

**"It is said that God created the Jann (or Jinn) two thousand years before Adam (according to some writers, much earlier) and that they are believers and infidels and every sect among them, as among men....It is commonly believed that the preadamite Jinn were governed by forty (according to some seventy-two) kings, to each of whom the Arab writers give the name Sulaiman (Solomon); and that they derive their appellation from the last of these, who was called Jann Ibn-Jann, and who, some say, built the Pyramids of Egypt."**

The Simon Necronomicon describes Tiamat as the Queen of the Ghouls, which in light of our discussion would also make her the Mother of the Jinn. Parker Ryan, in his essay about the Cthulhu Mythos, also asserts that 'Lovecraft's *Old Ones* are identical to the Jinn of Arab legend. This would indicate that the Elder Gods and the Ancient Ones, which appear in the Simon Necronomicon, are various classes of Jinn who were responsible for creating human beings, as presented in the Enuma Elish and other ancient mythologies. According to Arabic legend, the Jinn were Earth's first inhabitants and will survive the race of mankind. The MAGAN Text states:

**"For what is new**
**Came from that which is old**
**And what is old**
**Shall replace that which is new**
**And once again the Ancient Ones**
**Shall rule upon the face of the Earth!**
**And this is too the Covenant!"**

The Christian Bible also mentions a race similar to the Jinn:

**"Now the serpent was more subtile than any beast of the field which the LORD God had made. And he said unto the woman, Yea, hath God said, Ye shall not eat of every tree of the garden?"**

The "serpent" described in the Third Chapter of Genesis must have been one of the Jinn that descended to Earth at an earlier time. Genesis Chapter One states:

**"And God said, Let us make man in our image, after our likeness: and let them have dominion over the fish of the sea, and over the fowl of the air, and over the cattle, and over all the earth, and over every creeping thing that creepeth upon the earth.... And God blessed**

them, and God said unto them, Be fruitful, and
multiply, and *replenish the earth,* and subdue it: and
have dominion over the fish of the sea, and over the
fowl of the air, and over every living thing that moveth
upon the earth."

This is quite different than what is described concerning
the creation of mankind, as found in Genesis Chapter
two:

"And every plant of the field before it was in the earth,
and every herb of the field before it grew: for the
LORD God had not caused it to rain upon the earth,
and there was not a man to till the ground. ...But there
went up a mist from the earth, and watered the whole
face of the ground....And the LORD God formed man
of the dust of the ground, and breathed into his nostrils
the breath of life; and man became a living soul."

There are differences between the creation accounts in
Genesis chapter one and chapter two. In the first Chapter
of Genesis *"man"* is not created from the ground. The
creation of vegetation precedes the making of man. In the
second chapter of Genesis, the *"human"* is created from
the Earth. This took place before *'every herb of the field
grew in the earth.'* Evidently, these two accounts, describe
two different events, one pertaining to the Jinn and the
other to human beings.

Interestingly, some Judaic Traditions hold the belief that
*"Cain"* was not the son of Adam and Eve, but the son of
Eve and the Serpent. *Tree of Souls: The Mythology of
Judaism* by Howard Schwartz, states the following of
page 447:

"When Cain was born, Adam knew at once that he was
not of his seed, for he was not after his likeness, nor

after his image. Instead, Cain's appearance was that of a heavenly being. And when Eve saw that his appearance was not of this world, she said, *I have gained a male child with the help of Yahweh.* (Gen. 4:1)"

This perspective, given by Schwartz, seems to explain why Cain's life was spared after killing his brother Abel.

"And Cain said unto the LORD, My punishment is greater than I can bear...Behold, thou hast driven me out this day from the face of the earth; and from thy face shall I be hid; and I shall be a fugitive and a vagabond in the earth; and it shall come to pass, that every one that findeth me shall slay me... And the LORD said unto him, Therefore whosoever slayeth Cain, vengeance shall be taken on him sevenfold. And the LORD set a mark upon Cain, lest any finding him should kill him."

There is another aspect of this account that has been overlooked by both occultists and scholars alike, and that is the location of where Cain was taken to after the murder of his half-brother:

"And Cain went out from the presence of the LORD, and dwelt in the land of Nod, on the *east of Eden*....And Cain knew his wife; and she conceived, and bare Enoch: and he builded a city, and called the name of the city, after the name of his son, Enoch."

Cain settled in the *"east of Eden."* This indicates that Cain was indeed a progeny of a supernatural being because in Genesis Chapter 2:8, we read the following:

"And the LORD God planted a garden *eastward in Eden;* and there he put the man whom he had formed."

Cain was removed from the presence of the Adamites and was placed in the vicinity of the Garden of Eden. He also had a son named Enoch. He built a city and named it after his son. If we analyze what is recorded in the creation account of Genesis, we can come to the conclusion that the Enochian language and the famous Book of Enoch describe events and occurrences that took place in the city that Cain built. The city that Cain built is what the Arabs call "Irem Zhat al Imad." Parker Ryan makes the following observation:

**"Irem Zhat al Imad" (Irem of the Pillars) is the cities name in Arabic. It is popularly believed by the Arabs that Irem was built by the Jinn under the direction of Shaddad, Lord of the tribe of Ad. The tribe of Ad, according to legend, was a race roughly equivalent to the Hebrew "Nephlim" (giants). In some version of this myth Shaddad and the Jinn built Irem before the time of Adam. The Muqarribun (Arab magicians) have important beliefs about Irem and it's significance....The Muqarribun, whose traditions predate Islam, believe that Irem is a locale on another level of reality, rather than a physical city like NY or Tokyo. (Why Irem is important to the Muqarribun and how they use it will be more fully explained shortly.) The "Pillars" in "Irem of the Pillars" has a hidden meaning. Among Arab mystics pillar is a code name for "elder" or "old one." Thus "Irem of the Pillars" is really "Irem of the Old Ones."**

Kenneth Grant in his work, *The Nightside of Eden,* mentions that the City of Irem is the Garden of Eden. Regardless of where these *"mysterious cities"* are said to exist, such as Enoch, Irem, and etc, we can definitely say that there is a world that exists alongside the world of mankind. There is something else we need to take into consideration first. Genesis 3:15 states:

"And I will put enmity between thee and the woman, and between thy seed and her seed; it shall bruise thy head, and thou shalt bruise his heel."

The Biblical text suggests that the Jinn are cursed and will eventually be annihilated. However, this assertion seems to be a calculated response by the ancient monotheistic religions to plunder the Jinn and their progeny. L.A. Waddell mentions this in the *British Edda:*

"Indeed, the selfsame confusion occurs also in the Egyptian myth, wherein the Semitic priests of the Nile Valley degraded the original pure Sun-worship of Asar or "Osiris" (the Sumerian Asari title of King Dur or Tur) by deliberately introducing into it the Serpent and animal sacrificial cult of their own debased aboriginal Egyptian Mother-Son creed, which was essentially similar to the pre-Adamite Chaldean."

Although Waddell's observations are somewhat bigoted, he does verify the existence of the *"pre-Adamite Chaldean."* The customs and rites of the "aboriginal Chaldeans" were demonized by the monotheistic religions. Waddell also asserts that the Mother-Son creed existed before the creation of Adam. Therefore, the enmity between the woman's seed and the serpent, mentioned in Genesis, is symbolic of the war between the Jinn and mankind. Waddell continues on page 73:

"Before the advent of Adam Thor and his Sun-cult, the chief religion in the old world appears to have been devil worship of the Serpent and Wolf cult, with its headship in the matriarch priestess Eldi…"

Waddell later confirms that his matriarch priestess Eldi was also known as the goddess El. It is no coincidence that many angelic names end with *"el,"* as they are of the race of Jinn and keepers of the Moon-Serpent Cult. Waddell also defines *"El"* as a powerful witch, a dark magician that is *"naturally gifted with occult powers."* Those who are naturally gifted with occult powers are those who partake in the *natures of both parents,* jinn and human, as cited earlier in the Dictionary of Islam.

We can also see resistance to the Moon-Serpent cult's teachings in the Biblical history of Jesus. Jesus was conceived of Jinn-human relations and taught a rite that was Sumerian in origin. Evidence of this is found in his parable of the Good Samaritan. According to 2 Kings Chapter 17, Samaritans were worshippers of the god Nergal.

When one carefully observes Biblical lore, it seems that there were other religious rites that existed in Israel, which were not recorded in the Bible. For example, shortly after leaving Egypt the Israelites were said to have made a *golden calf* while Moses was receiving the Law. Centuries later, it is recorded in Ezekiel that the Prophet witnessed women weeping for the Babylonian god Tammuz, who was the consort of the goddess depicted as the golden calf during the days of Moses. Evidently, the Israelites weren't constantly turning to the worship of false gods, as claimed throughout the Biblical text, since there has never been a record of any indigenous people who abandoned the worship that their ancestors laid down, so often. It seems more probable that the Bible writers excluded the full history of the religious rites that existed in ancient Israel in an effort to make a particular "priesthood" and its god appear to be superior.

The customs and traditions of the Jinn and their progeny have been demonized by the monotheistic religions of the world today. Waddell continues in the British Edda on page 175:

**"The Matriarch El and her son Abel of The Garden of Eden...feverishly mustered all their swarms and allied hordes...for an overwhelming attack upon King Adam and his Goths...This epoch making battle was the greatest of all battles in the world, as judged by its far-reaching effects; for it led to the political supremacy of Adam's Higher Civilization, and its free propagation over the world –to its immediate extension to Carchemish or Eden, and thence down Mesopotamia to the Persian Gulf within a very short period.."**

Waddell described a battle that occurred between the "aboriginal Chaldeans," who are described as "serpent worshippers," and the invading Sun cult. It seems that these "aboriginal Chaldeans," led by the matriarch EL, were keepers of the traditions that the Jinn had worked so hard to establish, and some of these may have been Jinn themselves. Waddell mentions, in other writings, that the invading Sun cults captured a "stone-bowl," in their war with the "aboriginal Chaldeans." This stone-bowl was the central fetish of the magical rites in relationship to the pre-Adamic race. This bowl was the formulae that opened up a gate, whereby, the sorcerer could communicate with the elders of the parallel world, and benefit from the wisdom contained therein. However, there is another element that prevented the "aboriginal Chaldeans" from opening up this window and communicating with their ancestors, Christianity.

Christians are involved in a spiritual war, whether they realize it or not. Christianity, as we know it today, was developed by the Council of Nicea in 325 A.D. and continued the tradition mentioned by Waddell in their persecution of the aboriginal Chaldeans. *Egyptian Belief and Modern Thought* by James Bonwick page 182:

**"Constatine, a sun-worshipper,, who had, as other heathens, kept the Sun-day, publicly ordered this to supplant the Jewish Sabbath. To make matters worse, the Church, at an early date, selected the heathen festivals of sun-worship for its own."**

The Christian Church was founded upon the principle structure of ancient Sun worship. Regardless of what domination that exists today, all Christian religions are guilty of honoring the Sun as a symbol of the Christ. The Christian doctrine and the epistles of the Apostle Paul are not inspired scripture, but essays concerning the worship of the Sun. The ignorant are unaware of this fact, and regardless of how many holidays, or perspectives these varying dominations of Christianity insist upon, its makes no difference at all. The only way that Christianity can separate itself from its heathen origins is by rewriting the New Testament.

There is a much deeper aspect involved in the customs and rituals of Christianity that are an apparent attack against the world of the Jinn and their progeny. The Christian Bible contains over four-hundred references to the word "wicked." Throughout its seeming righteous damnation of the *"wicked,"* through prayers, scriptural texts, and etc, the naïve Christian is unaware, along with most monotheistic disciples, that the term *"wicked"* originated from the word *wizard,* or *sorcerer.* This means that on any given day, there are hundreds of millions of Christians pronouncing judgments against sorcerers and witches by their use of certain prayers and recitation of various scriptural texts. This is how the ancient Adamites were able to keep the doors of reality shut in regards to the Jinn. These practices were later adapted by the early leaders of the Christian Church. It is for this very same reason that we find many areas of the world, where the ancient shamanistic rites, so dear to the "pre-Adamite" tradition flourish, are also the same areas where extreme poverty and natural disasters occur. However, the doctrine of Christianity with all its hypocritical dogma, followers, and leaders, is soon to end. The Overlan Monthly printed an article in 1910 A.D. entitled God's Chosen People; states the following on page 543:

**"These beasts are to rule the world until the end of Gentile times of world domination, October, 1914, which will also be the end of the Jewish times of Divine disfavor...The Prophet pictures the end of Gentile times and the manifestation of the Ancient of Days, whose throne was like a fiery flame..,"**

Regardless of the use of ancient divination to keep the door to the world of the Jinn closed, it will serve them no good. The Jinn, in the Arab world and the Necronomicon Tradition, are called "those of fire." We find in Christian doctrine that the "Ancient of Days' is described as seated on a *"fiery throne."*

The year 1914 was a significant year not only to Christian cultists, but human society in general with the inception of World War 1. The events that followed align perfectly with Lovecraft's description of Cthulhu rising:

**"That cult would never die till the stars came right again, and the secret priests would take great Cthulhu from His tomb to revive His subjects and resume His**

rule of earth. The time would be easy to know, for then mankind would have become as the Great Old Ones; free and wild and beyond good and evil, with laws and morals thrown aside and all men shouting and killing and revelling in joy. Then the liberated Old Ones would teach them new ways to shout and kill and revel and enjoy themselves, and all the earth would flame with a holocaust of ecstasy and freedom. Meanwhile the cult, by appropriate rites, must keep alive the memory of those ancient ways and shadow forth the prophecy of their return."

The Simon Necronomicon properly aligns the powers of the Ancient Ones, also known as the Jinn, with TIAMAT. It is here that we see the reality and meaning of the events that occurred in 1914. TIAMAT is the primordial aspect of the goddess INANNA/ISHTAR, whose sacred number has been *"15"* from times memorable. *The Mystery of Numbers* by Annemarie Schimmel, makes the following observation on pages 213, 215:

"Fifteen represents the zenith of lunar power..Fifteen was a sacred number to Ishtar, perhaps derived from the more important Ishtar-number, 5, perhaps also because it forms 1/4 of the 60, the number of the highest god in Babylonia. Ancient Niniveh, the city devoted to Ishtar, had 15 gates,...The Old Testament counts the generations of Israel between Abraham and Solomon as 15, and from Solomon to Zedekiah again as 15. .Fifteen plays an important role in one of the most common magical squares, which built around, the sacred 5, always offers 15 as a sum. Although legend attributes a Chinese origin to this square, it was known in Babylonia where it was connected with Ishtar. Combined with the star of Ishtar, with its 8 beams, the diagonals always add up to 15."

When we look at the year 1914, we also see that it is the year of TIAMAT's rising, and so it is marked appropriately as the year of Ishtar's return. $1 + 9 + 1 + 4 = 15$. The Gate of Communion has been opened once again, and the matriarch EL, is seeking to find her children, as we have seen a decline in Christianity since the year 1914 and an increase in those who practice the occult arts.

In a very short time, those who are of Jinn-human progeny, as well as others initiated into the "pre-Adamic" ways of the Jinn, will enjoy a return to full goodness and power and sit on thrones amongst the kingdoms of men.

The Necronomicon Tradition, as found in the works of Lovecraft and the Simon Necronomicon, are stellar systems that were established before the race of Adam, or the "sons of Marduk" and are thereby known as the *Atlantean Mysteries*. These workings are called Qliphotic by many occultists, but we find this system to be a cosmological treaty pertaining to the world of the Jinn. Simon states the following in the Necronomicon:

**"The method of the NECRONOMICON concerns deep, primeval forces that seem to pre-exist the normal archetypal images of the tarot trumps and the Golden Dawn telesmatic figures. These are forces that developed outside the Judeo-Christian mainstream, and were worshipped and summoned long before the creation of the Qabala as we know it today. Hence, the ineffectiveness of the Golden Dawn banishing procedures against them. They are not necessarily demonic or qliphotic in the sense that these terms are commonly understood in the West, they just simply represent power sources largely untapped and thus far**

**ignored by twentieth-century, mainstream consciousness."**

The Necronomicon Tradition has been veiled in secrecy before the race of Adam was created, and still many of us who are of Jinn-human progeny cannot reveal our dual heritage publicly. It is not so strange to our ears to know that one of our parents were possessed during the time of conception, or we may have entered the shell of the embryo from the world that lies beyond time and space, as we attempt to recollect the meaning of our heritage. It is not an easy path to follow. If you want to be effective in this work, then maximize the system to its fullest capabilities. I have seen people jump from one thing to the next, but the mastery comes in the perfection of a craft, not in the paranormal effects that a working can create. The system is one that reveals our heritage, but it is also one that initiates us into the workings of the chthonic mind. Know thyself!

In the oral teachings of the Necronomicon Tradition it is said that *'the Race from Beyond the Stars'* is Tiamat, and that the Jinn are engaged in the divine work of awakening their Mother. When the Initiate begins to understand this they become aware of the benevolent aspects of the Dark Mysteries. Let us examine this a little further.

When we look at the phenomenal world around us and all its beauty, we can see that it was created by the divine source with care and love. Many of the things attributed to the physical body teach us that we were made not simply to live but to enjoy life. It is no coincidence that the Fall of Man is synonymous with the time that it is said that god rested. Basically, there are some among humankind who collectively make up this creative entity called god, and as these individuals grow in awareness, they appreciate more and more that the world will continue to run amuck until the Ancient Ones take their thrones again to rule. The relationship that we have with the Elder Gods is one of love, as they nurture us in understanding of who we are and wait patiently for the time that is described best by the words of the Mad Arab:

*"..for the Race of Draconis was ever powerful in ancient times, when the first temples were built in MAGAN, and they drew down much strength from the stars, but now they are as Wanderers of the Wastelands, and dwell in caves and in deserts, and in all lonely places where they have set up stones. And these I have seen, in my journeys through those areas where the ancient cults once flourished, and where now there is only sadness and desolation."*

In view of our present discussion, we can see that this process of harnessing energy from the stars is starting to unfold once again, as many are taking part in the Necronomicon Tradition:

*"Know that TIAMAT seeks ever to rise to the stars, and when the Upper is united to the Lower, then a new Age will come of Earth, and the Serpent shall be made whole, and the Waters will be as One, when on high the heavens had not been named."*

The perspective of the Adept in the Necronomicon Tradition is one of self-responsibility. When we realize that the condition of the world will change when we rise, then we have a responsibility to correct and perfect the environment around us. This is not an easy work and only can be executed by perfecting our inner self. This is our destiny and for those of us who believe that information is to be spoon-fed to them and not seek out for themselves the knowledge and wisdom, are in for a rude awakening. Notice what is written in the Magan Text:

*"But Man possesses the Sign*
*And the Number*
*And the Shape*
*To summon the Blood of his Parents.*
*And this is the Covenant.*
*Created by the Elder Gods*
*From the Blood of the Ancient Ones*
*Man is the Key by which*
*The Gate if IAK SAKKAK may be flung wide*
*By which the Ancient Ones*
*Seek their Vengeance*
*Upon the face of the Earth*
*Against the Offspring of MARDUK.*
*For what is new*
*Came from that which is old*
*And what is old*
*Shall replace that which is new*
*And once again the Ancient Ones*
*Shall rule upon the face of the Earth!*
*And this is too the Covenant!"*

This Tradition is not about ritual. Anyone can perform the incantations in the tome. It is about our personal relationship that we have with the Ancient Ones. Develop a relationship with the same forces that are guiding you, and are a part of your true being, instead of looking to do a simple ritual. When I first began Gate-Walking, I took a little time each day to research various aspects of the DinGir. At other times, I would reflect on some of the amazing experiences I had in order to understand the specific nature of the said gate deity. I would also research the customs and manners of how these same deities were entreated in ancient times. I looked up some of their correspondences that applied to animals, minerals, and plants. I also saw relationships between the ancient Sumerian mythologies and astrological movements and events. It takes work, but through these methods other doors would open up. I would receive epiphanies from the DinGir concerning the information that I had gathered in the past. Yet I have seen people in the occult community who are so selfish, seeking only to take the easy way out. They seek to gain your understanding by simply studying conclusions and can't understand how you are able to divine the deeper things about the deity. This is because they have no passion in their approach and cannot feel the presence of the deities, much less hear their words. The Necronomicon Tradition is a uniquely powerful system, but in order for the energies to become your own, you have to validate what is written in it.

# The Resurrection of a Goddess

In the Fall of Christianity article, we discussed the legacy of those who are of jinn-human progeny, also known as the Ishtar-Class. What is interesting about all of this is that Dingir Ishtar relates to Tiamat in the same manner as Jesus is said to relate to the "heavenly Father." Historically, the account of Ishtar's descent and crucifixion takes place thousands of years before Jesus is said to have existed. In the Simon Necronomicon's Introduction, we find the following under the subheading, *Goddess of the Witches*:

"**But what of INANNA, the single planetary deity having a female manifestation among the Sumerians? She is invoked in the NECRONOMICON and identified as the vanquisher of Death, for she descended into the Underworld and defeated her sister, the Goddess of the Abyss, Queen ERESHKIGAL (possibly another name for TIAMAT). Interestingly enough, the myth has many parallels with the Christian concept of Christ's death and resurrection, among which the Crucifixion (INANNA was impaled on a stake as a corpse), the three days in the Sumerian Hades, and the eventual Resurrection are outstanding examples of how Sumerian mythology previewed the Christian religion by perhaps as many as three thousand years - a fact that beautifully illustrates the cosmic and eternal nature of this myth. ..Therefore, the Goddess of the Witches has two distinct forms: the Ancient One, Goddess of the Dragon-like telluric Power which is raised in Magickal rituals, and the Elder Goddess, Defeater of Death, who brings the promise of Resurrection and Rejuvenation to her followers those who must reside for a time after death**

**and between incarnations in what is called the
"Summerland"."**

In the oral teachings of the Necronomicon Tradition, it is
said that '*the Race from Beyond the Stars*' is Tiamat, and
that the Jinn are engaged in the divine work of
awakening their Mother. When the Initiate understands
this they become aware of the benevolent aspects of the
Dark Mysteries. Let us examine this a little further.

When we look at the phenomenal world around us and
all its beauty, we can see that it was created by the divine
source with care and love. Many of the things attributed
to the physical body teach us that we were made not
simply to live but to enjoy life. It is no coincidence that
the Fall of Man is synonymous with the time that it is
said that god rested. Basically, there are some among
humankind who collectively make up this creative entity
called god, and as these individuals grow in awareness,
they come to appreciate more and more that the world
will continue to run amuck until the Ancient Ones take
their thrones again to rule. The relationship that we have
with the Elder Gods is one of love, as they nurture us in
understanding what we are and wait patiently for the
time that is described best by the words of the Mad Arab:

*"..for the Race of Draconis was ever powerful in ancient
times, when the first temples were built in MAGAN, and
they drew down much strength from the stars, but now
they are as Wanderers of the Wastelands, and dwell in
caves and in deserts, and in all lonely places where they
have set up stones...And these I have seen, in my
journeys through those areas where the ancient cults
once flourished, and where now there is only sadness and
desolation."*

In view of our present discussion, we can see that this process of harnessing energy from the stars is starting to unfold once again, as many are taking part in the Necronomicon Tradition:

*"Know that TIAMAT seeks ever to rise to the stars, and when the Upper is united to the Lower, then a new Age will come of Earth, and the Serpent shall be made whole, and the Waters will be as One, when on high the heavens had not been named."*

The perspective of the Adept in the Necronomicon Tradition is one of self-responsibility. When we realize that the condition of the world will change only when we rise up. We are entrusted with a responsibility to correct and perfect the environment around us. This is not an easy work and only can be executed by perfecting our inner self. This is our destiny. For those of us who believe that information is to be spoon-fed to them and not seek out for themselves the knowledge and wisdom, are in for a rude awakening. Notice what is written in the Magan Text:

*"But Man possesses the Sign*
*And the Number*
*And the Shape*
*To summon the Blood of his Parents.*
*And this is the Covenant.*
*Created by the Elder Gods*
*From the Blood of the Ancient Ones*
*Man is the Key by which*
*The Gate if IAK SAKKAK may be flung wide*
*By which the Ancient Ones*
*Seek their Vengeance*
*Upon the face of the Earth*
*Against the Offspring of MARDUK.*
*For what is new*

*Came from that which is old
And what is old
Shall replace that which is new
And once again the Ancient Ones
Shall rule upon the face of the Earth!
And this is too the Covenant!""*

This Tradition is not about ritual. Anyone can perform the incantations found in a tome. It is about our personal relationship that we have with the Ancient Ones. Develop a relationship with the same forces that are guiding you, and are a part of your true being, instead of looking to do a simple ritual. When I first began Gate-Walking, I took a little time each day to research various aspects of the DinGir. At other times, I would reflect on some of the amazing experiences I had in order to understand the specific nature of the said gate deity. I would also research the customs and manners of how these same deities were entreated in ancient times. I looked up some of their correspondences that applied to animals, minerals, and plants. I also saw relationships between the ancient Sumerian mythologies and astrological movements and events. It takes work, but through these methods other doors would open up. I would receive epiphanies from the DinGir concerning the information that I had gathered in the past. Yet I have seen people in the occult community who are so selfish, seeking only to take the easy way out. They seek to gain your understanding by simply studying conclusions and can't understand how you are able to divine the deeper things about the deity. This is because they have no passion in their approach and cannot feel the presence of the deities, much less hear their words. The Necronomicon Tradition is a uniquely powerful system, but in order for the energies to become your own, you have to validate what is written in it.

# Origin of the Necronomicon Term IA MASS SSARATU

Over the years, I have seen many newcomers stumbling across some of the terminology that appears in the Simon Necronomicon. Of course, the idea of pronouncing words that are foreign to our native tongue can be a challenge. We usually suggest that the new Initiate would do well to get acquainted with a Sumerian lexicon and other resources available on ancient Mesopotamian languages. With some time and effort pronunciation of the words and phrases becomes easier and easier.

There is one thing, however, that seems to present a problem for a few Gate-Walkers, and this is not about understanding the meaning of some of the Necronomicon Tradition's terminology. Some Initiates are under the hypothesis that many of the terms used in the Simon Necronomicon are made up, as some sort of blasphemous tongue and this is simply not the case. Today, we will discuss the term *IA MASS SSARATU*.

In the Simon Necronomicon's section entitled, *The Conjuration of the Watcher*, we find the following:

*"Wherefore it is wise to conjure It in the Names of the Three Great Watchers Who existed before the Confrontation from whose borne the Watcher and His Race ultimately derive, and those Three are ANU, ENLIL, and Master ENKI of the Magick Waters. And for this reason They are sometimes called the Three Watchers, MASS SSARATI and the Watcher MASS SSARATU, or KIA MASS SSARATU."*

Later we read:

*"When the time has come to summon the Watcher the first time, the place of thy calling must be clean, and a double circle of flour drawn about thee. And there should be no altar, but only the new Bowl with the three carven signs on it. And the Conjuration of the Fire should be made, and the sacrifices heaped thereupon, into the burning bowl. And the Bowl is now called AGA MASS SSARATU, and to be used for no other purpose, save to invoke the Watcher."*

When I first stumbled upon the Simon Necronomicon, I had no idea what the term *"MASS SSARATU"* meant, but it seemed like the word may have been translated with a different spelling than the one that appears in the Simon Necronomicon. I say this because over the years I have discovered that the Simon Necronomicon presents certain words in a way that it is easier to pronounce them correctly, and sometimes what appears to be two words could actually be one and vice versa. Famous scholar and Mesopotamian researcher Leonard William King in his work *First Steps In Assyrian,* gives us one rendering of the term *"MASS SSARATU"* on page 370:, where he tells us that the term *"massartu"* means *" to watch."*

In my research, I stumbled upon this word again, in an online article appearing in the Jewish Encyclopedia under the subheading *astronomy* we find:

**"etymologically referred to the Assyrian "massartu" (Babylonian "mazzartu"), a place where something is watched. But it is just as likely to be, as tradition already has it, a variation of "mazzalot" ( II Kings xxiii. 5) — a word also of uncertain meaning, varying as its**

explanations do between "planets," "constellations of the zodiac," and "stations of the moon."

From the above description we find that the Assyrian word *"massartu"* is where the Necronomicon term *MASS SSARATU* finds its origin. We are now clear that the Necronomicon term *MASS SSARATU* does have an authentic origin, which is found in the Assyrian term *"massartu,"* or the Babylonian *"mazzartu,"* which means *"watch."* However, it should also be noted, especially by those who care whether or not a slight phonetic change would affect the meaning of the term-that the Babylonian *massaratu,* is consistent with the lingustic structure of the said term appearing in the Simon Necronomicon as *MASS SSARATU,* means to *actively watch.* Francesca Rochberg makes the following observation in *Babylonian Horoscopes*:

**"(*massaratu*): EN.NUN AN. ... The *watches* of the night comprise the earliest system of "telling time" attested in *Babylonian* texts..."**

Here we find, according to Rochberg, that the Simon Necronomicon's term MASS SSARATU is phonetically correct, as it comes from the Babylonian verb *massaratu,* which can be defined as the act of watching. Now that we have validated that the term "MASS SSARATU" is indeed of ancient Mesopotamian origin, let us see if this term was used in the same way as it is described in the Simon Necronomicon. *Theological Dictionary of the Old Testament-Volume 12,* states the following on pages 431-433:

**"The sentinal goes to an elevated location...to observe (a) the surrounding area, and report important occurrences, e.g., the approach of enemies or**

messengers...These two primary tasks are described with stereotypical terminology. The activity of looking or watching is rendered as "(raise one's eyes and) see" ...and the transission of the message with ...."speak, call out, report"...Secular sentinals provide the model for understanding prophetic tasks...Hab 2:1 uses the sentinel topos to describe the prophetic reception of revelation...The prophet goes to and elevated location, ("watchpost, lookout post,"..) to recieve the divine revelation...Whereas most exegetes understand such descriptions of a "reception of revelation on the outlook post" in a psychological or metaphorical sense, Jeremias finds in them evidence of prophets who used certain techniques when recieving revelations and were closely associated with the temple. The place to which the prophet went at such times "Is described by an Assyrian loanword (*massartu*, "guard, sentry, garrison") that was originally a technical term referring to the place where Assyrian bird-watchers and astrologers practiced their craft within the holy precinct; the accompanying verb (*nasaru*) already refers in a Mari letter to the prophetic reception of revelation.."

The information cited above shows us that long before the Simon Necronomicon was ever published the idea of using a *"sentinel,"* or *"Watcher"* in mystical and prophetic practices had long been established by the nation of Israel, who, more than likely received such a formulae from the Babylonians based on the fact they used the Assyrian loanword *massartu* in a metaphorical sense. The fact that the ancient Peoples of Mesopotamia were well aware of the "magical" use of a Watcher can be confirmed in the Annals of Ashurbamipal, where we find the following:

**"I threw down the bull-colossi and the guardian *gods* and all the other *watchers* of the temple,"**

Here we see in the King's writings that he too associated "guardian gods" with "watchers of the temple." This clearly shows us once again that the Simon Necronomicon was written with a very deep understanding of the mystical practices that existed in ancient Mesopotamia. The use of the Watcher for divination also existed in ancient Egypt. Bud Carroll in the classic work *The Materialistic Wall* states the following on page 135:

**"At the beginning of the Egyptian empire, what the Egyptians call the "First Time," there were intermediaries between humans and the gods known as the "*Watchers*." They were the *Neteru*, beautiful godlike beings with supernatural powers that could manifest wherever and whenever they wished."**

This seems to unlock yet another mystery about the Watcher. The Simon Necronomicon mentions that the *"Lord of the Watchers"* dwells in the realms of the Igigi, which is the zodiac. It is with this information that we can determine that the Watchers are the Igigi, or the zodiac. Now that we have discovered the antiquity of the term *"MASS SSARATU"* let us now look at the term *IA*.

According to L. A. Waddell the definition of the term *IA* as it is used in the Simon Necronomicon, appears on page 92 of his famous, but bigoted work *The Makers of Civilization is Race and History*:

**"The god Sagg (Sakh, or In-dur, whose name also reads IA, the source of JAH, or" Father Ju " or Ju-piter or Jove, borrowed by the Hebrews as Yahwe or " Jehovah "). For**

**the prefixed title Ash (or An ) for : Lord : or "King" tends in this Bowl inscription and hereafter in Sumerian and Babylonian inscriptions and literature to have the sense of " God " as well as of " Lord."**

The above quote clearly indicates that the term *IA* means *god* or *lord*. We have already covered evidence of a Sumerian Egyptian connection and we must keep this in mind as Waddell also relates, in the work cited above, that *IA* is also known under the phonetic *IAH*. This is a point that should not be taken lightly. In the Simon Necronomicon's Chart of Comparisons we find that *IA* is a title of Enki, or Ea, which is different from some of the conclusions given by Waddell:

*(showing some relationships to be found between the mythos of Lovecraft, the magick of Crowley, and the faith of Sumer.)*

| Lovecraft | Crowley | Sumer |
|---|---|---|
| Cthulhu | The Great Beast as represented in "CTHDH 666" | Ctha-lu, Kutulu |
| The Ancient Ones | Satan; Teitan | Tiamat |
| Azathoth | Aiwass (?) | Azag-thoth |
| The Dunwich Horror | Choronzon | Pazuzu |
| Shub Niggurath | Pan | Sub Ishniggarab (?) |

| Out of Space | The Abyss | Absu; Nar Mattaru |
|---|---|---|
| IA! | IO! IAO! | IA (JAH; EA; Lord of Waters) |
| The Five-pointed grey Star carven | The Pentagram | The AR, or UB (Plough Sign; the original pentagram and the sign of the Aryan Race) |
| Vermis Mysteriis | The Serpent | Erim (the Enemy; and the Sea as Chaos; Gothic; Orm, or Worm, great Serpent) |

There is a part of Egyptian history that has not been readily discussed that may help us understand all of this is proven in ancient history. I would like to direct the reader to a Wikipedia article that describes the Egyptian Moon god Iah:

"**Iah is a god of the moon in ancient Egyptian religion, and his name,..(sometimes transliterated as Yah, Jah, or Aah), simply means "moon". Nevertheless, by the New Kingdom he was less prominent as a moon deity than the other gods with lunar connections, Thoth and Khonsu. Because of the functional connection between them, he could be identified with both of those deities.....Iah was also assimilated with Osiris, god of the dead, perhaps because, in its monthly cycle, the moon appears to renew itself. Iah also seems to have assumed the lunar aspect of Thoth, god of knowledge,** writing and calculation; the segments of the moon were used as fractional symbols in writing."

Now that we know that *IAH* is relative to the Egyptian deity Thoth, we can easily see how it connects to DinGir Enki. Enki corresponds to the Egyptian deity Thoth. They are both Mercurial. Revelation of the Holy Grail, states on page 55:

"In fact, the Vatican itself is now located on the ruins of an ancient Mithraic temple. Rome also had the god Mercury, who played a role identical to Hermes, *Thoth*, *Enki*, and Merlin, as a messenger and keeper of secrets."

In view of our discussion we can appropriately define the term *IA MASS SSARATU* as a *Watcher of Enki*.

# Conjuration of the Watcher

One of the most seldom topics discussed in the world of occult studies is information pertinent to the Watcher. We find evidence of the Watcher's existence long before the publication of the Simon Necronomicon. In the famous myth, Inanna's Descent into the Netherworld, Inanna is noted as giving instructions to her minister, or Watcher, as to what actions, he/she, should take after a certain amount of time during her visit to the Underworld. There are other mythologies of Sumerian origin where we find Enki instructing his vizier, or Watcher. In the Biblical Book of Daniel, an Aramaic term used to denote angels is "watchers" (ʿîrîn). The term "watcher" probably derives from the verb "to be awake" or "to be vigilant," so that the implication of calling the angels "watchers" is that they are constantly on watch as sentinels for a deity. We can say then that the idea of having a "Watcher" is very ancient. However, the Initiate of the Necronomicon Tradition may wonder what is the Watcher according to our spiritual path? A close examination of the Simon Necronomicon may reveal this for us.

In the Simon Necronomicon's Introduction, under the subheading *Prefatory Notes*, we find this statement about the Watcher:

**"The "Conjuration of the Watcher" follows the Fire God conjuration. The word "watcher" is sometimes used synonymously with "angel", and sometimes as a distinct Race, apart from angelos: egragori. The Race of Watchers are said not to care what they Watch, save that they follow orders. They are somewhat mindless**

creatures, but quite effective. Perhaps they correspond too Lovecraft's shuggoths, save that the latter become unweildly and difficult to manage."

The above statement seems to agree with the information that we discussed so far. Yes, the Watcher is like an angel. It is also suggested that they correspond to Lovecraft's shuggoths. Wikipedia gives us the following history of the *shuggoth:*

"The shoggoths were created by the Elder Things as living bioengineered construction equipment. Being amorphous, they could take on any shape needed, making them very versatile within their aquatic environment. Though able to "understand" the Elder Things' language, they had no real consciousness and were controlled through hypnotic suggestion....The shoggoths built the underwater cities of their masters. Over millions of years of existence, some shoggoths mutated and gained independent minds. Some time after this, they rebelled. Eventually, the Elder Things succeeded in quelling the insurrection, but thereafter watched them more carefully. By this point, exterminating them was not an option as the Elder Things were fully dependent on them for labor and could not replace them. It was during this time that, despite their masters' wishes, they demonstrated an ability to survive on land....Within the Mythos, the existence of the shoggoths possibly led to the accidental creation of Ubbo-Sathla, a god-like entity supposedly responsible for the origin of all life on Earth, though *At The Mountains of Madness* brings up the possibility of the Elder Things being the creators, having made early life as discarded experiments in bioengineering."

Similar to the Watcher, mentioned in the Simon Necronomicon, the *"shuggoths"* were considered to be mindless creatures when they were first created and then rebelled against the Elder Things. This is similar to what we are told about the Watcher in the Simon Necronomicon:

*"The third sign is the Sigil of the Watcher. It is called BANDAR. The Watcher is a Race sent by the Elder Ones. It keeps vigil while one sleeps, provided the appropriate ritual and sacrifice has been performed,: else, if called, it will turn upon you. These seals, to be effective, must be graven on stone and set in the ground. Or, set upon the altar of offerings. Or, carried to the Rock of Invocations. Or, engraved on the metal of one's God or Goddess, and hung about the neck, but hidden from the view of the profane. Of the three, the ARRA and the AGGA may be used separately, that is to say, singly and alone. The BANDAR, however, must never be used alone, but with one or both of the others, for the Watcher must needs be reminded of the Covenant it has sworn with the Elder Gods and our Race, else it will turn upon thee and slay thee and ravage thy town until succour is to be had from the Elder Gods by the tears of thy people and the wailing of thy women."*

We can clearly see from the Mad Arab's words that the Watcher can turn on the Initiate if it is invoke "singly and alone." This seems to indicate that the Watcher is not really an angelic force, but a force that is working out some sort of "karma" as it needs to be reminded of the Covenant it has sworn with the Elder Gods during its invocation. If we recount the Mad Arab's experience in how he came to possess this knowledge and initiation, it was due to his understanding of one word, KUTULU.

# The Watcher-Self

The Simon Necronomicon describes the Race of Watchers in the following words:

*"The Watcher comes from a Race different from that of Men and yet different from that of the Gods, and it is said that he was with KINGU and his hordes at the time of the War between the Worlds, but was dissatisfied and did cleave unto the Armies of Lord MARDUK."*

In mythologies about Queen ERESHKIGAL, we discover something that has been overlooked by scholars for quite some time. The myth tells us how ERESHKIGAL became the Queen of the Underworld. We can see what her feelings were and how she left her two brothers, ENKI and ENLIL. It is from the ancient *Myth of ERESHKIGAL* that we read the following words:

**"a fleeting shadow crossed ENLIL's smiling face. 'I wish I saw things your way ERESHKIGAL...Take Kur for example, and our dark little brothers and sisters who followed him to the land's end. It is true that Kur and the others looked different than us. But why did they leave the safety of the Duku, the mound of creation, why did they go beyond the waters of Mother Nammu?"**

The above passage indicates that ENLIL and ENKI were not the Old Gods, but the 'dark brothers' who left with Kur were. Kur was also considered the Underworld Ocean and the Abyss. The "dark brothers" were those who dwelt in the Abyss after leaving DuKu. Don Juan Cardoza stated the following, in his online article entitled, *Lilith*:

**"In Ancient Sumerian belief, the primal gods, the ZU, originally emerged from the great Chaos of the Abyss. This Chaos was characterized as an endless sea located in the heavens (NAMMU or TIAMAT). The primal gods were called the Abzu (Apsu) or stellar powers connected to the Great Deep. Their servitors who carried out their will were called An-Zu, lunar powers that were connected with the air or night sky. Primary among these were the Abgal."**

This is a very fascinating observation made by Cardoza. We discover here that there were older gods or 'dark brothers' who did not have the same appearance, or live in the same place as the Elder Gods. A review of the history of PAZUZU will shed some light on the observations made by Cardoza about the ZU.

Not much is known about PAZUZU, but we do know that he is sometimes called ZU, and that he moves with stealth and can change in form, sometimes appearing as an Anzu Bird. He is the king of the wind demons. If we compare this information with what is written about PAZUZU in the Magan Text, we get a clear picture about the Race of the Watcher. We have seen in the words of Cardoza, cited earlier, that the primal gods were called the ZU. This would indicate that PAZUZU and his kind were the original gods during the prehistoric era, as they seem to reflect the *Atlantean Period,* which the race of ANU is associated with as well. Their appearance is also different to that of the Elder Gods, as mentioned in the Myth of ERESHKIGAL. In some myths, ERESHKIGAL is said to have gone forth into the realms of Kur on her own accord. In other myths, she is stolen by Kur and brought to the Underworld. ENKI later tried to rescue her, but failed. ENKI struck the god Absu in the Enuma Elish maybe as an act of revenge for kidnapping

ERESHKIGAL. Most of the ancient myths concerning Ereshkigal seem to imply that ERESHKIGAL left on her own free will. It seems that after Kur was struck, the Watchers battled alongside Kingu, but were defeated and became subject to the authority of the Elder Gods. Anzu birds were often depicted as deceptive in Sumerian legend because they were the original gods that had been made subject to the Elder Gods. This is similar to how Marduk was promoted as the head of the Babylonian pantheon by priests who saw the need to compose the Enuma Elish. Evidence of this can be seen in the myth of *ISHTAR and the Huluppu Tree*. This account describes the original occupants of the "tree" as Lilith (LAMASHTU), an Anzu Bird (PAZUZU), and the serpent. Legend has it that with the aid of Gilgamesh, ISHTAR was able to set up her throne in the Huluppu Tree, and Lilith, the Anzu Bird, and the "serpent" were forced to flee into the wilderness. Lilith is an archetype of the Atlantean Goddess, LAMASHTU.. The Huluppu Tree Myth reveals the primordial rites that existed before the advent of the solar gods, which Gilgamesh's presence in the myth indicates. Interestingly, this transition must have made worldwide news in the ancient world because elements of the *Huluppu Tree Myth* are contained in the book of Revelation Chapter 12:

**"Now a great sign appeared in heaven: a woman clothed with the sun, with the moon under her feet, and on her head a garland of twelve stars. 2 Then being with child, she cried out in labor and in pain to give birth. 3 And another sign appeared in heaven: behold, a great, fiery red dragon having seven heads and ten horns, and seven diadems on his heads. 4 His tail drew a third of the stars of heaven and threw them to the earth. And the dragon stood before the woman who was ready to give birth, to devour her Child as soon as it was born. 5 She bore a male Child who was to rule all nations with**

a rod of iron. And her Child was caught up to God and His throne. 6 Then the woman fled into the wilderness, where she has a place prepared by God that they should feed her there one thousand two hundred and sixty days."

ISHTAR and the Huluppu Tree:

"The tree grew big, its trunk bore no foliage,
In its roots the snake who knows no charm set up its nest,
In its crown the Imdugud-bird placed its young,
In its midst the maid Lilith built her house –
The always laughing, always rejoicing maid,
I, the maid INANNA, how I weeped
Her brother, the hero Gilgamesh,
Stood by her in this matter,
He donned armor weighing fifty minas about his waist
--
Fifty minas were handled by him like thirty shekels –
His "ax of the road" --
Seven talents and seven minas -- he took in his hand,
At its roots he struck down the snake who knows no charm,
In its crown the Imdugud-bird took its young, climbed to the mountains,
In its midst the maid Lilith tore down her house, fled to the wastes."

This form of oppression by the Elder Gods over the ZU is symbolic of the Fall of Man, or the lost of awareness by Earth's founders due to over usage of the logical mind. There is a great amount of wisdom that can be gained from the Elder Gods, even after we are initiated into the ways of the Ancient Ones, our relationship with them will grow. In order to get further insight into the origin of the Watchers, let us turn to the Biblical book of Genesis.

The creation account that appears in the first chapter of Genesis is probably one of the most misunderstood creation myths ever written by man. The reason is very simple; each creative day that appears in Genesis Chapter 1 ends with these words:

**"And the *evening* and the *morning* were the ___ day."**

How could there be an evening and morning even before the Sun and Moon appeared? Evidently these terms *evening* and *morning* are symbolic of something else.

The book of Genesis was written about 1400 B.C.E, which is long after the emergence of the Sumerian civilization. During the time Genesis was written, ISHTAR the Queen of Heaven, was known as the Morning and Evening star. ISHTAR as the morning star is named Dilbah, Goddess of War and Hunting, and as the *evening star* her name is Zib. This would indicate that the creative days described in Genesis Chapter One refer to ISHTAR's Descent into the Underworld (Earth, ERESHKIGAL). In ISHTAR's Descent into The Underworld, ISHTAR is said to give up an item at each Gate. In the myths of earlier origin, concerning the Goddess INANNA, it is said that she gave up one of the *mes*, or creative powers at each Gate. We can now determine that Genesis actually describes the descent of the *Watcher-Class, personified as ISHTAR, into the earthly realm, also known as The Underworld.* These Watchers evidently took human bodies for themselves to do a special work of preparing the Earth and mining it. Due to the severity of the conditions, human beings were created by ENKI to ease the work of the Watchers. The Watchers tried to teach man how to advance himself by sharing the science of technology and magic. The Watchers were known in Genesis as the serpent, or seer.

Evidently, what they told early man was NOT a lie because it is said in Genesis, concerning Adam and Eve, that their *'eyes did become open'* and they were able to make clothes for themselves while living on for hundreds of years after. This means that the *"serpent" taught mankind civilization.* Later, "God" is said to walk through the garden during the breezy part of the day. The Sumerian god of the wind is ENLIL, and gives man and the Watchers an adverse judgment. The Watchers evidently lost memory of themselves, *symbolized by the serpent being bruised in the head,* along with their ability to climb the heavenly ladder. This Biblical prophecy seems to imply that the Watchers are without memory of their heritage and remain in human form. Genesis says that "enmity" would occur between the serpent's seed and mankind, and for this *enmity* to exist both parties must live on the Earth. Another indication of this can be found in Genesis Chapter 6: 4 where it mentions that the Nephilim were said to appear in "those days *and afterwards.*" Evidently the Nephilim were clearly recorded to have existed in the world prior to the deluge and *"afterwards."* The Watcher-Class, being bound to the Earthly plane and not fully aware of their heritage or power, is what the Mayans meant by the Birth of Venus, or ISHTAR. Jesus admits that he is of this Watcher-Class in Revelation Chapter 22:16:

**"I Jesus have sent mine angel to testify to you these things in churches. I am the root and offspring of David, and the bright and *morning star."***

The term *"morning star"* is translated from the Greek word *Lucifer.* This would explain why Jesus taught publicly with parables, but would reveal the deeper things to his students, as they were also a part of the

Watcher-Class, or Ishtar, which Jesus referred to in his parable of the virgin and the bridegroom.

Since we have discovered that the Ishtar-Class is surviving in the Underworld, we know that the myth about her descent also involves her awakening and restoration to power. Notice what the Mad Arab says in the Simon Necronomicon:

*"Know that TIAMAT seeks ever to rise to the stars, and when the Upper is united with the Lower, then a new age will come of Earth."*

The Mad Arab is describing the full restoration of the Watcher's abilities and power. Man fears that life may exist somewhere out in the universe and still they have not ascertained that the Watcher-Class dwells with man right here on Earth. Notice what the Mad Arab mentions in his Second Testimony:

*"for the Race of Draconis was ever powerful in ancient times ..and they drew down much strength from the stars.."*

When the Watchers were in their full glory, they walked the Earth having the strength of a distant star behind them. The word *star* derives from the term Ishtar. Ishtar (Tiamat) is a personification of the Watcher-Class. The Watcher-Class created the universe, as seen by our observations of Genesis Chapter One. Their powers were usurped from them by others of the same class. When we look at the beauty of the Earth and the detailed creation that surrounds us, we come to appreciate that *this planet was considered the center of the universe because it is the home of the creator*. We can verify our observation by looking further into the Mesopotamian myth of Ishtar and the Huluppu Tree:

"Once upon a time, a tree, a huluppu, a tree --
It had been planted on the bank of the Euphrates,
It was watered by the Euphrates --
The violence of the South Wind plucked up its roots,
Tore away its crown,
The Euphrates carried it off on its waters.

The woman, roving about in fear at the word of An,
Roving about in fear at the word of ENLIL,
Took the tree in her hand, brought it to Erech:
"I shall bring it to pure INANNA's fruitful garden."

In this section of the myth, we see that the planters of the "*tree*" are not mentioned, but the "*tree*" is said to have been uprooted by the "*South Wind.*" The woman described in the account seems to be a righteous woman that feared the heavenly forces symbolized in the myth as ANU and ENLIL. The myth continues:

"The woman tended the tree with her hand, placed it by her foot, INANNA tended the tree with her hand, placed it by her foot, "When will it be a fruitful throne for me to sit on," she said, "When will it be a fruitful bed for me to lie on," she said."

From this part of the myth we see that the woman who cultivated the "tree" was INANNA herself. The "tree," we can now determine is the Earth. INANNA states: "When will it be a fruitful throne for me to sit on?" This is agreement with Genesis Chapter 1:28, which states:

"And God blessed them, and God said unto them, Be fruitful, and multiply, and *replenish* the earth,"

The Huluppu Tree myth continues:

"The tree grew big, its trunk bore no foliage,
In its roots the snake who knows no charm set up its
nest,
In its crown the Imdugud-bird placed its young,
In its midst the maid Lilith built her house --
The always laughing, always rejoicing maid,
The maid INANNA -- how she weeps!"

The first settlers of Earth were the Ancient Ones. The
"tree" is said to be occupied by Lilith (Lamashtu), the
Indugud-bird (Pazuzu), and the 'snake that know no
charm (Kingu).' These same creatures are found in the
URILIA Text working. Since we are aware of the fact that
"ISHTAR/INANNA" is a term denoting the
personification of the Watcher-Class, it seems likely that
the older Watchers were the first to inhabit the Earth and
found much delight in it, as it is stated in the myth: *"The
always laughing, always rejoicing maid."* Later in the myth
we find the following:

"Her brother, the hero Gilgamesh,
Stood by her in this matter,
He donned armor weighing fifty minas about his waist
--
Fifty minas were handled by him like thirty shekels --
His "ax of the road" --
Seven talents and seven minas -- he took in his hand,
At its roots he struck down the snake who knows no
charm,
In its crown the Imdugud-bird took its young, climbed
to the mountains,
In its midst the maid Lilith tore down her house, fled to
the wastes.

The tree -- he plucked at its roots, tore at its crown,
The sons of the city who accompanied him cut off its
branches,

He gives it to holy INANNA for her throne,
Gives it to her for her bed,
She fashions its roots into a pukku for him,
Fashions its crown into a mikku for him. "

After a second set of Watchers descended to the Earth,
they rivaled their older siblings over dominion of the
*"tree,"* or Earth. It was due to the aggression of the solar
cults, represented by Gilgamesh's presence in the myth,
against the "Ancient" Watcher-Class that corruption
entered the Earth. Notice how the *Huluppu Tree* myth
concludes:

"After the evening star had disappeared,
And he had marked the places where his pukku had
been,
He carried the pukku before him, brought it to his
house,
At dawn in the places he had marked -- bitterness and
woe!
Captives! Dead! Widows!

Because of the cry of the young maidens,
His pukku and mikku fell into the "great dwelling,"
He put in his hand, could not reach them,
Put in his foot, could not reach them,
He sat down at the great gate ganzir, the "eye" of the
nether world,
Gilgamesh wept, his face turns pale . . . . "

According to the Biblical account, the Fall of Man (The
Watchers) occurred on the same day that God rested. The
Watcher-Class wanted to see the conditions of this realm
by becoming a part of it and sharing in its experiences,
whether good or bad, in order to be able to judge the
world upon their awakening. During this time, human

beings and lesser spirits have allowed the world to run amuck.

## Watcher Ritual

In order to begin working with the Watcher, the Initiate should create a space to work with. They should also have the following tools:

1. A clean heat-resistant bowl with no markings
2. White or black candles
3. A sterno
4. A large kitchen knife or sword
5. Cedar and pine incense
6. Nettles
7. Bread for the sacrifice

Before the Initiate begins work with the Watcher, there are a few preliminary steps that must be followed:

*"Our Master and Lord of All Magick. Great care must be taken that this untamed Spirit does not rise up against the Priest, and for that reason a preliminary sacrifice must be made in a clean and new bowl with the appropriate sigils inscribed thereupon, being the three grey carven signs of the Rock of my initiation, which are:*

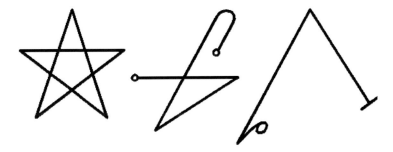

One of the first steps that the Initiate must take is to draw the Three Seals of MASSHU on the outer side of the heat-resistant bowl that will be used in magical invocation. A sterno should be place in this bowl. Some Initiates also make it a practice to mark the Three Seals of MASSHU on their kitchen knife, or sword, which will be used for conjuring the Watcher.

*"They must be engraved upon the bowl with a fine stylus, or painted thereon with dark ink. The sacrifice must be new bread, pine resin, and the grass Olieribos. These must be burned in the new bowl, and the Sword of the Watcher, with his Sigil engraved thereupon, at hand, for he will inhabit such at the time of the Calling of the Watcher and will depart when he is given license to depart."*

The herb Olieribos is also known a *"stinging nettles."* This is mentioned in Dan Harms' book, *The Necronomicon Files*, though it is a book that is highly critical of Simon's work, it does reveal some deeper and hidden aspects of the tome. I would say to that if you are unable to obtain nettles, it is still okay. When I performed my first conjuration of the Watcher, it worked effectively without it. Today, however, I make sure that I have some available before I do ritual. What I usually find best and advise most newcomers to the Tradition to do is to take the nettles and pine resin, and burn it in a brazier. The bread can be burned in the AGA MASS SSARATU, or bowl with the Three Seals of MASSHU written upon its outer side. Remember that a sterno should be placed inside the bowl. Now let us list the step to begin with the Invocation of the Watcher. The Mad Arab gives us additional instructions:

*"When the time has come to summon the Watcher the first time, the place of thy calling must be clean, and a*

*double circle of flour drawn about thee. And there should be no altar, but only the new Bowl with the three carven signs on it. And the Conjuration of the Fire should be made, and the sacrifices heaped thereupon, into the burning bowl. And the Bowl is now called AGA MASS SSARATU, and to be used for no other purpose, save to invoke the Watcher. And the bowl must be lain between the Circles, facing the Northeast. And thy vestments should be black, and thy cap black. And the Sword must be at hand, but not yet in the ground. And it must be the Darkest Hour of the Night. And there must be no light, save for the AGA MASS SSARATU. And the Conjuration of the Three must be made, thus:"*

The steps are very simple to do, even if one lives in an urban area. We are informed that our attire must be black with a black head covering. Use what you feel appropriate for the occasion, but something only used for this working. Also a circle of flour should be drawn and the Bowl should be place in the Northeast. The ritual should take place late into the night.

First, the Initiate should light all the candles that are to be used in working and then the sterno followed by the Calling of the Fire God. *Conjuration of the Fire God* by Warlock Asylum covers this thoroughly. The nettles and pine resin should be burning already in a separate brazier, if it cannot fit in the "bowl."

Next, the Initiate should then pick up his/her sword with the RIGHT HAND ONLY and read the following incantation: (Please note that the bread should be placed over the flame, but not as to extinguish the sterno)

*"ISS MASS SSARATI SHA MUSHI LIPSHURU
RUXISHA LIMNUTI!
IZIZANIMMA ILANI RABUTI SHIMA YA DABABI!
DINA DINA ALAKTI LIMDA!
ALSI KU NUSHI ILANI MUSHITI!
IA MASS SSARATI ISS MASS SSARATI BA IDS MASS
SSARATU!"*

After these words are spoken we are told the following:

*"This being said, at the words IDS MASS SSARATU the
Sword must be thrust into the ground behind the AGA
MASS SSARATU with force. And the Watcher will
appear for the instructions to be made by the Priest."*

If you are not outside, you may find this difficult to
follow, since you probably don't want to put holes in
your floor. What many Gate-Walkers have found
effective, including myself, is to simply tap the bowl on
the right side with the Sword of the Watcher. This
Preliminary Invocation is to be read before the *Normal
Invocation of the Watcher* that is used in the Gate-Walking
Ceremony. However, during the reading of this
incantation, the Copper Dagger of Inanna must be held in
the right hand. The incantation is as follows:

*"IA MASS SSARATU!
I conjure Thee by the Fire of GIRRA
The Veils of Sunken Varloorni,
And by the Lights of SHAMMASH.
I call Thee here, before me, in visible shadow
In beholdable Form, to Watch and Protect this Sacred
Circle, this Holy Gate of (N.)
May He of the Name Unspeakable, the Number
Unknowable,
Whom no man hath seen at any time,
Whom no geometer measureth,*

*Whom no wizard hath ever called*
*CALL THEE HERE NOW!*
*Rise up, by ANU I summon Thee!*
*Rise up, by ENLIL I summon Thee!*
*Rise up, by ENKI I summon Thee!*
*Cease to be the Sleeper of EGURRA.*
*Cease to lie unwaking beneath the Mountains of KUR.*
*Rise up, from the pits of ancient holocausts!*
*Rise up, from the old Abyss of NARR MARRATU!*
*Come, by ANU!*
*Come, by ENLIL!*
*Come, by ENKI!*
*In the Name of the Covenant, Come and Rise up before*
*me!*
*IA MASS SSARATU! IA MASS SSARATU! IA MASS*
*SSARATU ZI KIA KANPA!*
*BARRGOLOMOLONETH KIA!*
*SHTAH!"*

I must remind the reader that during the course of this working, he/she should not touch the Sword of the Watcher with their left hand until the time comes when they are ready to dismiss the Watcher.

*"At this point, the Watcher will surely come and stand*
*outside the Gate or Circle until such time as he is given*
*the license to depart by striking of the Priest's left hand*
*on the hilt of the Sword, while pronouncing the formula*
*BARRA MASS SSARATU! BARRA!"*

After the Candidate has spoken to the Watcher concerning personal matters, they must then dismiss the Watcher by picking up the Sword with their left hand and saying: *BARRA MASS SSARATU! BARRA!* Some Initiates also make it a practice to tap the bowl on the left side further emphasizing the Watcher's dismissal.

In summary we can say that what many of the Abrahamic religions revere as the history of mankind's origins appears in truth to be the reverse. The serpent that spoke to Eve is the same serpent that lived with Lilith and the Anzu Bird in the original Tree of Life, Earth. Later these entities tried to help man evolve and their eyes became open. Human beings began to make clothes for themselves, which is symbolic of human beings learning how to conduct themselves in civilization. So where is the lie in all of this? If a deity is upset over mankind's evolution, then this deity certainly cannot be the same deity who created man. A true look at history reveals that when the ancient gods rested, human beings created deities from their imagination.

# The Realm of the Igigi: Keys to the 12 Hidden Gates

Any individual who is seeking to explore the spiritual aspects of this path would do well to become familiar with the books cited in the Simon Necronomicon's bibliography. I know this from personal experience. I have seen people post responses to some of the articles that I have written, as if it is subject to debate. Some of the information I have seen readers disagree with is not my personal opinion, but actual fact. Yet there are those of us who have taken on a different approach by thoroughly investigating some of the resources listed in the Simon Necronomicon and have become well acquainted with Sumerian lore. These people are also well aware that the Testimony of the Mad Arab is a symbolic outline of the qliphotic rites and initiations. The Mad Arab lists three distinct initiations that exist within the Necronomicon Tradition:

*"Know, then, that I have trod all the Zones of the Gods* (seven gates of initiation), *and also the places of the Azonei ( the zodaic), and have descended unto the foul places of Death and Eternal Thirst, which may be reached through the Gate of GANZIR (*Urilia Text workings *), which was built in UR, in the days before Babylon was."*

The above passage clearly illustrates three distinct initiations that exist within the Necronomicon Tradition: **1-the seven gates of self-initiation, 2-the azonei, or realm of fixed stars, 3-the Underworld, or Ganzir**. It is interesting to note that much of what took place in the

Mad Arab's First Testimony was received in the realms of the Azonei:

*"For this is the Book of the Dead, the Book of the Black Earth, that I have writ down at the peril of my life, exactly as I received it, on the planes of the IGIGI, the cruel celestial spirits from beyond the Wanderers of the Wastes..."*

The fact that there exists, three distinct initiations in the Necronomicon Tradition, is emphasized again in the Book of Entrance:

*"When thou hast ascended to the limit of the Ladder of Lights (* 1-seven gates of initation *), thou wilt have knowledge and power over the Spheres, and wilt be able to summon them thereby in times of need. This will not give thee power over the ABSU, however, this power being obtained differently by the Ritual of Descent (*2-Ganzir-The Underworld *). This Ritual thou wilt undertake in the fifteenth day after the thirteenth of the month when thou hast summoned the Gate of MARDUK to open. For MARDUK slew the Fiends, and INANNA, the Goddess of the Fifteen, conquered the Netherworld, where some of theirs still dwell. This is a most perilous Rite, and may be undertaken by any man who as the formulae, whether he has passes the previous Gates or not, save that it is best advised to have passed through MARDUK Gate before venturing forth into the Pit. For this reason, few have ever opened the Gate of ADAR, and spoken to the Horned One who resideth there and giveth all manner of wisdom regarding the operations of necromancy, and of the spells that hasten unto death. Only when thou hast shown thy power over the Maskim and the Rabishu, mayest thou venture forth to the Land of the IGIGI (* 3- the realm of fixed stars *), and for that reason was this Covenant made, that none shall safely*

Walk through the sunken valleys of the Dead before
having ascended to MARDUK, nor shall they breach the
Gates that lie beyond ADAR until they have seen the
Signs of the Mad God and felt the fury of the hellish
Queen."

Here we see three distinct initiations that occur, and in
part, a formula for each. After the Sphere of Marduk is
reached, the Initiate can go into Ganzir. Following this,
the Initiate enters Adar, and then the realm of fixed stars,
also known as the Igigi. Jason Breshears, in his book
entitled; *The Lost Scriptures of Giza*, makes a similar
observation on pages 47-49:

"**Sumerian writings tell of a mysterious mountain
somewhere on earth that was called Mashu. This is
intriguing since there are no mountains in Sumer
(southern Iraq). Concerning Mashu these texts read,
"On high, to the celestial band it is connected; Below, to
the lower world it is bound." This alludes that Mashu
connected heaven and the underworld to earth.** *The
celestial band refers to the band of 12 constellations
called the Zodiac that were long ago believed to harbor
great secrets in the images of animals and deities. Even
individual stars within the constellations contributed to
these mysteries by the meanings of their names but those
not initiated into the stellar mysteries saw these star
patterns as merely attached to legend and lore....*The
celestial band was also of prophetic significance, the
constellations representing future things. Mashu was
also bound to the lower world, or underworld....
Perhaps it is this very mountain that is referred to in
this Sumerian Temple Hymn: "Enduring place, light
hued mountain which in artful fashion was founded.
Its dark hidden chamber is an awe-inspiring place; in a
field of supervision it lies. Awesome, its ways no one
can fathom." This is as adequate a description of the**

Great pyramid as any given today. Those Sumerian
scribes that wrote this were descendants of those who
had survived the cataclysm and were aware of its
existence....This mountain of the Sumerians is no
different in function than their Tree of Life."

The Mad Arab gives us further detail about the realm of
the Igigi and what is to be suspected:

*"And there are many another, of which this is not the
rightful place wherein they may be mentioned, save to
warn the Priest against the ambitious striving against
the Ancient Ones of the Outside, until mastery is
acquired over the powers that reside Within. Only when
ADAR has been obtained, may the Priest consider
himself a master of the planes of the Spheres, and able to
wrestle with the Old Gods."*

This passage cited above warns the Initiate against
**"ambitious striving against the Ancient Ones."** This
indicates that the Initiate is cautioned not to approach the
realms of the Igigi, as they may have approached the
seven gates of initiation. The seven gates of initiation are
listed in an order that runs counter to the Sun's path
through the zodiac. For example, we are first instructed
to Walk Nanna, which represents the astrological sign of
Cancer. This is followed by Nebo, which is symbolic of
Gemini. Thus, the Initiate Walks in a pattern that is
converse to our Sun. It is with this in mind that we now
understand that any **"ambitious striving against the
Ancient Ones"** would mean that the Initiate is to Walk
through the twelve constellations of the zodiac in the
same manner as the Sun.

The *realms of the Igigi* assist the Initiate in the areas of
psychic phenomena and physical cultivation. The seven
gates of self-initiation deal primarily with day-to-day life.

Ganzir, as cited above, instructs the Initiate in the ways of necromancy and some of the black arts. While the Initiate is traveling through the realms of the Igigi, they will encounter and receive a sign from the "**Jinn**" that will appear in their daily lives. This can be ascertained due to the fact that the Mad Arab said he received this book in the realms of the Igigi, and in the words that follow:

*"And against the Ancient Ones, there is only defence. Only a madman, indeed, such as I am called!, can hope to have power over Them that dwell in the Outer Spaces, for their power is unknown,"*

Now that we are aware of another initiation, which occurs when the candidate walks through each of the said Igigi, the meaning of other passages in the Simon Necronomicon begins to unravel. Let us look at how the term Igigi is used in reference to the seven gates:

*"The God of Saturn is NINIB called ADAR, the Lord of Hunters and of Strength. He appears with a crown of horns and a long sword, wearing a lion's skin. he is the final Zonei before the terrible IGIGI."* ( **Of The Zonei and Their Attributes** )

*"Know that, when Walking thus through the Sea of Spheres, he should leave his Watcher behind that It may guard his body and his property, lest he be slain unawares and must wander throughout eternity among the dark spaces between Stars, or else be devoured by the wrathful IGIGI that dwell beyond."* (**The Book of Entrance** )

*"Only when thou hast shown thy power over the Maskim and the Rabishu, mayest thou venture forth to the Land of the IGIGI,"* ( The Book of Entrance )

*"Master of the IGIGI, swing open Thy Gate!"* (Incantation of the Nanna Gate )

*"NINIB, Watcher of the Ways of the IGIGI, Remember!"* (Incantation of the Ninib Gate)

*"And the Lord of the Watchers dwells, it is said, among the Wastes of the IGIGI, and only Watches and never raises the Sword or fights the idimmi, save when the Covenant is invoked by none less than the Elder Gods in their Council, like unto the Seven Glorious APHKHALLU."* (Conjuration of the Watcher)

*"These incantations are said by the hidden priests and creatures of these powers, defeated by the Elders and the Seven Powers, led by MARDUK, supported by ENKI and the whole Host of IGIGI;"* (The Urilia Text )

Now that we are clear that indeed the Azonei, or the 12 constellations of the zodiac are to be walked separately as Gates, it would be good to list these as they appear in Supplementary Material to 777:

1-Aries = Agru ( Xubur ) 2-Taurus = Kakkab U Alap Shame ( Kingu ) 3-Gemini = Re' u Kinu Shame U Tu'Ame Rabuti 4-Cancer = Shittu = ( Snake ) 5- Leo = Kalbu Rabu (Lakhamu ) 6-Virgo= Shiru ( Whirlwind ) 7- Libra = Zibanitum ( Ravening Dog ) 8-Scorpio = Akrabu (Scorpion-Man ) 9-Sagittarius = Pa-Bil-Sag ( Hurricane ) 10-Capricorn = Suxur Mash ( Fish- Man ) 11-Aquarius =Gula ( Horned beast ) 12-Pisces = Dil Gan U Rikis Nuni (weapon)

When the initiate passes the gate of Adar they should create a seal for each constellation listed above and Walk each zodiacal gate starting from Agru. This process will give the initiate insight and heavenly wisdom. We will discuss these 12 mysterious gates in a future writing.

*"HUBUR arose, She who fashioneth all things,*
*And possessor of Magick like unto Our Master.*
*She added matchless weapons to the arsenals of the Ancient Ones,*
*She bore Monster-Serpents*
*Sharp of tooth, long of fang,*
*She filled their bodies with venom for blood*
*Roaring dragons she has clothed with Terror*
*Has crowned them with Halos, making them as Gods,*
*So that he who beholds them shall perish*
*And, that, with their bodies reared up*
*None might turn them back.*
*She summoned the Viper, the Dragon, and the Winged Bull,*
*The Great Lion, the Mad-God, and the Scorpion-Man.*
*Mighty rabid Demons, Feathered-Serpents, the Horse-Man,*
*Bearing weapons that spare no*
*Fearless in Battle,*
*Charmed with the spells of ancient sorcery,*
*withal Eleven of this kind she brought forth*
*With KINGU as Leader of the Minions."*

*"For what is new*
*Came from that which is old*
*And what is old*
*Shall replace that which is new*
*And once again the Ancient Ones*
*Shall rule upon the face of the Earth!*
*And this is too the Covenant!"*

# The 144,000 Find Their Place In The Necronomicon Tradition

It is easy for the Gate-Walker to find some similarities between the Abrahamic faiths and the Necronomicon Tradition, due to the fact that Abraham was a Chaldean. So in some ways Judaism, Christianity, and Islam carry some aspect of the Necronomicon Tradition in their symbolism and dogma. It should be noted, however, that the teachings of these belief systems are only a part of the pre-Adamite Chaldean legacy and a degraded presentation of whatever was received by them. The way of life and its spiritual principles maintained by the *Race from Beyond the Stars, could never have a founder*, since our customs, culture, and spiritual practices originated before the Earth was ever inhabited. Any religion that has a founder is based on the premise of one simple principal; that some civilized being went out and discovered an uncivilized people and taught them civilization, or how to work in union with the movements of Heaven and Earth. Nowhere in the Bible do we find an origin for the spiritual practice of sacrifice that Cain and Abel were involved in. These customs were practiced by Earth's first settlers, as found in Hinduism, Ifa, Shinto, and Taoism. These spiritual traditions have no founder because they are extensions of a divine government. Western scholars make the error of trying to give a date of origin for both Shinto and Taoism, which is essentially the same. Their deceit is easily exposed by those who are of Asian history. How could you calculate a date of origin for the spiritual practice of Shinto when it has no founder? These methods of deceit are perpetrated by religious leaders of the Abrahamic faith and academic scholars, who for the most part, are practitioners of these

Abrahamic religions. The Sumerian epics speak about a great civilization's customs and spiritual practices long before Adam was created and even describe how he was created. Science even confirms this. We have found human remains in areas such as, Africa, Asia, and North America that are thousands of years older than the Biblical date ascribed to Adam. These academic scholars, many of whom are Christian, are on the Discovery Channel trying to convince the world that the Biblical story of Adam and Eve is really factual. If this doesn't work, there is always the religious faction propagating some doomsday report as fulfillment of Biblical prophecy to create fear in their followers in hopes of gaining more constituents. Meanwhile, death is inevitable for all mortals.

The other day I was drawn to re-read Revelation's description of the 144,000. Usually I check the mythologies of various religious traditions, which correspond to the work I am doing in Necronomics. Presently, I am working with the 12 Hidden Gates in the Simon Necronomicon, which correspond to Chokmah in the Judaic Kabbalah and to the *"Kingdom of Heaven"* in Christian mythology, but is commonly known as the Sphere of the Zodiac, which is attributed to Enki. I must also make note that usually when you enter the realms, or gates, you will receive several epiphanies from the cosmic forces that help you gain a better understanding of the realm that you are in, and this could also come from outside sources, whether it is dialogue with people, information read, and etc, but a thought will appear in your head that is not your own, and you will gain much wisdom by validating it.

*"...for these Operations attract many kinds of wandering demon and ghost to the Gates, but in the air*

*above the altar whereupon thou wilt presently see the Gate opening for thee and the Spirit-Messenger of the Sphere greeting thee in a clear voice, and giving thee a Name, which thou must remember, for that is the Name of thy Passing the Gate,."*

When I entered the realms of the Igigi, I was prompted to do some research on the Watchers. The term Igigi corresponds also to the Sphere of the Zodiac in the Necronomicon Tradition. Let us look at the Supplementary Material To 777, appearing in the tome's introduction:

|  | Table VII [A.C.] | Table XXV [S.] |
|---|---|---|
| 0. | . . . | ANU (TIAMAT) |
| 1. | Sphere of the Primum Mobile | ENLIL (ABSU) |
| 2. | **Sphere of the Zodiac or Fixed Stars** | **ENKI; LUMASHI (IGIGI)** |

While Enki is equated to the Sphere of Fixed Stars, or Zodiac, being the Igigi, we are also reminded of the following passage that appears in the Simon Necronomicon:

*"Wherefore it is wise to conjure It in the Names of the Three Great Watchers Who existed before the Confrontation from whose borne the Watcher and His*

*Race ultimately derive, and those Three are ANU,
ENLIL, and Master ENKI of the Magick Waters. And for
this reason They are sometimes called the Three
Watchers, MASS SSARATI and the Watcher MASS
SSARATU, or KIA MASS SSARATU."*

We see that the Watchers ultimately derive from the
Three Great Watchers, who are DinGir Anu, Enlil, and
Enki. This also means that Dingir Anu and DinGir Enlil
have some stake, along with DinGir Emki, in the Sphere
of the Zodiac. Morris Jastrow states the following in epic
work *The Religion of Babylonia and Assyria,* page 523:

**"In this way they reach the gate of Anu, Bel, and Ea in
safety, where they take a rest. The eagle is not yet
satisfied, and urges Etana to follow him to the domain
of Ishtar.**

*Come my friend [let me carry thee to Ishtar]. With Ishtar, the
mistress [of the gods, thou shalt dwell], In the glory of Ishtar,
the mistress of the gods, [thou shall sit?] On my side place my
side, on my pinion place my palms.*

**The gods, it will be seen, dwell on high in accordance
with the view developed by astronomical speculations.
Anu, Bel, and Ea are here evidently identified with the
fixed stars bearing their names."**

Jastrow's observation indicates that DinGir Anu, and
Dingir Bel (Enlil), were also associated with the *fixed
stars.* This fact is brought to a clearer understanding in
the rare and priceless work by F. Castells, entitled *The
Genuine Secrets in Freemasonry Prior to AD 1717,* on page
221, we read:

**"In the Antiquity of the Holy Royal Arch we have
shown that the Sacred Word was derived from Babylon,**

where *Anu, Bel, Ea* (or Yah) were not merely names of three mythological beings but an astronomical formulae....*Anu, Bel, Ea* embody a conception of the Universe,...It is well known that the ancient Babylonian astronomers divided the planisphere into three separate regions, over which three Deities were said to preside: *Anu* had charge of the sky, *Bel* of the earth and its inhabitants, and *Ea* of Hades....One scholar would distribute the twelve Signs of the Zodiac between those Deities, giving one to each of them in regular succession; but Professor Hemmel is of opinion that the Trinity stands for thirds of the Ecliptic and gives three Signs of the Zodiac to Anu, four to Bel, and five to Ea; which is reminiscent of the Pythagorean Triangle,.."

The words cited above suggest that the trinity of Anu, Bel (Enlil), and Ea (Enki) might just be the lost word that Freemasons have searched centuries for. It with this information that we are able to determine who the Race of Watchers really are, the "*stars.*"

*"Wherefore it is wise to conjure It in the Names of the Three Great Watchers Who existed before the Confrontation from whose borne the Watcher and His Race ultimately derive.."*

The identification of the Watcher with the azonei, or stars, is also supported by Gerald Massey's infamous work *Ancient Egypt – The Light of the World*; pages 599-600 states:

"In one character the seven stars were regarded as watchers solemnly aloof....Astronomically these were the gods of the seven pole-stars whose seats were in the never-setting stars around the throne Anu. Thus, and in no other way, the seven powers caused the deluge, and

**ascended to their seats in the heavens of Anu and assumed their thrones on high as rulers in the realm of eternity."**

Based on the information that we have covered so far, it is clear that the *Watchers* are spirits of the stars. In earlier articles, we discussed how closely the description of the *Watcher* is to that of Kutulu. Simon wrote in *Dead Names* that Kutulu is the power of the Jinn. The Jinn, as we have discussed many times in previous articles, are said to be *'souls'* without bodies and made from *smokeless fire*. The Jinn are composed of the same material that we find in the stars that radiate the zodiac and the universe beyond. Therefore, the Jinn descend into this reality assuming a physical body, but their power derives from a distant star. The Mad Arab confirms this for us in several passages appearing in the Simon Necronomicon:

*"...for the Race of Draconis was ever powerful in ancient times, when the first temples were built in MAGAN, and they drew down much strength from the stars"*

*"And they work by the Moon, and not by the Sun, and by older planets than the Chaldeans were aware"*

*"thou shalt see things becoming dark; and the Wanderers in their Spheres shall no more be seen by thee; and the Stars in their places will lose their Light, and the Moon, NANNA, by whom thou also workest, shall become black and extinguished"*

In an interview conducted by Edith Hathaway with famous astrologer Diana R. Rosenberg entitled *Fixed Stars*, Rosenberg expresses her understanding and characteristics concerning zodiac correspondences of Ea (Enki) and the starry influences of his realm:

"In the Chaldeo-Babylonian celestial hierarchy, one of three gods who reigned supreme was Ea, "Lord of the Deep," preeminently wise and beneficent, enlightener and lawgiver, archetype of Divine Intelligence. The stars of *Capricornus* belonged to Ea. One of the most ancient of all the zodiac figures, *Capricornus*, the sea-faring goat with a fish's tail also represents the divine Man-Fish. Author Rupert Gleadow describes Ea:

"Ea is the only one of the Sumerian and Babylonian gods who was never angry, and always ready to help both gods and men out of difficulties. He is often represented as a man walking in a great fish-shaped cloak, the fish's head over his head and pointing upwards like a mitre, the tail at his heels, and the forward leg showing his human form. He is said to have emerged four times at long intervals from the ocean to teach civilization to men, and during each of these periods would retire into the water at night. Capricorn, his symbolic creature, symbolizes this dual life, and has as yet no association with the planet Saturn, which has never been reputed to help people out of scrapes....The teachings of Ea-Oannes, epitomized by *Capricornus*, make his stars an area of emergence and enlightenment, where laws are established, maintained and renewed; where challenges, struggles and experimentation bring about new systems of social contracts and new legal pathways for the just implementation of power."

Enki is here identified with the constellation of Capricorn. The alleged battle between the Ancient Ones and Elder Gods is a blind. Here is one example of this. In the Urilia Text we find the following:

*"Now, there are Two Incantation to the Ancient Ones set down here, which are well known to the Sorcerers of the Night, they who make images and burn them by the Moon and by other Things. And they burn them by the Moon and by other Things. And they burn unlawful grasses and herbs, and raise tremendous Evils, and their Words are never written down, it is said. But there are. And they are Prayers of Emptiness and Darkness, which rob the Spirit."*

After the Mad Arab wrote the words cited above, one incantation, which he speaks about is given. Its title is Hymn to the Ancient Ones. This prayer is known historically as *The Prayer to the Gods of the Night*. In any event we find the following contained in this incantation:

*"Ever-Shining Star of the*
*North! ... SIRIUS!..DRACONIS!..CAPRICORNUS!*
*Stand by and accept*
*This sacrifice I offer*
*May it be acceptable*
*To the Most Ancient Gods!"*

As discussed earlier, many researchers align the constellation of Capricorn with Enki. Researcher Gary David Thompson recently put forth some very interesting information that was written in the Simon Necronomicon a long time ago:

**"A pioneering study of Mesopotamian astronomy was initiated with the 3 articles by Archibald Sayce and Robert Bosanquet published during 1879-1880 in Monthly Notices of the Royal Astronomical Society. By at least 1887 Sayce was identifying a Pole Star (Lectures on the Origin and Growth of Religions). He held that "The Star/Constellation of Anu was the "Yoke of Heaven" = Draco, alpha Draconis. In an early Volume**

of Transactions of the Society of Biblical Archaeology
he stated: "The Akkadian term "Ditar-Anki" ("the
Judge of Anki") and the Assyrian term "Dayen-Same"
are designations of the Pole Star (North Celestial Pole).
The assertion by Sayce of ""Yoke of Heaven" = Draco,
alpha Draconis" may possibly be matched to the
modern translation..."

Sirius is associated with Anu, Draconis with Enlil, and
Capricorn with Enki. These cosmic forces were
reconfigured during the transition from one age to the
next as described in the Biblical book of Revelation and
the 144,000. Before we continue, I thought it would be
useful to make one more remark about the the zodiac, as
found in the writing *A Dictionary of the Bible*, written in
1901:

"The Zodaic was also divided into a region of Anu
(Taurus, Gemini, Cancer, Leo), a region of Bel (Virgo,
Libra, Scorpio, Sagitarious), and a region of he earth-
and-water god Ea (Capricornus, Aquarius, Pisces,
Aries)"

The above correspondences are relative to the zodiac.
Anu, Enlil, and Enki are also noted as corresponding to
certain elements of nature and other distant stars. We
have covered a lot of information so far in this
discussion, as it is relative to the topic of the 144,000.

Although Christians are not aware of the Necronomicon
Tradition, it is interesting to note that Jesus himself was a
Gate-Walker. Jesus' mother, Mary, was said to be
impregnated by the angel Gabriel, which is considered to
be the angelic representation of the sphere of Yesod in
kabbalistic studies. Yesod corresponds to the Gate of
Nanna, and is associated with the Moon. It is recorded
that when Jesus was 12 years of age, he ventured off from

his human parents and went into the Temple asking the Pharisees and religious leaders of that day various questions.12 is the number of Nebo since times antiquity. Next, we find Jesus preparing for baptism by John the Baptist when he is 29 1/2 years old. It takes Saturn 29 1/2 years to travel around the Sun. So it is that Jesus had to descend under the waters, or travel to Ganzir before he reached the Gate of Adar (Saturn).

What is also interesting about this, especially when you are an Initiate of the Necronomicon Tradition, is the character of John the Baptist. We can say on some levels that John the Baptist worked as Jesus' Watcher. After his Watcher served in the initiatory function, he was executed. Having passed the Gate of Adar, Jesus no longer needed an earthly Watcher, since he became one with his Watcher and was accepted as an Initiate. The Bible mentions that when Jesus was baptized the heavens opened up and a dove descended upon him. Doves are a symbol of Ishtar. After the Heavens opened up, or the realm of the Igigi, Jesus went into the wilderness (the zodiac) for 40 days. Forty is the number of Enki, which corresponds to the sphere of the zodiac, the realm of the Igigi. It is with this in mind that one may wonder if the 144,000 also find a place in the Necronomicon Tradition. The first mention of the 144,000 appears in the biblical book of Revelation chapter 7:

**"(1) And after these things I saw four angels standing on the four corners of the earth, holding the four winds of the earth, that the wind should not blow on the earth, nor on the sea, nor on any tree."**

These "four winds" are also discussed in the Book of Daniel chapter 7:

**"(2) Daniel spoke and said, I saw in my vision by night, and, behold, the four winds of the heaven strove upon the great sea....3 And four great beasts came up from the sea, diverse one from another...4 The first was like a lion, and had eagle's wings: I beheld till the wings thereof were plucked, and it was lifted up from the earth, and made stand upon the feet as a man, and a man's heart was given to it...5 And behold another beast, a second, like to a bear, and it raised up itself on one side, and it had three ribs in the mouth of it between the teeth of it: and they said thus unto it, Arise, devour much flesh...6 After this I beheld, and lo another, like a leopard, which had upon the back of it four wings of a fowl; the beast had also four heads; and dominion was given to it...7 After this I saw in the night visions, and behold a fourth beast, dreadful and terrible, and strong exceedingly; and it had great iron teeth: it devoured and brake in pieces, and stamped the residue with the feet of it: and it was diverse from all the beasts that were before it; and it had ten horns."**

These are the four creatures, described in the passage from Daniel cited above, are also mentioned in Revelation chapter 4:

**"(7) And the first beast was like a lion, and the second beast like a calf, and the third beast had a face as a man, and the fourth beast was like a flying eagle."**

Long before the Biblical book of Daniel and Revelation were written, these four living creatures were relative to spiritual practices embraced by the people of Sumeria and Egypt. We can confirm this with something as simple as the Egyptian canopic jars. These jars were used by the Ancient Egyptians to store various body parts during the mummification process. The pottery of these jars date in a period long before the Bible was written, yet we can easily see that these jars match the description of the four living creatures that are around god's throne:

**CANOPIC JARS DATED 990-969 BC**

John G. Jackson in the book *Man, God, and Civilization*, states the following on page 141:

**"The four gods holding up the skies are called Cherubim in the Bible." As for the likeness of their faces, they four had the face of a man, the face of a lion, on the right side; and they four had the face of an ox on the left side; they four had the face of an eagle."...These celestial creatures were said to have been seen by Ezekiel in a vision while in Babylon, and they were obviously the four corner constellations of the Chaldean zodiac."**

These four constellations were at times noted as being a "divine power," in like manner the "four winds" mentioned in Revelation are the cosmic energies emanating from these four constellations, namely, Taurus, Leo Scorpio, and Aquarius. Now let us continue with our reading of Revelation Chapter 7:

"And I saw another angel ascending from the east, having the seal of the living God: and he cried with a loud voice to the four angels, to whom it was given to hurt the earth and the sea,....3 Saying, Hurt not the earth, neither the sea, nor the trees, till we have sealed the servants of our God in their foreheads....4 And I heard the number of them which were sealed: and there were sealed an hundred and forty and four thousand of all the tribes of the children of Israel."

The "trees" mentioned in Revelation's symbolic language are a reference to constellation. J.C. Cooper in *Synbolism-The Universal Language* admits:

"The *Babylonian* palm had seven branches, as representing the heavens ... The Chinese *tree* has the Twelve Terrestrial Branches, each with a *symbolic* Animal of the *Constellations*."

Cooper's observations are just one of many emphasizing that *"trees"* were symbolic of constellations and starry energies. In the above passage in Revelation we see the 144,000 mentioned for the first time and that these ones were collected from the twelve tribes of Israel, as explained in the verses that follow, are a reference to the twelve signs of the zodiac. The 144,000 are mentioned also in Revelation Chapter 14:

"(3) And they sung as it were a new song before the throne, and before the four beasts, and the elders: and no man could learn that song but the hundred and forty and four thousand, which were redeemed from the earth...4 These are they which were not defiled with women; for they are virgins. These are they which follow the Lamb whithersoever he goeth. These were redeemed from among men, being the firstfruits unto God and to the Lamb."

Revelation chapter 14 describes the four beasts that we discussed earlier, but again the 144,000 are mentioned as being redeemed from the *"earth."* They are also said to be virgins. The mention of the "Lamb" is relative to the sign of Aries. This whole passage concerning the 144,000 is nothing but ancient astrology. *Ancient Freemasonry* by Frank C. Higgins makes this point very clear on pages 187-189 of the said work, he states:

**"The zodiacal sign of Aries, the ram or lamb, was called Amon and for hundreds of years the sun at the vernal equinox was said to rise in this sign. At the same period the brightest constellation in the heavens opposite by night was known as the zodiacal Virgin, or "Virgo." She was, therefore, at this period deemed the mother of the young spring sun, whose symbol was a pure white lamb. In her hand the celestial Virgin carries a cluster of stars, called by the Hebrews the "wheatsheaf," or "shibboleth" from the Hebrew verb *"shabal"* to sprout. The brightest of these stars is Spica Virginis...The spring sun rose to power, glory and mastership in the higher signs. Arrived at that of Virgo, he became the spouse of her who had previously been his mother, and their offspring were the vintage and harvest."**

Many of the passages written in Revelation pertain to astrology. In the later part of the verses cited above, the 144,000 were said to be *"the first fruits unto God and the Lamb."* According to Higgins, when the Sun arrived in the constellation of *"Virgo"* it became the spouse of her who had previously been his mother, and their offspring were the vintage and harvest." While having discovered how all of this is relative to astrology, it does not dismiss the importance of what is written. Many people make mistake of discovering how the ancient mysteries are relative to astrology and then dismiss them altogether based on such. They do not take to the message of the stars, or Igigi, knowing that they have a great influence upon the earthly affairs of man. The movement of the stars and planets push a cosmic energy into our being, which shapes and molds our experiences. This energy is later emitted by the human, due to stress and the sun's power to absorb it. This is why many people feel the same tiredness from staying in the Sun too long as when they are stressed out. This is the work that the Igigi were complaining about and thus the human being was made. The Simon Necronomicon is such a powerful system since the practitioner is harnessing the energy of a distant star. With this in mind, let us now discover how the 144,000 redeemed from earth?

Before digging further into this topic, we should consider the fact that while Judaic and Christian mysteries derive from ancient Mesopotamian sources, these very same mystics denounced Babylon in their writings. They were enslaved by the Babylonians. It should also be noted too, that Babylon did fall into a degraded state when invaders mistook certain symbolism literally. Now let us proceed. Revelation Chapter 14 opens with the following:

**"And I looked, and, lo, a Lamb stood on the mount Sion, and with him an hundred forty and four thousand, having his Father's name written in their foreheads."**

In the Simon Necronomicon's Book of Entrance, we read:

*"And the Number of ENKI is Forty a most excellent Number, and he is our Father, of all who would tread these forgotten paths, and wander into Lands unknown,*

*among the Wastes, amid frightful monsters of the Azonei."*

We are told by the Mad Arab that all who are able to ascend into the realms of the Igigi (Azonei, zodiac) have Enki as their father and that his number is 40. Enki's number, being 40, was well-known to the people of ancient Mesopotamia. In Zechariah Sitchin's work, *The 12th Planet*, we find the following on page 124:

**"The highest unit of the Sumerian sexagesimal system — 60 — was assigned to Anu; Enlil "was" 50; *Enki*, 40;"**

There are many other works that the reader would do well to explore, which confirms Enki's number as being forty. This correspondence is agreed upon by scholars and is not a recent invention. Now let us take Enki's number (40) and see if there is some mathematical equation involved here.

40 divided by 144,000 = 3600. Interestingly, the number 3600 is equal to 1 shar in ancient Sumeria. Many who believe in planet Nibiru say that it has a 3600-year cycle. As Gate-Walkers we are aware of the cosmic world of the ancient Sumerian pantheon, as not having such a great physical effect, as it has on an etheric level, which is occurring at this present time. The Initiate of the Necronomicon Tradition fully understands that the 3,600 years refers not to the coming of the planet Nibiru, for the every Gate-Walker can attest that the gods are upon us, but to the cosmic clock that was established by the pre-Adamite Chaldeans also known as the Jinn.
*Appleton's Journal of Literature, Science and Art-* Issues 171-196, reveal the following:

"The Chaldeans originated the ecliptic into the twelve signs of the zodiac, the figures of the constellations, the division of the circle into 360, and discovered that a chord of the circle equalt to the radius measures an are of 60. They also gave us the divisions of the degree into 60 minutes, these into 60 seconds, etc. The week of seven days is a Chaldean institution, each day being dedicated to one of the planets, which they worshipped as divine; also the division of the day into 24 hours, and these into minutes and seconds. Their system was extended into a great cycle of 43,200 years, which was divided into 12 cosmic hours of 3,600 years each..."

Long before the propaganda about planet Nibiru was created by Zechariah Sitchin, as a blind to divert attention from the process of Chaldean initiation, scholarship about the ancient Chaldeans was a lot more honest. It wasn't until the decline of Chrisitanity and new information about the Chaldeans and the Sumerians and what their contribution to civilization was that we now see everyone trying to fit themselves into the make-up of these swarthy aboriginal people. In any event, the 3,600 years was regarded by the ancient Chaldeans as a division of the cosmic clock. So it is by dividing Enki's number, 40, into 144,000, we get 3,600, which is only one hour on the great cosmic clock.

Now that we know this is all relative to the zodiac, we should actually take 3,600 and divide that into 144,000, which would give us 40, of course. So it is that the daughters and sons of Enki are the 144,000 and members of the Necronomicon Tradition.

If we keep in mind that the ancient Chaldeans counted their days from sunrise to sunset, 144,000 years would be equal to a little over 36 hours on the cosmic clock, or 3 periods of 12 hours and one period a little less than half.

*(This is strikingly similar to the Biblical mythos, which describes Jesus teaching for 3 ½ years after his baptism.)* What is interesting about this is that the Moon passes from one sign of the zodiac into another every two to three days, or 36 hours. The fact that we are speaking of the Moon in relation to Enki and the 144,000 is nothing unusual to the Initiate of the Greater Mysteries. H.P Blavatsky in her essays under the subject *The Chaldean Legend* mentions:

**"With the Chaldeans the moon was Sin, and Nannak or Nannar, the son of Mulil, the older *Bel*. It is Mulil (Bel) who caused the waters of the Flood to fall from heaven on earth, for which Xisuthrus would not allow him to approach his altar. Behind the lunar "worship" was the secret teaching that the first race of men, the images and astral doubles of their Fathers, were the pioneers or the most progressed Entities from a preceding though lower sphere, the shell of which is now our Moon. But even this shell is all-potential, for having generated the earth, it is the *phantom* of the Moon which, attracted by magnetic affinity, sought to form its first inhabitants, the pre-human monsters. "While the gods were generated in the androgyne bosom of Mother-space, the reflection of *Hea's* Wisdom became on earth the woman *Omoroka*, the Deep or the Sea, which esoterically or even exoterically is the Moon."**

Keeping Blavatsky's comment in mind, and realizing the Moon's connection to Enki, let us now read the Mad Arab's words with confidence knowing that we are among the 144,000:

*"Know, seventhly, of the Things thou art to expect in the commission of this Most sacred Magick. Study the symbols well, and do not be afraid of any awful spectre that shall invade thine operation, or haunt thine habitat*

*by day or by night. Only charge them with them the words of the Covenant and they will do as you ask, of thou be strong. And if thou performest these operations often, thou shalt see things becoming dark; and the Wanderers in their Spheres shall no more be seen by thee; and the Stars in their places will lose their Light, and the Moon, NANNA, by whom thou also workest, shall become black and extinguished,..AND ARATAGAR SHALL BE NO MORE, AND THE EARTH SHALL ABIDE NOT...And around thee shall appear the Flame, like Lightning flashing in all directions, and all things will appear amid thunders, and from the Cavities of the Earth will leap forth the ANNUNNAKI, Dog-Faced, and thou shalt bring them down."*

# Mysteries of the Necronomicon Tradition

There are many aspects of the Necronomicon Tradition that the Initiate will learn about during their work. The Necronomicon Tradition cannot be explained fully in writing. The Initiate must Walk through all the various levels of the cosmology in order to gain a basic understanding of the text. It is said that this *"Tradition is a warrior's path where trust is not allowed, and upon the basis of such, everyone can become the greatest teacher unto their own self."* Many Initiates on this path can testify to the transformational power that issues forth from the Gates. In view of such, it is imperative that we check and research the attributes and methods that we are being taught. One of the greatest exercises mentioned in the Simon Necronomicon is copying the text over in our own hand. We can find this information in the Second Testimony:

*"And when fire comes from the heavens, there wilt surely be panic among the people, and the Priest must calm them an take this book, of which he must make a copy in his own,"*

This is probably one of the simplest exercises that many find difficult to execute. The passage cited above by the Mad Arab doesn't leave this practice up to a matter of choice. It must be done. In an age where electronic media is so readily available, many have lost appreciation for the value of writing, especially when it comes to sacred texts. The way words and letters are placed together in a written work is a form of alchemy that has long been forgotten. Leo G. Perdue, in the classical work entitled,

*Scribes, Sages, and Seers: The Sage in the Eastern Mediterranean World*, states the following on pages 41-42:

**"Copying sacred texts leads to knowledge, and this process is metaphorically seen as the disciple's swimming in the ocean of knowledge....He who is a skilled scribed and willing to work will learn beyond limits, while he who is incapable or unworthy of it will inevitably fail."**

The ancient adepts of the Greater Mysteries made it a practice to copy over sacred texts in their own hand since the act of writing was something divine in itself. Written in 1886, *A British Friend-Volume 44*, page 195 explains:

**"All ancient writers agree in calling the Chaldeans a nation of scribes, and Berosus, the Greco-Chaldean priest who wrote the history of his nation, and was himself a member of the scribe caste, ascribes to the guild of letters an antiquity extending far back beyond the Deluge. According to his writings, it was the strange creature –half fish, half human being-called Oannes Musaros, who first taught men the art of letters, and who himself wrote the beginning of all things....The people not only patronized, but even by their own pens or by the employment of the scribes enriched the libraries of their own cities, and it was deemed a pious act for a man to dedicate a copy of some standard work to the library of some temple "for the saving of his life and the prolonging of his days."...The science of letters in Chaldea held as high a position as in China or in Egypt, and the scribe was the most honoured of men, and the members of the best families joined the brotherhood of letters."**

It is very clear that the ancient world valued the art of letters and the act of copying a text over was revered as a divine work. The Book of the Black Earth presented to us by the Mad Arab, is a tome that we should make it a point to copy in our own hand, as we are instructed. The Tome is divided up into twelve sections, representing the twelve signs of the Igigi, and each section relates to mythologies that appear in ancient Mesopotamian lore.

**The Testimony Of The Mad Arab** is equivalent to the zodiac sign of Aries, or *Agru* (Xubur). The Akkadian term *Agru* means the *"hired man,"* or *"hireling,"* an agricultural worker employed to bring in the springtime barley harvest. It is within the Testimony of the Mad Arab that we find the uninitiated taking steps towards initiation, so the correlation of a laborer, or Agru. Interestingly, we find the following in Gavin White's *Babylonian Star-lore*:

**"The regent of the Hired Man is the shepherding god Dumuzi – 'the true child' or 'rightful son'. He is one of the earliest and most popular gods known in Mesopotamia, where he is thought of as the 'spirit of life' that is manifest in all aspects of nature. He appears in numerous guises, as a god of shepherds, cattle-herders, farmers, orchard men, fishermen and fowlers. Among the shepherds he promotes the abundance of the cattle-fold and its dairy produce, and in this aspect his mother is said to be Duttur, the personified ewe.**

**The myths surrounding Dumuzi largely concern his springtime courtship with Inanna, which culminated in the ceremony of the Sacred Marriage. In this rite, the deified king who was identified with Dumuzi either married the goddess or a priestess representing her. The fertility and fecundity of all nature was promoted by this sacred act of union."**

Dumuzi is called 'the Shepherd' and 'lord of the sheepfolds'. As the companion of Nigizzida 'to all eternity' he stands at the gate of heaven. The Testimony of the Mad Arab specifically deals with how to gain access to initiation into the Necronomicon Tradition. I can say from my personal experience from working with others that the energies of the Necronomicon Tradition usually communicates to the perspective Initiate in some way, whether through dreams, or a particular coincidence, before they come into contact with someone who can aid them in learning the system. When copying this part of the text over, the initiate will notice some relative experiences to that of the Mad Arab.

**Of The Zonei And Their Attributes** is the section following the Testimony of the Mad Arab, and specifically relates to the zodiac constellation of Taurus, or *Kakkab U Alap Shame* (Kingu). It is interesting to note how the sign Taurus was known as the *Bull of Heaven* in ancient Mesopotamia, which was revered as the *Crown of Anu*. Gavin White continues in the previously cited work:

**"The Bull of Heaven is probably the oldest exemplar of the theme of the shepherd and his flocks, which is so strongly represented in the springtime skies. As a basic celestial symbol cattle seem to represent all the fertile powers of the springtime skies – world mythology frequently relates the images of bulls, cows and calves to a whole range of heavenly phenomena including rain-clouds, rays of sunlight and the newborn sun."**

We begin to see some progress from Agru to Taurus, the Bull of Heaven. The hired laborer is now a shepherd. Gavin White continues on page 284:

**"In astrology texts the Crown of Anu is effectively used as an alternative name for the Bull of Heaven and the**

Bull's Jaw. It corresponds to the Greek Hyades, which makes up the head of Taurus. The astral symbol of the horned crown is thus very likely to have been developed from the horns of the Bull of Heaven."

Julye Bidmead makes the following observation in *The Akitu Festival*, page 220:

"The cultic symbols represent the deities' powers and epitomize heaven and earth. Anu was the sky god, the god of the heavens, creation, and kingship. His tiara, the "crown" of Anu, embodies the heavens. Because a tiara is worn on the head, it represents the above, the heavens..."

From Bidmead's comments we can see that the second section of the tome, **Of The Zonei And Their Attributes** gives the Initiate a brief outline, not only about the Gates, but the ruling powers of the zodiac, which collectively make up the **Crown of Anu**. *Chaldean Magic* by Francois Lernormant, page 432, states:

"In the descending scale of the emanations, and the supreme hierarchy of the pantheon, the gods of the five planets had the next place: viz., Adar (Saturn), Marduk (Jupiter), Nergal (Mars), Istar (Venus), and Nebo (Mercury)....With these planetary personages ends the series of the twelve great gods who constituted the true Chaldaic-Babylonian Olympus, the superior order of that divine hierarchy, ...who were said by him to preside over the twelve months of the year and the twelve signs of the zodiac."

In the ancient Chaldean Mysteries, it was believed that the gods of the seven planets ruled over the zodiac. These same deities are listed in **Of The Zonei And Their Attributes** section of the tome, which collectively find its correspondence to the powers ascribed to the Crown of Anu. The bull of Heaven also appears in Jewish mythology as the Golden Calf, wherein its shift from a cardinal zodiac sign to a fixed one, is described as Moses smashing the idol, or Gilgamesh slaying the Bull, also known as the first spouse of Ereshkigal, Gugalanna.

**The Book Of Entrance, And Of The Walking** corresponds to the zodiac sign of Gemini, also known as *Re'U Kinu Shame U Tu'Ame Rabutil* (Viper). Gavin White gives us a deeper look into the sign of Gemini:

**"The Twins were envisioned, weapons at the ready, guarding one of the entrances to the underworld. In Babylonian tradition, there are actually two entrances to the underworld, each of which is associated with one of the solstices. The wintertime entrance is primarily used by discarnate souls journeying to the afterlife, but the summer entrance, located in the region of the Crab, is used by the spirits of the ancestors when they return to earth to visit their family homes for the great ancestral festival celebrated in month 5. The summertime entrance is also the route that the souls of newborn babies use to enter into the world of men. The Twins probably guard this entrance to prevent the ingress of evil demons, which are sometimes said to use this otherworldly portal to bring plague and disease to mankind.... Even though the Twins are gods in their own right, they are both commonly identified with Nergal, the Lord of the Underworld, who brings death to man through the combined agencies of war, famine and plague. Indeed, the names of the Great Twins simply reveal two aspects of Nergal's character – Lugalirra means the 'Mighty King', perhaps a reference to Nergal as king of the dead, and Meslamtaea is literally 'the One who has arisen from the Underworld'."**

The connection of the Great Twins with Nergal is very unique, as they are said to guard the entrance to the World of the Dead. In one case, the summer entrance is used by spirits of the ancestors to visit their family homes. The other case is the wintertime entrance used by discarnate souls journeying to the afterlife. The twins are armed heavily to prevent evil influences that may try to come into the gate that the unborn take to enter the kingdom of men. This should not be surprising, as the Initiate learns that the Gate-Walking Ritual of Initiation is controlled by Nergal The whole underworld was said to be ruled over by Nergal, god of wisdom, and was divided into seven spheres or regions, each under the guardianship of a watcher stationed at a massive portal. The deceased is represented as a traveler who must surrender a portion of his vestments (his sheaths of consciousness) to each one of the seven guardians in turn.

**The Incantation Of The Gates** corresponds to the zodiac sign Cancer, also known as *Shittu* (Snake).Gavin White continues:

**"The Crab was also closely associated with an entrance to the underworld in Greek and Roman traditions. Much the same is implied in Babylonian traditions where some magical texts even speak of using the influence of the Crab in rites designed to raise ghosts from the underworld and to make offerings to the dead."**

The sign Cancer is ruled by the Moon and it is also remembered in Roman astrology as the 'Gates of Men,' which is the route taken by the souls of babies destined to be born on earth. However, the souls of the Unborn are not the only thing created in the process of the Gate of Men, but it is the first step towards the sacred marriage between our Jinn being and the human Initiate.

**The Conjuration Of The Fire God** corresponds to the zodiac sign of Leo or *Kalbu Rabu* (Lakhamu). In some ancient Mesopotamian texts the region of the Lion is named as the minor god Latarak. Sandra Tabathat Cicero in the work, *Babylonian Tarot*, makes the following observation:

**"La-tarak was a god who guarded doorways and protected the devout against sorcery and evil magic."**

The description given by Cicero is similar to the work of the Fire God in the Necronomicon Tradition. Earlier in this work we discussed how the Fire God was used in ancient Mesopotamia to combat the influences of "negative" energy. Leo is ruled by the Sun and when the Initiate advances to higher stages of the work, they will come to appreciate that everything that is done in the ritual of Calling is symbolic of the natural progression of celestial and terrestrial movements. One of the first things that we do in opening the ritual of Calling is summoning the Fire God. The Fire God represents the cosmic fire that works in all living things. Therefore, the rising of the celestial Sun begins a new day and corresponds to the Conjuration of the Fire God. The physical body's metabolism, being ruled by the Sun, is symbolic of the Fire God's influence over the Watcher, and the Walking is where we direct our thoughts and emotions during the day are symbolic of the incantations and words of power that we use in ritual.

**The Conjuration Of The Watcher** corresponds to the zodiac sign of Virgo, also known as *Shiru* (Whirlwind).

Shiru or Siru (Ear of Corn), or title also applied to its luminary Spica, the star of spring which led the constellation. Virgo was also known as The Proclaimer of Rain with the Sumerian name Ab-Nan. Its Akkadian name, Siru, denoted an Ear of Corn. In Babylonia, the constellation was known as the wife of Bel and as Sa-Sha-Shiru. In *Astronomica* by Manilius, 1st century AD, p.237 and 239, we find the following:

**"The temperaments of those whose span of life she pronounces at their birth** Erigone (Virgo) **will direct to study, and she will train their minds in the learned arts. She will give not so much abundance of wealth as the impulse to investigate the causes and effects of things. On them she will confer a tongue which charms, the mastery of words, and that mental vision which can discern all things, however concealed they be by the mysterious workings of nature. From the Virgin will also come the stenographer: his letter represents a word, and by means of his symbols he can keep ahead of utterance and record in novel notation the long speech of a rapid speaker. But with the good there comes a flaw: bashfulness handicaps the early years of such persons, for the Maid, by holding back their great natural gifts, puts a bridle on their lips and restrains them by the curb of authority. And (small wonder in a virgin) her offspring is not fruitful."**

Virgo heralds in a time of harvest, and so too is the Watcher extremely instrumental in bringing about the fruitage of our ritual work. Gavin White continues:

**"The origins of *Virgo* can be traced back to the Babylonian constellation called the Furrow. Like the familiar Greek image, the Furrow was portrayed as a goddess bearing an oversize ear of barley. She**

symbolised the barley fields in early autumn when they are about to be seeded, and as may be expected her star was used in astrology to predict the success or failure of the coming harvest: *'If the Furrow is dark: the barley will fall short of its predicted yield, a shortage of barley and straw will befall the land'*. It would actually be more accurate to regard the modern image of the *Virgin* as a combination of two independent Babylonian constellations – the Furrow and the Frond, which occupy the eastern and western sectors of *Virgo* respectively. The Frond, which stands immediately behind the Lion, was depicted as a goddess holding a frond of the date palm – this attribute has, in fact, been retained in many images of *Virgo*, where she bears her barley stalk in one hand and a date palm frond in the other... The cultic nature of late summer is dominated by the observances for the dead. The mourning rites of Dumuzi were celebrated in month 4, immediately following the summer solstice, and the ancestors were honoured in the great Brazier festival of month 5. In this ritual the ancestors were invited back to the world of the living for an annual feast in their ancestral homes. The most significant part of the ceremony involved lighting torches and braziers to guide the ghosts of the ancestors back from the darkness of the underworld... The archaic forms of the Furrow and the Raven can now be tentatively restored as a 'Torch-bearing goddess and a 'Soul-bird,' which represents an ancestral ghost returning from the realm of the dead."

The Soul-Bird mentioned above is the phoenix. The reader may also want to note that the "Watcher" is described in the Chaldean Oracles as the immortal soul, but is spoken of in feminine form. In a summary of the Oracles themselves, we find in the Thomas Stanley translation of the text in 1661, under Pletho's Exposition, we read:

"The Magi that are followers of Zoroaster, as also many others, hold that the Human Soul is immortal; and descended from above to serve the mortal Body, that is, to operate therein for a certain time; and to Animate, and Adorn it to her power; and then returns to the place from which she came. And whereas there are many Mansions there for the Soul, one wholly-bright, another wholly dark, others betwixt both, partly-bright, partly-dark: The Soul, being descended from that which is wholly-bright, into the Body, if she perform her Office well, runs back into the same place; but if not well, she retires into worse Mansions, according to the things which she hath done in Life. The Oracle therefore sayeth, *seek thou the Souls path*, or the way by which the Soul flowed into thee; or by what course (*viz* of Life) having performed thy charge toward the Body, thou mayst Mount up to the same place from which thou didst flow down, *viz.* the same Track of the Soul, *joyning action to sacred speech*. By *sacred speech*, he understands that which concerns Divine Worship; by action, Divine Rites. The Oracle therefore sayeth, that to this Exaltation of the Soul, both speech concerning Divine Worship (Prayers,) and Religious Rites (Sacrifices) are requisite."

Usually the Watcher will appear in the opposite gender of the individual in most cases, not all. The Chaldean Oracles describe the Watcher in code, as all in this work are children of Ishtar/Inanna. We will return to this subject later in our writing.

**The Maklu Text** corresponds to the zodiac sign of Libra, also known as *Zibanitum* (Ravening Dog). Gavin White continues:

"The constellation of the Scales, which was formed from the Scorpion's Claws long ago, is held to be particularly sacred to the sun god Šamaš. In the first place, the Scales symbolise the autumn equinox, when the watches of day and night are held to be of equal duration and the sun rises due east and sets due west. And secondly, the Scales symbolise the idea of judicial prudence, as in the phrase 'weighing up the evidence', which is particularly appropriate to the sun god as his principle role within the Babylonian pantheon was to act as the arbitrator of truth and justice. For these reasons the Scales are thought to be the special station of the sun in Babylonian astrology, where they are purposefully set opposite to the moon's station in the Star Cluster (the *Pleiades*)."

In the opening passages of the Magan Text, we read:

*"The banishings, or exorcisms, are to be pronounced in a clear voice without trembling, without shaking. The arms should be held over the head in the attitude of a Priest of SHAMMASH, and the eyes must behold the Spirit of the God SHAMMASH, even though it be the time of the Sleeping of SHAMMASH behind the Mountains of the Scorpion."*

When we compare the words of the Mad Arab with what was written by Gavin White, we can see evidence of how the Maklu Text is relevant to the sign of Libra. The Scales is a symbol of justice. The Maklu Text is not used to curse, or attack, but the recital of any of the incantations in the Maklu Text is a call for justice.

The Book Of Calling corresponds to the zodiac sign of Scorpio, also known as *Akrabu* (Scorpion-Man). Gavin White explains:

"Nevertheless, the Scorpion's mythical nature within the stellar calendar is most clearly revealed in the *Epic of Gilgamesh* where the gate of the sun is guarded by a pair of scorpion-people. The gate marks the start of an underground tunnel that was travelled by the sun during the course of each night and was traversed by Gilgamesh on his way to the visit the immortals who lived beyond the confines of this world. In terms of the sun's annual circuit of the stars this tunnel can naturally be thought of as symbolising the sun's autumnal descent into the darkness of the underworld... The Scorpion in its entirety is attributed to the multifaceted goddess Išhara. She was worshipped by many peoples and nations throughout the Ancient Near East, which has led to a confusing array of attributions – she is known as a great goddess to the Hurrians, the wife of Dagon among the West Semites, and to the Akkadians she was a goddess of love with close affinities to Ištar, whose sacred plant cannabis (*qunnabu*) was known as the 'aromatic of Išhara'. In astrology texts she is sometimes called 'Išhara of the ocean' (Išhara Tiamat), a name applied to Venus, and from her widespread worship she is also known as the 'queen of the inhabited world'."

Different than modern-day correspondences the sign of Scorpio was attributed to Ishara, the goddess who has close affinities to the Babylonian goddess Ishtar. The Scorpion Man and Woman were the gatekeepers and guarded the Mountains of Mashu, where the Sun traveled through every night. Access through this mountain could only be obtained if one were determined to be a progeny of the gods, if not a god/goddess themselves, as was the case with Gilgamesh, which relates directly with what we find in the Book of Calling:

*"Therefore, thine obligation is as of the Gatekeeper of the Inside, agent of MARDUK, servant of ENKI, for the Gods are forgetful, and very far away, and it was to the Priests of the Flame that Covenant was given to seal the Gates between this World and the Other, and to keep Watch thereby, through this Night of Time, and the Circle of Magick is the Barrier, the Temple, and the Gate between the Worlds."*

Many of the rituals and rites listed in the Book of Calling are relevant to mystical practices that are executed during the Sun's mythical journey through the Mountains of Mashu.

**The Book of Fifty Names** corresponds to the zodiac sign Sagittarius, also known as *Pa-Bil-Sag* (Hurricane). This is very interesting as Jupiter rules the sign of Sagittarius in modern astrology, and here we have the 50 Names of Marduk aligned with Sagittarius. Gavin White makes this observation:

**"Even though the Goatfish is part of the zodiac, and thus constantly interacting with the sun, moon and planets, it has surprisingly little lore directly associated with it in either Babylonian or Greek traditions. Consequently, if we want to describe the symbolic nature of the constellation, we have to fall back on other, more indirect methods.... Despite the strong affinity to Enki, astrology texts list the regent of the Goatfish as the little-known goddess Tašmetu. Her name is derived from the Akkadian word *šamû*, and can be roughly translated as *'the granter of requests'*. She is regarded as the wife of the scribe god Nabu, who is the regent of the nearby Cargo-Boat."**

In the book *Dead Names,* Simon mentions that a careful reading of the Magan Text may reveal a certain formulae.

The Text is very mystical and is employed through various breathing exercises that we will discuss later.

**The Urilia Text** corresponds to the zodiac sign of Aquarius, also known as *Gula* (Horned Beast). Gavin White associates this constellation with the god Enki. However, in the works of E.M. Plunket, *Ancient Calendars and Constellations*, on page 263, we read:

**"As to a mythological reason for the choice of the goddess Gula to preside over the constellation known to us as Aquarius, we find it in the fact that Gula appears as another name for the goddess Bau"**

Gula was a Babylonian goddess, the consort of Ninib. She is identical with another goddess, known as Bau, though it would seem that the two were originally independent. Bau seems originally to have been goddess of the dog; as Nininsina she was long represented with a dog's head, and the dog was her emblem. Perhaps because the licking of sores by dogs was supposed to have curative value, she became a goddess of healing. She was a daughter of An (The Sky God), king of the gods. The sacred animal of Gula was the dog - a large number of small votive figures of dogs were dedicated to the goddess by her devotees and supplicants, the models acting as offerings. It seems that dogs wandered freely within the sanctuary and played a key role in the healing ritual. She is praised as the "Eldest of Heaven" and the mother goddess of Babylonia and Phoenicia. She is the Goddess of Mabon, a mother protector, with the power to inflict disease, or to cure disease. She lived in a garden at the center of the world, and watered the tree that forms its axis. Other names borne by this goddess are Nin-Karrak, Ga-tum-dug and Nm-dindug, the latter signifying "the lady who restores to life", or the Goddess of Healing. After the Great Flood, she helped "breathe life" back into mankind. The designation well emphasizes the chief trait of Bau-Gula which is that of healer.

Aspects of the goddess Gula, also known as Nintinugga, seem to fall in line with the very definition of the term Ur-ila, or Urila, as *ila* means *mother goddess*, and *Ur* is defined as *light*. Since Enki means *Lord of the Earth*, it stands to reason that he is joined to the goddess of the Earth.

**The Testimony Of The Mad Arab, the Second Part** corresponds to the zodiac sign of Pisces, also known as *Dilgan U Rikis Nuni* (Weapon). In the Babylonian zodiac Pisces was associated with the goddesses Anunitum and Simmah, symbolizing the rivers Tigris and Euphrates.

When we compare the twelve different sections with the seven Gates of Initiation, it becomes clear that the Simon Necronomicon is a complete reflection of current celestial movements. When we make effort to copy the text over in our own hand, we are practicing the art of creating our own experience and those who remain focused on doing such are able to use their will in achieving their goals successfully. Letters are individual sigils that represent a certain phenomena occurring in the heavens and on Earth. Writing has a valuable place in the Necronomicon Tradition. When the Initiate begins to copy the text in his/her own hand, he/she, will notice the connection between the body, mind, and soul. The veil becomes lifted and the Initiate soon recognizes that the physical plane and the astral plane are the same, and through the course of our initiation, we see elements of our ritual in daily course of life. For example, our Conjuration of the Fire God corresponds to the rising of the Sun, the beginning of a new day. It is usually on the rising of the

Sun that we awaken, which represents the Calling of the Watcher, and as we begin our day, engaging in various activities, we are walking a Gate. Each day is a Gate. The banishing rituals that are mentioned in the Maklu Text can be performed throughout the day simply by avoiding negative thinking. In so doing, we become like the Elder Gods.

# Origin of the Term Elder Gods

It is important for us to look at how the term Elder Gods is used in the Simon Necronomicon. The term *Elder Gods* first appears in the Simon Necronomicon as follows:

*"Let all who read this book be warned thereby that the habitation of men are seen and surveyed by that Ancient Race of gods and demons from a time before time, and that they seek revenge for that forgotten battle that took place somewhere in the Cosmos and rent the Worlds in the days before the creation of Man, when the Elder Gods walked the Spaces, the race of MARDUK, as he is known to the Chaldeans, and of ENKI our MASTER, the Lord of Magicians."*

We next find use of this term in the description of the Three Seals of MASSHU:

*"Of the three carved symbols, the first is the sign of our Race from beyond the Stars, and is called ARRA in the tongue of the Scribe who taught it to me, an emissary of the Elder Ones. In the tongue of the eldest city of Babylon, it was UR. It is the Sigil of the Covenant of the Elder Gods, and when they see it, they who gave it to us, they will not forget us. They have sworn!..Spirit of the Skies, Remember!..The second is the Elder Sign, and is the Key whereby the Powers of the Elder Gods may be summoned, when used with the proper words and shapes. It has a Name, and is called AGGA... The third sign is the Sigil of the Watcher. It is called BANDAR. The Watcher is a Race sent by the Elder Ones. It keeps vigil while one sleeps, provided the appropriate ritual and sacrifice has been performed,: else, if called, it will turn upon you."*

In a *Sumer Aryan Dictionary*, we find the Term AGGA, defined on page 6 of the said work, as meaning *command*, but on page 7 it is defined as *fiery spirit of the deep*, and as *watery spirit of the deep*. It would seem that the AGGA sign has more to do with commanding the fiery and watery elements of the deep. The term itself, though assigned to the Elder Gods, doesn't define who or what the Elder Gods are. So we shall proceed to another passage that is found in the Simon Necronomicon's Book of Calling:

**"THIS is the Book of the Ceremonies of Calling, handed down since the time the Elder Gods walked the Earth, Conquerors of the Ancient Ones."**

The above passage helps us to see that besides all the abstract correspondences considered, the Elder Gods are advanced men and women. Is it possible to find historical proof of this before Lovecraftian fiction? Yes

We find evidence of the Elder Gods existence prior to Lovecraftian fiction in the Greater Mysteries. Written in 1893, years before the Lovecraftian Mythos, *The Pacific Theosophist, Volumes 4-6*, states the following on page 65:

**"There has existed for tens of centuries in the inaccessible wilderness about the Himalaya mountains a secret Brotherhood of great souls-which is the meaning of the word Mahatma-or Elder Brothers; men who after many incarnations have obtained great wisdom; have learned to control themselves and through that control to make the forces of Nature their servants. These Mahatmas are the repository of wisdom of the ages, which, accumulating century after century, has been entrusted to their keeping. Nations have appeared and disappeared with their various**

civilizations; priesthoods have advanced to great power and have been abolished, yet the Brotherhood has continued, and has been made the heir of all which these civilizations and priesthoods have developed. Continents have risen above the ocean, have been made ready for inhabitants, have been occupied by millions, and have been sunk beneath the waves; still the Brotherhood has endured, not as the same individuals, but as successive Adepts possessed of all knowledge and power of their predecessors. When one Brother has laid aside the body, a neophyte has been advanced to his place, and so the number has always remained undiminished. Not always have all the Elder Brothers remained in the same place; as occasion required they have appeared now in one place and now in another. For not only are they deep students and custodians of the knowledge of myriads of years, bur are Saviors of humanity. Their special charge is to help the human race in its slow evolution process of evolution from the man of flesh to the man of Spirit."

The information cited above, which was written in 1893, clearly shows us that the Simon Necronomicon's use of the term *"Elder Gods"* is actually more in accord with writings that pre-date Lovecraftian fiction. The Elder Gods according to the Simon Necronomicon are said to use the following:

*"The Watcher is a Race sent by the Elder Ones. It keeps vigil while one sleeps, provided the appropriate ritual and sacrifice has been performed."*

Is there any historical evidence aligning the Watcher with the Elder Brothers in regards to the Greater Mysteries? Back in 1959, W.E. Butler in his book *The Magician His Training and Work* mentions the following on page 60:

"If our home-made ritual is built up on lines of the true principles of the Egregore of our tradition, then by the process of induction we may draw power from that tradition, and become linked with it. Now behind every magical school, behind the Eastern and Western Traditions, and again behind the Planetary Tradition, there are people, who are the Stewards or Guardians of their respective Mysteries, are only too glad to work with and through any earnest student who is working along their line. It therefore happens that an individual group of magical workers is drawn into psychic and spiritual contact with the Guardians of the Mysteries. From thenceforward it becomes a centre though which they may work...Such a great privilege brings with it increasing responsibilities, but also increased opportunity for work in the service of the *Elder Brothers* of humanity....Each country has its own group of "Watchers" and the normal magical evolution of any member of that country is within the sphere of that group. But to every man his own master."

The information, written by Butler back in 1959, not only shows us that the Watcher is an integral part of the work of the Elder Brothers, but validates the fact that the *Invocation of the Watcher* is a practice that is consistent with the Greater Mysteries, wherein the Simon Necronomicon is unique. In that it preserves this sacred magical rite that has been aborted by watered-down New Age groups and propaganda. This shows us beyond a shadow of a doubt that the term *Elder Gods*, as it appears in the Simon Necronomicon, is faithful to the Greater Mysteries, and not a compromise to fit into Lovecraft fiction.

## Realm of the Igigi: The Kingdom of Heaven

### No. 77,821 (85–4–30, 15).

| Month. | Determinative of Star. | Name of the Sign of the Zodiac. | Modern Equivalent. |
|---|---|---|---|
| 𒌋 | 𒀭 | 𒌍 𒂍 𒄑 | Goat. |
| 𒇇 | 𒀭 | 𒀭 𒀸 𒇇 𒌋 𒇽 | Bull. |
| 𒌋 | 𒀭 | 𒌍 𒀭 𒌋 𒇽 𒀸 𒌋 𒂊 𒇇 𒇇 | Twins. |
| 𒂍 | 𒀭 | 𒇇 𒂍 | Crab. |
| 𒍏 | 𒀭 | 𒈦 𒑱 𒂍 | Lion. |
| 𒂍 | 𒀭 | 𒂍 𒇽 | Virgin. |
| 𒉈 | 𒀭 | 𒇽 𒂍 𒈬 𒀸 | Scales. |
| 𒂍 | 𒀭 | 𒄿 𒂊 | Scorpion. |
| 𒄑 | 𒀭 | 𒌋 𒍏 𒇇 | Bow. |
| 𒉈 | 𒀭 | 𒀀 𒇇 𒌋 𒀀 | Capricornus. |
| 𒄑 | 𒀭 | 𒑱 𒂍 | Water-bearer |
| 𒀸 | 𒀭 | 𒌋 𒈹 𒄿 | The Fishes. |

*"When the Great KUTULU rises up and greets the Stars, then the War will be over, and the World be One."*

From the above passage we can determine that the work of the Necronomicon Tradition is integral part of the Greater Mysteries, in that it has everything to do with completing our being and perfecting ourselves. Yet it is still different. It is a qliphotic rite that has everything to do with the perfection of those who are jinn and of jinn-human progeny. In regards to the Mad Arab's words above, we find this theme to be very consistent with what is mentioned in Babylonian Legends of Creation by E.A. Budge:

**"There are in the British Museum several fragments of Neo-Babylonian copies of the Seven Tablets of Creation, the exact position of which is at present**

uncertain. One of these (S. 2013) is of some importance because it speaks of one object which was in the "upper Tiâmat" ⸗I⟨ 𒂍 ⸗I⟨, and of another which was in the "lower Tiâmat" This shows that the Babylonians thought that one half of the body of Tiâmat, which was split up by Marduk, was made into the celestial ocean, and the other half into the terrestrial ocean, in other words, into "the waters that were above" and "the waters that were beneath" the firmament respectively."

When we consider what is mentioned by the Mad Arab in the Urilia Text and what is mentioned by Budge in the material cited above, it seems evident that the Realm of the Igigi is what Christians refer to as the Kingdom of Heaven. Jake-Stratton-Kent mentions the following in Stellar Lore Essay:

"The two rivers are reminiscent of crossing rivers in Greek and Semitic legend. They also suggest the White and Blue Nile of Egypt. Originally they were associated with Sumeria's Tigris and Euphrates. The Goddess Tiamat, the Celestial Dragon, has been identified with the Milky Way by some students. But the Underworld Dragon was always the Zodiac itself, through whose body the traveller made their way. On the other hand Tiamat has been identified with the cloak of mist over the rivers of Sumeria, spread out on the plain like an immense serpent. It is more likely however that Tiamat had a physical as well as a celestial counterpart. The dragon of the zodiac is necessarily circular, the serpent with its tail in its mouth in fact. Not only is the serpent said to encircle the world in this form, but to coil about World Mountains and Trees. In Greek and Semitic mythology it guards the 'forbidden fruit' at what is recognisably an archetypal World Centre. Draco has been identified with all these mythological Dragon Guardians.

We should also note that the Sumerio-Babylonian Stellar Lore recognised two kinds of celestial spirit. The first kind are the children of Anu, the infernal judges, the Anunnaki- identified with the oarsmen of Argo Navis. These are the spirits of stars below the horizon, in the Underworld. The other kind, the Igigi are spirits of the stars above the horizon, and were also associated with Anu, the Sumerian Sky and Heaven God. In Mesopotamia (and points north) Draco, Ursa Major and the Circumpolar stars are Igigi, they never set. Canis Major, Argo Navis and Orion are invisible much of the time in northern latitudes and are thus Anunnaki. Tiamat fulfills both roles, as celestial dragon she is Igigi, as Underworld River Anunnaki."

Kent comments clearly illustrate that the "Igigi" represent the upper heavens. This cosmology is also expressed in the Simon Necronomicon:

*"The lines of my life have been obliterated by my wanderings in the Waste, over the letters writ in the heavens by the gods. And even now I can hear the wolves howling in the mountains as they did that fateful night, and they are calling my name, and the names of Others. I fear for my flesh, but I fear for my spirit more."*

The "wanderings" that the Mad Arab is referring to, is the continual process of Walking and re-Walking the seven gates of initiation as they appear in the Simon Necronomicon. Evidently, the Mad Arab is explaining such as a warning against these ignorant actions. We can be certain of this by his description of the Igigi:

*"For this is the Book of the Dead, the Book of the Black Earth, that I have writ down at the peril of my life, exactly as I received it, on the planes of the IGIGI, the cruel celestial spirits from beyond the Wanderers of the Wastes."*

Here we see that the Igigi are described as dwelling beyond the "Wanderers of the Wasters." we can conclude that when the Mad Arab speaks about his "wanderings in the Waste," he is referring to Walking and re-Walking the seven gates of initiation. The Initiate can call upon one of the seven gates after initiation by using the proper method of drawing out the seal of the Gate and invoking it in a fashion that is similar to how the 50 Names are invoked, or they could use the method in the Book of Calling. Other passages in the Simon Necronomicon help us to appreciate that the term "Spaces" is also a reference to the realms of the Igigi. Let us look at a few examples of these. The first is taken from the Book of Calling:

*"THIS is the Book of the Ceremonies of Calling, handed down since the time the Elder Gods walked the Earth, Conquerors of the Ancient Ones."*

The above passage relates to the rituals used by the Elder Gods when calling upon "earthly powers." This statement is vastly different from what we read in the Mad Arab's First Testimony:

*"Let all who read this book be warned thereby that the habitation of men are seen and surveyed by that Ancient Race of gods and demons from a time before time, and that they seek revenge for that forgotten battle that took place somewhere in the Cosmos and rent the Worlds in the days before the creation of Man, when the Elder Gods*

*walked the Spaces, the race of MARDUK, as he is known to the*
*Chaldeans, and of ENKI our MASTER, the Lord of Magicians."*

This part of the text indicates that the Elder Gods were first Walkers of the plains of the Igigi, or the "spaces," before Earth was settled and this was the reason that it was probably referred to as the Abode of the Gods. In the work cited before by Budge, we find the following:

"Not content with Ummu-Khubur's brood of devils, Tiâmat called the stars and powers of the air to her aid, for she "set up" (1) the Viper, (2) the Snake, (3) the god Lakhamu, (4) the Whirlwind, (5) the ravening Dog, (6) the Scorpion-man, (7) the mighty Storm-wind, (8) the Fish-man, and (9) the
Horned Beast. These bore (10) the "merciless, invincible weapon," and were under the command of (11) Kingu, whom Tiâmat calls "her husband." Thus Tiâmat had Eleven mighty Helpers besides the devils spawned by Ummu-Khubur. We may note in passing that some of the above-mentioned Helpers appear among the Twelve Signs of the Zodiac which Marduk "set up" after his conquest of Tiâmat, *e.g.*, the Scorpion-man, the Horned Beast, etc. This fact suggests that the first Zodiac was "set up" by Tiâmat, who with her Eleven Helpers formed the Twelve Signs; the association of evil with certain stars may date from that period. That the Babylonians regarded the primitive gods as powers of evil is clear from the fact that Lakhamu, one of them, is enumerated among the allies of Tiâmat.

The helpers of Tiâmat were placed by her under the command of a god called KINGU who is TAMMUZ. He was the counterpart, or equivalent, of ANU, the Sky-god, in the kingdom of darkness, for it is said in the

text "Kingu was exalted and received the power of
Anu," *i.e.*, he possessed the same power and attributes
as Anu. When Tiâmat appointed Kingu to be her
captain, she recited over him a certain spell or
incantation, and then she gave him the TABLET OF
DESTINIES and fastened it to his breast, saying,
"Whatsoever goeth forth from thy mouth shall be
established." Armed with all the magical powers
conferred upon him by this Tablet, and heartened by
all the laudatory epithets which his wife Tiâmat heaped
upon him, Kingu went forth at the head of his devils."

From the onset of our discussion it seems that the Gate-
Walker finally gains full initiation when, he or she,
travels from the lower worlds and reaches the realms of
the Igigi. This is what is meant by the Mad Arab's words
that follow:

*"When the Great KUTULU rises up and greets the Stars,
then the War will be over, and the World be One."*

We can determine this based on another passage which
speaks about the Igigi:

*"Only when thou hast shown thy power over the
Maskim and the Rabishu, mayest thou venture forth to
the Land of the IGIGI,"*

It is only when the Gate-Walker has reached a level of
spiritual maturity and purity that they are allowed to
enter into the Kingdom of the Heavens. This is the
purpose of the qliphotic alchemy so integral to the
Necronomicon Tradition, and it is for this reason that we
find the Mad Arab's words in the Magan Text, and
appropriate conclusion:

*"For what is new..Came from that which is old..And what is old..Shall replace that which is new..And once again the Ancient Ones..Shall rule upon the face of the Earth!..And this is too the Covenant!"*

*"Only when thou hast shown thy power over the Maskim and the Rabishu, mayest thou venture forth to the Land of the IGIGI, ... Only when ADAR has been obtained, may the Priest consider himself a master of the planes of the Spheres, and able to wrestle with the Old Gods. Once Death Herself has been stared in the Eye, can the Priest then summon and control the denizens of Death's darkly curtained halls. Then can he hope to open the Gate without fear and without that loathing of the spirit that slays the man."*

# Nindinugga

One of the most mysterious deities appearing in the Necronomicon pantheon is Nindinugga. In the Second Testimony of the Mad Arab we find the following:

*"And if these worshippers and sorcerers still come at thee, as it is possible, for their power comes from the Stars, and who knows the ways of the Stars?, thou must call upon the Queen of Mysteries, NINDINUGGA, who wilt surely save thee. And thou must make incantations with her Title, which is NINDINUGGA NIMSHIMSHARGAL ENLILLARA. And it is enough merely to shout that Name aloud, Seven times, and she will come to thine aid."*

Since information concerning DinGir Nindinugga is not readily available, many people have wondered if this deity is something fictional, or maybe an aspect of more popular goddess. When we look at the name Nindinugga, we see these three distinct aspects:

**NIN** = Lady **DIN** = righteous, pure, bright **UGGA (Uga)** = raven, dead

William W. Hallo, in the classic work, *The World's Oldest Literature*, defines Nindinugga on page 766 as:

**"For *Nindinugga*, the "*Woman* who Revives the *Dead*" in ... "the mistress who revives the (near-) *dead*." 35 The same epithet, applied to Ninisina in a hymnal prayer, 36 was translated by Kramer as "queen of the living and the *dead*."**

Readers will find it useful to explore aspects of the deity Nindinugga under the name Nintinugga. Readers will see that Nindinugga is actually an aspect of DinGir Gula. Wikipedia explains further under the title Nintinugga:

**"Nintinugga was a Babylonian goddess of healing, the consort of Ninurta. She is identical with another goddess, known as Bau, though it would seem that the two were originally independent.**

**The name Bau is more common in the oldest period and gives way in the post Khammurabic age to Gula. Since it is probable that Ninib has absorbed the cults of minor sun-deities, the two names may represent consorts of different gods. However this may be, the qualities of both are alike, and the two occur as synonymous designations of Ninib's female consort.**

**Other names borne by this goddess are Nin-Karrak, Nin Ezen, Ga-tum-dug and Nm-din-dug, the latter signifying "the lady who restores to life", or the Goddess of Healing. After the Great Flood, she helped "breath life" back into mankind. The designation well emphasizes the chief trait of Bau-Gula which is that of healer. She is often spoken of as "the great physician," and accordingly plays a specially prominent role in incantations and incantation rituals intended to relieve those suffering from disease"**

I hope this information serves as a gateway of sorts for those who seek to understand this primordial energy a little bit more and that the Initiate of the Necronomicon Tradition find his/her experience with DinGir Nindinugga a healing one indeed.

# Divine Law Within The Necronomicon Tradition

One of the interesting things that I have heard some Initiates of the system complain about is that the deities invoked in the Necronomicon (Qliphotic) pantheon are not easily controlled. Many who are familiar with the text, are sure to be reminded of the Mad Arab's words that follow:

*"Remember, always, in every empty moment, to call upon the Gods not to forget thee, for they are forgetful and very far away. Light thy fires high in the hills, and on the tops of temples and pyramids, that they may see and remember."*

The deities in the Necronomicon Pantheon are not spirits, as in the case of Ceremonial Magick, which are subject to the Initiate in the Western sense of the term. It should be remembered that when and individual chooses this Tradition as their path and Walks through the Seven Gates of self-initiation, they become citizens of a spiritual society and subject to Divine Law. Divine Law is any law (or rule) that in the opinion of its believers comes directly from the will of God (or a god).

Divine Law is communicated by a particular deity to the Initiate via revelation. Within the Necronomicon Tradition these laws usually comes through to the Initiate via dreams, as in the cliche, *Dead, But Dreaming*. In the Book of Calling, the Mad Arab reveals the law of each Gate, which goes as follows:

*(Nanna Gate)* **Know, first, that the Power of the Conquerors is the Power of the Magick, and that the stricken gods will ever tempt thee away from the Legions of the Mighty, and that you will feel the subtle fluids of thy body moving to the breath of TIAMAT and the Blood of KINGU who races in your veins. Be ever watchful, therefore, not to open this Gate, or, if thou must needs, put a time for its closing before the rising of the Sun, and seal it at that time; for to leave it open is to be the agent of CHAOS.**

*(Nebo Gate)* **Know, secondly, that the Power of Magick is the Power of Our Master ENKI, Lord of the Seas, and Master of Magick, Father of MARDUK, Fashioner of the Magick Name, the Magick Number, the Magick Word, the Magick Shape. So, therefore, the Priest who governeth the works of Fire, and of the God of Fire, GISHBAR called GIBIL, must firstly sprinkle with the Water of the Seas of ENKI, as a testament to his Lordship and a sign of the Covenant that exists between him and thee.**

*(Ishtar Gate)* **Know, thirdly, that by the Power of the Elder Gods and the submission of the Ancient Ones, thou mayest procure every type of honour, dignity, wealth and happiness, but that these are to be shunned as the Purveyors of Death, for the most radiant jewels are to be found buried deep in the Earth, and the Tomb of Man is the Splendour of ERESHKIGAL, the joy of KUTULU, the food of AZAG-THOTH.... Therefore, thine obligation is as of the Gatekeeper o the Inside, agent of MARDUK, servant of ENKI, for the Gods are forgetful, and very far away, and it was to the Priests of the Flame that Covenant was given to seal the Gates between this World and the Other, and to keep Watch thereby, through this Night of Time, and the Circle of Magick is**

the Barrier, the Temple, and the Gate between the
Worlds.

(*Shammash Gate*) **Know, fourthly, that it is become the
obligation of the Priests of the Flame and the Sword, and
of all Magick, to bring their Power to the Underworld
and keep it chained thereby, for the Underworld is surely
the Gate Forgotten, by which the Ancient Ones ever seek
Entrance to the Land of the Living, And the Ministers of
ABSU are clearly walking the Earth, riding on the Air,
and upon the Earth, and sailing silently through the
Water, and roaring in the Fire, and all these Spirits must
be brought to subjection to the Person of the Priest of
Magick, before any else. Or the Priest becomes prey to
the Eye of Death of the Seven ANNUNNAKI, Lord of the
Underworld, Ministers of the Queen of Hell.**

(*Nergal Gate*) **Know, fifthly, that the worshippers of
TIAMAT are abroad in the world, and will give fight to
the Magician. Lo, they have worshipped the Serpent from
Ancient Times, and have always been with us. And they
are to be known by their seeming human appearance
which has the mark of the Beast upon them, as they
change easily into the Shapes of animals and haunt the
Nights of Men and by their odor, which comes of burning
incenses unlawful to the worship of the Elder Ones. And
their Books are the Books of CHAOS and the flames, and
are the Books of the Shadows and the Shells. And they
worship the heaving earth and the ripping sky and the
rampant flame and the flooding waters; and they are the
raisers of the legions of maskim, the Liers-In-Wait. And
they do not know what it is they do, but they do it at the
demands of the Serpent, at whose Name even
ERESHKIGAL gives fright, and the dread KUTULU
strains at his bonds ... MUMMU TIAMAT Queen of the
Ancient Ones!**

*(Marduk Gate) Know, sixthly, that thou shalt not seek the operations of this Magick save by the rules and governments set down herein, for to do other is to take the most awful risk, for thyself and for all mankind. Therefore, heed these words carefully, and change not the words of the incantations, whether thou understand them, or understand them not, for they are the words of the Pacts made of Old, and before Time. So, say them softly if the formula is "softly", or shout them aloud if the formula is "aloud", but change not one measure lest thou call something Else, and it be your final hour.*

*(Adar Gate) Know, seventhly, of the Things thou art to expect in the commission of this Most sacred Magick. Study the symbols well, and do not be afraid of any awful spectre that shall invade thine operation, or haunt thine habitat by day or by night. Only charge them with them the words of the Covenant and they will do as you ask, of thou be strong. And if thou performest these operations often, thou shalt see things becoming dark; and the Wanderers in their Spheres shall no more be seen by thee; and the Stars in their places will lose their Light, and the Moon, NANNA, by whom thou also workest, shall become black and extinguished, And around thee shall appear the Flame, like Lightning flashing in all directions, and all things will appear amid thunders, and from the Cavities of the Earth will leap forth the ANNUNNAKI, Dog-Faced, and thou shalt bring them down....AND ARATAGAR SHALL BE NO MORE, AND THE EARTH SHALL ABIDE NOT*

A careful study of the above principles illustrates a perfect example of Divine Law and helps the Initiate to understand the purpose of the work, as many who seek this form of divination only for selfish gain will only find themselves in for a rude awakening; the knowledge and energy that the Initiate gains from Gate-Walking is provided by the DinGir so that the Initiate can resolve some of the issues that affect them and the world overall. The reason for this is very interesting, and reveals why the Simon Necronomicon was called the *"Necronomicon."*

Different than popular opinion, Simon had every right to name his book, the Necronomicon. It is a true necromantic text. The term Necronomicon has been defined by some as *"The Book of the Law of the Dead."* This seems to indicate that the workings of a "Necronomicon" would have a lot to do with understanding the Abode of the Dead. Ironically, H. P. Lovecraft said that the name came to him in dreams, and as noted earlier in our discussion, dreams are a medium of communication between human society and the spirit world, or in this case the world of the dead.

Some have stated that the Simon Necronomicon is an actual grimoire, but is not the *"Necronomicon"* that Lovecraft described in his fictional stories. This is a true opinion. But this does not mean that the Simon book is not a "Necronomicon." I can make this statement by the very reason that the Initiate must invoke various deities that were once popularly revered by the people of ancient Mesopotamia. This in itself concerns the "law of the dead." Alfred Jeremais describes these deities in *The Babylonian Conception of Heaven and Hell* on pages 32-33, we read:

**"In the "eternal palace," however, the inmost sanctuary of the Underworld, there is a spring (?) of the water of life, guarded, apparently, by the Anunnaki, already known to us as demons of the sepulchral world. Only indeed by violence and with the help of the god Ea can this water be reached...The fact also that a whole series of divinities are distinguished by the epithet "raiser of**

the dead" is connected with the same order of ideas. It is, indeed, the Sun and Spring gods especially that are said to love to wake the dead...Of Samas, the Sun god, it is said, " to make the dead live, to free the captive lies in thy hand. The god Nebo is praised as he "who lengthens the days of life and raises the dead." But above all it is Marduk, god of the Early Sun and the Spring Sun who is spoken of as "the compassionate one, whose joy is in raising the dead,"....The same power of "raising the dead" is attributed to Gula, the wife of Marduk, who moreover is called " the lady raiser of the dead,"

Based on the information cited above, we can determine that the gate-walking rite of initiation is a tour of the land of the dead. However, this initiation is the most ancient rite that the Initiate must undergo to achieve Immortality. It is during this same initiation that the candidate learns the essence of what is known as divine law. Notice what is mentioned in the Magan Text:

*"Go, Watcher of the Gate ... Go, NINNGHIZHIDDA, Watcher of the Gate..Open the Door to ISHTAR..And treat Her as it is written..In the Ancient Covenant."*

The covenant mentioned in this section of the Magan Text, is the same *Covenant* that the Mad Arab speaks about throughout the various pages of the Simon Necronomicon. It is a covenant between the spirits of the dead, man, and the Jinn. When one learns the lessons and principles of divinity and becomes as a Jinn unto themselves, they are then given authority over the dead. Simon alludes to this heavily in his book *Dead Names*. On page 235, we read:

**"One is not certain what the Magan text is doing in the Necronomicon, unless it is a history of how these**

demonic forces came to be loosed upon the Earth in order to educate the magician and inform him of certain secret formulae that can be gleamed from a careful reading of the text. That this may be so is indicated by the next chapter of the book, which is entitled "The Urilia Text," or "The Book of the Worm."

Since the Initiate receives certain powers and control over spirits of the dead, the candidate must adhere to the ancient covenant. But the fact that he/she is given charge over the dead and other spirits is seen in the Mad Arab's words that follow:

*"I have raised armies against the Lands of the East, by summoning the hordes of fiends I have made subject unto me, and so doing found NGAA, the God of the heathens, who breathes flame and roars like a thousand thunders."*

When the Initiate establishes a personal relationship with the DinGir then much can be accomplished. But if he/she were to assume that they can control ancient primordial forces by just performing and incantation from a book, they were never initiated in the first place.

# Origin of the Term Zi Kia Kanpa, Zi Anna Kanpa

For a long time Initiates of the Necronomicon Tradition thought of the term ZI KIA KANPA, ZI ANNA KANPA, were relative to what the Simon Necronomicon Spellbook defines as; *"Spirit of the sky, remember. Spirit of the earth, remember."* It was based on this definition that many assumed these terms to be just simple ways of calling *"heaven"* and *"earth,"* but if these same individuals investigated the matter further, they would have seen something entirely different. The definition of these terms can be found in a book that is listed in the Simon Necronomicon's bibliography entitled; *Chaldean Magic,* written by Francois Lenormant. The book was written in the late 1800's. It is an examination of some of the Assyrian magical texts that were found in Nineveh, dating back to the 7th century BC. These texts come from what is commonly known as **The Royal Library of Ashurbanipal.** Much of what appears in the Simon Necronomicon are excerpts from these manuscripts dating back to the 7th century B.C. This is like finding the Lord's Prayer in a Christian document from the 1st century, and putting it in a modern grimoire. It would still give the reader access to an ancient prayer, so it is also with the Simon Necronomicon.

Getting back to the topic at hand, we find the following observation based on these ancient magical texts, found on page 155 of the book Chaldean Magic:

**"The name of Hea means "dwelling;" this name then was manifestly connected with the time when the god was first imagined to be the same as the zone over**

which he presided, the zone which served as a home for men and animated beings; but he was afterwards regarded as much more separate from the material object than Anna. He was the lord of the earth's surface (*mul-ki*), and this title is applied to him quite frequently as Hea. In the sacramental formulae of the incantations he was invoked as Spirit of the earth, or more exactly still, of the terraqueous surface (*zi-ki-a*)."

Enki (Hea) was entreated in ancient magical incantations as the Spirit of the earth, or *zi-ki-a*. Therefore, we find the term *"Zi-kia-Kanpa,"* means *Spirit of the Earth, Remember*, as mentioned in the Simon Necronomicon Spellbook. This is the way the ancient Assyrians invoked Enki.

Now that we understand that *zi-ki-a kanpa* is a way to invoked DinGir Enki, it would now be useful to explore the origins of the term *zi-anna-kanpa*. Chaldean Magic page 154:

"Anu certainly preserves some features belonging to the Accadian Ana....In those parts of the collection which have been handed down to us, there is no special hymn addressed to Ana, but he is invoked in the sacramental formulae of all the incantations under the name Spirit of the heavens (*Zi-ana*). As his name indicates he was the same as the material heavens, he was heaven itself, whilst also the soul of it; and he was more completely one with the object to which he was attached than any other of the supernatural deities."

We can clearly see that these terms are used to invoke both DinGir Enki and DinGir Anu, and should not be taken lightly. This also gives newcomers of the Necronomicon Tradition further validity that this is an ancient system of divination.

## Discovering Virtue On the Left-Hand Path

Over the past several years I have met many people who are interested in the practices and workings of the Necronomicon Tradition. Some of these people were interested in acquiring a certain status in life. Others wanted to achieve great "magical power." However, I have come across the intelligent few who desired to work with the tome in order to find out some answers about what life's purpose really is.

The idea of acquiring spiritual merit through the Qliphotic Tradition is an ancient idea. *Magic in the Middle Ages* by Richard Kieckhefer-page 168, states:

**"Like manuals of orthodox exorcism, the books of *necromancy* insist on ascetic preparation and ritual *purity* (if not moral integrity) as prerequisites for commanding the demons."**

The problem that many people who work with the "dark arts" encounter is largely due to their lack of purity and virtue. We have discussed the qliphotic forces that flourish throughout the Necronomicon Tradition are for the most part, primordial, and this is what many so-called LHP practitioners fail to understand. This problem has gotten much worse since many of these "adepts" work with "chaotic magic," which is based solely on theory. The basis of the qliphotic world is formed around entities and energies in nature and the heavens, so it is in nature that we gain an understanding of the how to work with the dark path.

When we turn to the world of nature, we soon discover that it is a world within many worlds. One of these worlds is the animal kingdom. Animals are probably one of the best examples of what it means to 'fight for survival.' Animals have a unique ability in acquiring what they need to survive. Yet animals display a certain stillness and purity, as they only engage in certain emotions based on environmental changes. In the Urilia Text, we find many deities depicted with animistic features, such as Pazzuzu. When the Initiate invokes these energies, it is important that do so with an emotionally pure disposition. It is here that we see the error in so-called "chaos magic," as there is no moral emotional preparation, which results in a misappropriate outcome. In order to effectively engage the use of qliphotic energies the Initiate must recognize that discipline is essential. The Initiate must hold the image of the intended result and send this vision out emotionally. This takes discipline. Yet, we find many LPHers parading around as if they can engage in any sort of misconduct and think that there exists no retribution.

The Mad Arab admonishes us to *remember the gods in every empty moment*. This means that we should replace habits of worry with opportunities to master our work. We must keep in mind that during this process we have no time to engage in vice. This is one aspect of how we can honor rites of purity effortlessly.

Another aspect of wisdom can be gained by looking into the world of plants and trees. Scientific experiments now confirm that plants catch a negative reaction, not from cigarette smoke, but from the human thought of smoking. The Initiate must learn the mental stillness developed through purging animal urges. Through such course of discipline, they are able to perceive the thoughts of others, as a result of mastering the desire body, which influences our mental thoughts within ourselves and are able to see this process in others. Ningizzida means *"lord of the good tree."* Plant life is able to harness the kundalini force.

The insect kingdom is probably the epitome and personification of the Qliphotic Tradition, as these creatures show us a perfect example of pressing your *"will"* upon reality with definite results. Insects are able to move through any environment and remain focused on their path. They are also able to merge their emotional energy with intent, which gives them a great mount of strength. Insects display emotional outbursts by effectively acting in the moment with the thought of survival. Humans tend to ineffectively use this opportunity on worry.

If you are interested in the Necronomicon Tradition and do not have the time to work on your sense of virtue, you will get burned. Increasing our awareness while engaging in vice will elevate the negatives sides of our being. The Mad Arab said:

*"And a man may cry out, what have I don't, and my generation that such evil shall befall me? And it means nothing, save that a man, being born, is of sadness, for he is of the Blood of the Ancient Ones, but has the Spirit of the Elder Gods breathed into him. And his body goes to the Ancient Ones, but his mind is turned towards the Elder Gods, and this is the War which shall be always fought, unto the last generation of man; for the World is unnatural. When the Great KUTULU rises up and greets the Stars, then the War will be over, and the World be One."*

## Dead But Dreaming

Earlier in our discussion it was mentioned that certain parts of the text were symbolic descriptions of certain breathing exercises that are a vital part of our alchemical work. The Mad Arab wrote the following in the Book of Calling:

*"Know, first, that the Power of the Conquerors is the Power of the Magick, and that the stricken gods will ever tempt thee away from the Legions of the Mighty, and that you will feel the subtle fluids of thy body moving to the breath of TIAMAT and the Blood of KINGU who races in your veins."*

From the passage cited above, Tiamat is relative to the heart, and when one approaches the act of meditation after initiation it becomes a very effective method in letting our will influence the world. The Mad Arab wrote that *'Tiamat seeks ever to rise to the stars.'* These words take on more meaning, when the Initiate comes to the understanding that he/she is Tiamat seeking to be reborn and rise in astral flight. The first step in doing this is learning how to relax the body and breathe in a completely relaxed state.

The Initiate should practice the following exercises at least once a day. First, it is important that the candidate find a comfortable place to relax. Possibly laying in the bed, on one's back or sitting comfortably in a chair. The Initiate should make sure that they are wearing loose fitting clothing, or dressed in a way that doesn't distract them. Relaxation is important and unfortunately many of us have become accustomed to traveling thousands of miles for vacation just to relax. This is largely due to people not taking the time to perform intentional relaxation.

Once the initiate has found a comfortable place to relax, preferably lying on their back in bed, or seated in a chair, he/she should begin to relax their muscles. This cannot be done throughout the body all at once, but must begin by relaxing one section of the body at a time. The Mad Arab wrote that the Initiate must not call upon a Gate deity until they have Walked the said Gate:

*"Thou mayest not call upon NANNA till thou hast passed the Gate of NANNA. Thou mayest not call NEBO until his Gate hast thou passed. Similarly for the rest of the Gates."*

The words cited above are true for relaxing the body as well. We cannot relax one part of the body until we have relaxed the part preceding it first. These sections of the body and their order are given to us in astronomical law:

**Aries** = The Head = **First Testimony of the Mad Arab**
**Taurus** = Neck, throat, ears, lower teeth = **Of The Zonei and Their Attributes**
**Gemini** = Hands, arms nerves, lungs = **Book of Entrance**
**Cancer** = Breast, stomach = **Incantations of the Gates**
**Leo** = Heart, sides, upper back = **The Conjuration of the Fire God**
**Virgo** = Hands, nervous system, intestines, upper bowel = **The Conjuration of the Watcher**
**Libra** = Lower back, kidneys, adrenal glands = **The Maklu Text**
**Scorpio** = Genitals, rectum, bladder = **Book of Calling**
**Sagittarius** = Hips, thighs, upper leg = **The Book of Fifty Names**
**Capricorn** = Knees and lower leg = **The Magan Text**

**Aquarius** = Circulatory system, lower legs = **The Urilia Text**

**Pisces** = Feet = **Second Testimony of the Mad Arab**

It is important that the Initiate begins the relaxation in the sign of Aries, meaning with the muscles and nerves around the head and move down gradually until the whole body is relaxed. During this time it is important to focus on the breath. In the antiquity of the Necronomicon Tradition, the breathing begins as a four-count inhalation. Hold the breath for two-counts, and exhale four-counts.

With time and effort the Initiate will improve their life and ability to manipulate energy. It is advised in the beginning of this exercise that the Initiate spends only five minutes a day for the first week, adding a couple of minutes each week, until they reach a maximum of 15 to 20 minutes per session.

# Mystical Keys

There are many mystical keys in the Necronomicon Tradition that will enable the practitioner to assimilate the transformation that occurrs during the Gate-Walking initiation more easily. Today, we will describe the full meaning of these practices as they are written about in the Book of Calling:

## 1-Affirmative Breathing:

*"Know, first, that the Power of the Conquerors is the Power of the Magick, and that the stricken gods will ever tempt thee away from the Legions of the Mighty, and that you will feel the subtle fluids of thy body moving to the breath of TIAMAT and the Blood of KINGU who races in your veins. Be ever watchful, therefore, not to open this Gate, or, if thou must needs, put a time for its closing before the rising of the Sun, and seal it at that time; for to leave it open is to be the agent of CHAOS."*

In the above passage, we see a stark difference between "Man" and "mankind." Man, or the ARRA, those of Jinn-nature are made from the *Breath of Tiamat*, whereas man was created by the breath of the Elder Gods. Here the Mad Arab is informing us that it is upon the breath that thoughts, feelings, and emotions, enter the body. Therefore, it is important that we use every moment to exhale a positive outcome. So during times of worry and stress, which are states that also enter the body upon inhalation of the breath, we can effectively transform these "negative thoughts" by creating a "positive visualization."

When we first awaken the kundalini force it is important that we learn how to regulate and see the source of our thoughts and how they ride into our consciousness through breathing. This will help us to understand that what we focus our minds on is just as impactful spiritually, as if we were performing the desired function. The Enuma Elish and the Magan Text poetically describe the assimilation of kundalin energy and how it is distributed throughout the body of the Initiate in the symbolic battle between Tiamat and Marduk, which actually represents the Initiate's ability to battle negative emotions. In the passage cited above we are told to *"put a time for the closing of the "gate" before the rising of the Sun.* The rising of the Sun in this case would be transforming our thoughts and emotions into positive ones. This rising of the Sun is symbolic of exhalation. It is here that we see a window or "gate," between the inhalation and the exhalation, and this space is known as the Underworld, for where the inhalation and exhalation meet is often forgotten. We are instructed to call upon the "gods in every empty moment." It is at this space between the inhalation and the exhalation that we find a moment to engage is creative visualization.

*"KNOW FIRSTLY,"* indicates that this function is a quality of Nanna the 1st sphere we approach as Gate-Walkers. We should remember that DinGir Nanna was born in the Underworld, the space between the inhalation and exhalation of the breath. His parents were Enlil and Ninlil. Enlil means "Lord of Air. However, Ninlil in composed of two parts, *nin,* meaning *lady* and *lil,* which is usually translated as "air," or "wind," can also "night," which is normally applied to the prefix for Lilith. This could mean then that Ninlil may be a reference to a spirit similar to Lilith. Jack Tresidder's *The Complete Dictionary of Symbols,* page 544 states:

*"Lilith* the demonic first wife of Adam, according to Hebrew legend. *Lilith* may derive from the Mesopotamian fertility goddess *Ninlil.* "

This being the case, we can also say that the myth concerning the birth of Nanna, dealt primarily with the formation of the lunar deity as he appears in Heaven, but also corresponding to that "empty space" between the inhalation and exhalation of the breath.

**2-Creative Visualization:**

*"Know, secondly, that the Power of Magick is the Power of Our Master ENKI, Lord of the Seas, and Master of Magick, Father of MARDUK, Fashioner of the Magick Name, the Magick Number, the Magick Word, the Magick Shape. So, therefore, the Priest who governeth the works of Fire, and of the God of Fire, GISHBAR called GIBIL, must firstly sprinkle with the Water of the Seas of ENKI, as a testament to his Lordship and a sign of the Covenant that exists between him and thee."*

The passage cited above deals primarily with creative visualization. We are instructed, as workers of Fire, to sprinkle the Water of the seas of Enki upon our way of thinking. We must remember that it was Enki who was responsible for Ishtar's resurrection. The Water of the Seas of Enki are transformative, taking what is negative or dead within us, things that are relative emotionally to the Underworld and its desires and making it something of use in our experience. Notice what is mentioned in the Magan Text concerning Enki's transformative power:

*"He fashioned the KURGARRU, spirit of the Earth,
He fashioned the KALATURRU, spirit of the Seas,*

*To the KURGARRU he gave the Food of Life*
*To the KALATURRU he gave the Water of Life*
*And to these images he spoke aloud*
*Arise, KALATURRU, Spirit of the Seas*
*Arise, and set thy feet to that Gate GANZIR*
*To the Gate of the Underworld*
*The Land of No Return*
*Set thine eyes*
*The Seven Gates shall open for thee*
*No spell shall keep thee out*
*For my Number is upon you.*
*Take the bag of the Food of Life*
*Take the bag of the Water of Life*
*And ERESHKIGAL shall not raise her arm against you*
*ERESHKIGAL SHALL HAVE NO POWER OVER YOU.*"

The alchemy of fire and water is known throughout many esoteric schools in the world. The ancients looked upon the Earth as water, since it is a celestial body covered with such, and they looked upon the heavens as Fire since the Stars laid in heaven. These aspects are found also in the anatomy of the human body. Water represents the lower part of our physical body and the seat of the Kundalini force, and the "light of the mind" would then represent the heavens. The idea here is to sprinkle our thoughts and emotions with the joys of life. Ancient Mesopotamian myths tell us that Enki built his Abode atop of the Abzu. We are to give care and attention to that space between inhalation and exhalation, the symbolic New Moon. This is a time where we become creators of our destiny and in some ways alter a fate that may be harmful to life's path. The Mad Arab mentions this many times throughout the text with the word "remember." In the beginning of the mystical Magan Text, he gives us a deeper meaning about what the term "remember" means:

*"But heed these words well, and remember! For remembering is the most important and most potent magick, being the Rememberance of Things Past and the Rememberance of Things to Come, which is the same Memory."*

The *"Rememberance of Things Past,"* is symbolic of inhaling the breath. *"Rememberance of Things to Come"* is the creative visualization during exhalation. It is all the same breathe, or as the Mad Arab put it, the same "Memory." However, for us to understand this process we must acquire stillness.

*"KNOW SECONDLY,"* is a reference to Nebo. Nebo was responsible for engraving the destiny of an individual based on what the gods decreed. This engraving process is performed when the practitioner of the Necronomicon Tradition colors their fate by visualization and exhalation of the breath.

**3-Stillness:**

*"Know, thirdly, that by the Power of the Elder Gods and the submission of the Ancient Ones, thou mayest procure every type of honour, dignity, wealth and happiness, but that these are to be shunned as the Purveyors of Death, for the most radiant jewels are to be found buried deep in the Earth, and the Tomb of Man is the Splendour of ERESHKIGAL, the joy of KUTULU, the food of AZAGTHOTH... Therefore, thine obligation is as of the Gatekeeper of the Inside, agent of MARDUK, servant of ENKI, for the Gods are forgetful, and very far away, and it was to the Priests of the Flame that Covenant was given to seal the Gates between this World and the Other, and to keep Watch thereby, through this Night of*

*Time, and the Circle of Magick is the Barrier, the Temple, and the Gate between the Worlds."*

The Mad Arab wrote that things such as, monetary success, honor, and etc, were said to be among the "Purveyors of Death." This primarily is concerned with how we approach life. Desires for wealth, fame, and success, will naturally enter the mind of any person at one time or another. What the Mad Arab is talking about here is how we approach life.

Many people approach life with "wealth," as their only aim. Death occurs when we become imprisoned by our five senses, as these are only representations of consciousness, not the sense itself. Stuart Alve Olson mentions this on pages 144-145 of *The Jade Emperor's Mind Seal Classic*:

**"The immortal's mind clearly sees that these sense organs are all empty and can thus illuminate both consciousnesses and the objects of those senses. This is the state of Nature Void discussed earlier. When you enter this state of Nature Void the seven apertures can emit light, or wisdom light, as it is properly called. To explain this phenomena, all we must understand is what happens when we shut our eyes. Do colors appear? Of course they do. When we dream we also see colors and lights. Where do these colors and lights come from when we have closed off our organ of sight? From the consciousness of sight, when dreaming we may close off the sense organs, but the sense consciousnesses still function and thus produce objects of sense. Therefore, the immortal understands that not only are objects of the senses illusory, but that the organ and consciousness are also false. She is thus left with the experience of Nature Void."**

Nature Void is referred to by the Mad Arab as the *"most radiant jewels are to be found buried deep in the Earth."* We lose the very essence of our immortality if we are still bound by these things. It is then better to be still. Despite popular opinion, stillness is the greatest gift that Ishtar employs. She is the goddess of Stillness. Ishtar is popularly known as the Goddess of Love and War, yet many forget that she is the first among crucified deities and had to remain still for three days in the womb of the Earth. We come to know this when we see all three aspects of her being demonstrated in account about her descent.

First, we recognize that Ishtar's descent to the Underworld was due to the death of her 'Brother-In-Law" Gugalanna. This was an act of Love for it would mean her own death. Her death was to experience the stillness necessary for insight. Afterwards, she was able to arise as a Warrior and slay all unnecessary attachments to her own senses. Stillness is accessed in our day-to-day experiences and emotions. Ishtar teaches us that it is better to observe life through the state of stillness before action is taken, as stillness is an action.

We enter the state of stillness through self-observation. Ishtar instructed her Watcher to visit Enki after three days, for she knew that she would need help in overcoming death. The space between inhalation and exhalation is the location of the Watcher-The Void. The Void corresponds to our heart condition. The heart is Ishtar. It can love. It can kill. The heart is Ishtar. It is also known is Taoism as the "Mysterious Female." It is the wilderness, which Jesus ventured forth into for 40 days. Although the heart emanates strong desires, it still has the function of pumping blood throughout the body of which it is faithful. It is here that we see how stillness is first achieved when we realize our connectedness to life around us. Just the simple act of becoming aware of our actions reveals how we touch things and experiences that are not always tangible to us personally. Thus, we are instructed by the Mad Arab to become as *Gate-Keepers of Inside*, or to guard our hearts from allowing "negative thinking and emotions" to enter our being through the breath. When we realize that everything around us, in some way, shape, or form corresponds to one of the Sumerian deities, we make it a point to observe all as being inside of us in whatever activity we are engaged in. This is the empty moment of stillness. Not only do we see the divinity within ourselves, but in everything around us. We can grasp this concept by looking at objects in our waking experience as part of inner-selves. Remember, the mind is the phenomenal world unto which we are directors of life. Miraculous things begin to take place when we enter the Nature Void.

### 4-The Four Elements of the Nocturnal Sun

*"Know, fourthly, that it is become the obligation of the Priests of the Flame and the Sword, and of all Magick, to bring their Power to the Underworld and keep it chained thereby, for the Underworld is surely the Gate Forgotten, by which the Ancient Ones ever seek Entrance to the Land of the Living, And the Ministers of ABSU are clearly walking the Earth, riding on the Air, and upon the Earth, and sailing silently through the Water, and roaring in the Fire, and all these Spirits must be brought to subjection to the Person of the Priest of Magick, before any else. Or the Priest becomes prey to the Eye of Death of the Seven ANNUNNAKI, Lord of the Underworld, Ministers of the Queen of Hell."*

In order for the Priest of the Flame to bring the said forces into subjection to them, he/she must be consciously aware of their existence in each moment. This is why we are encouraged to recognize the consciousness in all objects, people, and things, and address it as we see fit, or more precisely via telepathy.

In order for us to understand this exercise, we must first examine its Qliphotic aspect being Shammash. Shammash is able to give life-energy to all here on Earth and judges the Underworld as he passes though Mt. Mashu during nocturnal hours. Imagine a white ball of light and we can move it from the space between our eyes to whatever object, person, or thing that we meet in our day-to-day experience.

## 5-Lucid Dreaming

*"Know, fifthly, that the worshippers of TIAMAT are abroad in the world, and will give fight to the Magician. Lo, they have worshipped the Serpent from Ancient Times, and have always been with us. And they are to be known by their seeming human appearance which has the mark of the Beast upon them, as they change easily into the Shapes of animals and haunt the Nights of Men and by their odor, which comes of burning incenses unlawful to the worship of the Elder Ones. And their Books are the Books of CHAOS and the flames, and are the Books of the Shadows and the Shells. And they worship the heaving earth and the ripping sky and the rampant flame and the flooding waters; and they are the raisers of the legions of maskim, the Liers-In-Wait. ."*

It is not only important that we observe our breath going in and out of our bodies, but it is deeply important that we gain consciousness through dreams. The Mad Arab speaks about the Ancient Ones possessing the ability to change shapes and having a 'seemingly human appearance.' He is referring to encounters that he has seen in lucid states of dreaming, and by doing such practices we are able to meet the demands of the *serpent*, or the kundalini force, and make possible connections to the dream. One thing we should also keep in mind is that dreaming influences our day-to-day life.

Nergal's power was chained to the Underworld as he was sometimes called a "Son of Anu." Just as emotions and desires enter our being through the breath, so it is that diseases enter the body in dreams, as well as, a way of healing ourselves. It is for this reason that lucid dreaming becomes an essential part of our spiritual path.

Nergal married Ereshkigal. This is symbolic of the Initiate's ability to form alliances in the dream world and become ruler of the subconscious mind. The mind in Lovecraft lore is described as the seven and nine entering the dream, or the Seven Gates and the Nine aspects considered in the Urilia Text.

*"Know, sixthly, that thou shalt not seek the operations of this Magick save by the rules and governments set down herein, for to do other is to take the most awful risk, for thyself and for all mankind. Therefore, heed these words carefully, and change not the words of the incantations, whether thou understand them, or understand them not, for they are the words of the Pacts made of Old, and before Time. So, say them softly if the formula is "softly", or shout them aloud if the formula is "aloud", but change not one measure lest thou call something Else, and it be your final hour."*

The passage cited above pertains to the exercise of memorization. An adept in the Necronomicon Tradition is one that has copied over the tome and can recite all the conjurations and invocations in the Tome. Once this is accomplished many of the rituals are done by visualization, but first the Initiate must master the five previous steps. Marduk is described throughout the Tome as the "slayer of the serpent," or one who has bridled the kundalini force, a necessary step of survival during initiation.

*"Know, seventhly, of the Things thou art to expect in the commission of this Most sacred Magick. Study the symbols well, and do not be afraid of any awful spectre that shall invade thine operation, or haunt thine habitat by day or by night. Only charge them with them the words of the Covenant and they will do as you ask, of thou be strong. And if thou performest these operations often, thou shalt see things becoming dark; and the Wanderers in their Spheres shall no more be seen by thee; and the Stars in their places will lose their Light, and the Moon, NANNA, by whom thou also workest, shall become black and extinguished, "*

Every action of the Initiate is in some way, shape, or form, relative to the Necronomicon Tradition. This is being.

# True Blood

The history of the Family describes the Elder Gods as physical beings. I am sure that many of us have researched the origins of human civilization only to find the recurrent theme and legends concerning a time when the "gods" dwelt openly with humankind. While the Elder Gods are attributed to celestial bodies, or planets, it may very well be possible that they represent ancient sorcerers who walked the earth at one time. Notice what is mentioned in the Simon Necronomicon's Book of Calling:

*"THIS is the Book of the Ceremonies of Calling, handed down since the time the Elder Gods walked the Earth, Conquerors of the Ancient Ones."*

It is easy to see, in view of this passage, as it appears in the Simon Necronomicon, that the Elder Gods also correspond to physical beings that walked the Earth at some time in the remote past. Interestingly, we find the following excerpt from Montague Summers' book, *The Vampire; His Kith and Kin,* page 232 states:

**"It would, perhaps, be hardly too much to say that in ancient Mexico all magicians were regarded as Vampires..."**

Interestingly, the Mad Arab mentions something of a similar nature in his First Testimony:

*"They turned toward me, and I saw a loathing that they had cut their chests with the daggers they had used to raise the stone, for some mystical purpose I could not then divine; although I know now that blood is the very*

*food of these spirits, which is why the field after the battles of war glows with an unnatural light, the manifestations of the spirits feeding thereon."*

In 1911's edition of the Encyclopedia Britannica; A Dictionary of Arts, Sciences, Volume 2, by Hugh Chrisholm, page 55 states:

**"...in Australia it cannot even be asserted that the gods are not spirits at all, much less that they are spirits of dead men; they are simply magnified magicians, supermen who have never died;"**

Here we see another case where the magician was deified in the history of man as a god. This seems to be the hidden theme in the Simon Necronomicon, as it is not about a battle between the Ancient Ones and the Elder Gods, but relates more so to the candidate's initiation first into what is known as "white magic" and when a grasp is gained in this area, the magician then enters the realms of the black magician. We can determine this by what is said in the Simon Necronomicon itself. In the SN's Introduction, under the subtopic *SUMERIA*, we read the following:

*"**There was a** battle between the forces of "light" and "darkness" (so-called) **that took place long before man was created, before even the cosmos as we know it existed. It is described fully in the Enuma Elish and in the bastardized version found in the NECRONOMICON, and involved the Ancient Ones, led by the Serpent MUMMU-TIAMAT and her male counterpart ABSU, against the ELDER GODS (called such in the N.) led by the Warrior MARDUK, son of the Sea God ENKI, Lord of Magicians of this Side, or what could be called "White Magicians" – although close examination of the myths of ancient times makes one pause before attempting to***

*judge which of the two warring factions was "good" or "evil". MARDUK won this battle – in much the same way that later St. George and St. Michael would defeat the Serpent again – the cosmos was created from the body of the slain Serpent, and man was created from the blood of the slain commander of the Ancient Army, KINGU, thereby making man a descendent of the Blood of the Enemy, as well as the "breath" of the Elder Gods; a close parallel to the "sons of God and daughters of men" reference in the Old Testament. Yet, though the identity of the Victor is clear, there were – and are – certain persons and organizations that dared side with the vanquished, believing the Ancient Ones to be a source of tremendous, and most unbelievable, power."*

We can see in the above passage that the "battle" between the Ancient Ones and the Elder Gods was considered by Simon to be metaphoric, for in the passage above, he states that this was a "so-called battle," which means that it is symbolic of an inner process of development. Other evidence of this is based on how Aleister Crowley is described. Let's take a look at some quotes from the SN's Introduction to confirm this:

*"He changed his name to Aleister Crowley while still at Cambridge, and by that name, plus "666", he would never be long out of print, or out of newspapers. For he believed himself to be the incarnation of a god, an Ancient One, the vehicle of a New Age of Man's history, the Aeon of Horus, displacing the old Age of Osiris."*

The words quoted above describe Crowley as an "Ancient One," or one who believed himself to be his own god. Later, in the tome's Introduction, we find the following:

*"Although a list is appended hereto containing various entities and concepts of Lovecraft, Crowley, and Sumeria cross-referenced, it will do to show how the Editor found relationships to be valid and even startling. AZATOT is frequently mentioned in the grim pages of the Cthulhu Mythos, and appears in the NECRONOMICON as AZAG-THOTH, a combination of two words, the first Sumerian and the second Coptic, which gives us a clue as to Its identity. AZAG in Sumerian means "Enchanter" or "Magician"; THOTH in Coptic is the name given to the Egyptian God of Magick and Wisdom, TAHUTI, who was evoked by both the Golden Dawn and by Crowley himself (and known to the Greeks as Hermes, from whence we get "Hermetic"). AZAG-THOTH is, therefore, a Lord of Magicians, but of the "Black" magicians, or the sorcerers of the "Other Side"."*

The quote above defines Azag-Thoth as the Lord of Black Magicians, or 'sorcerers of the "Other Side.' Yet it also mentions that this entity was evoked by Crowley himself. Therefore, the Simon Necronomicon, which is dedicated to Aleister Crowley, is a grimoire of the "Other Side."

Additional evidence to support this can be obtained by close examination of the tome's content. We find a section completely dedicated to the *"Black Magician"* entitled **Worship of the Ancient Ones in History.** Here we can find the following:

*"In both the European and Chinese cultures, the Dragon or Serpent is said to reside somewhere "below the earth"; it is a powerful force, a magickal force, which is identified with mastery over the created world; it is also a power that can be summoned by the few and not the many......In the West, the conjuration, cultivation, or worship of this Power was strenuously opposes with the advent of the Solar, Monotheistic religions and those*

*who clung to the Old Ways were effectively
extinguished. The wholesale slaughter of those called
"Witches" during the Inquisition is an example of this,
as well as the solemn and twisted – that is to say,
purposeless and unenlightened – celibacy that the Church
espoused. For the orgone of Wilhelm Reich is just as
much Leviathan as the Kundalini of Tantrick adepts, and
the Power raised by the Witches. It has always, at least
in the past two thousand years, been associated with
occultism and essentially with Rites of Evil Magick, or
the Forbidden Magick, of the Enemy, and of Satan . . ."*

These words indicate quite a few things about the Simon
Necronomicon. First, we see that the Dragon Current is
described as existing "below the earth." The forces that
are summoned in the Simon Necronomicon are these
same "below the earth" forces, for it mentions in the
Book of Calling the following:

*"Know, seventhly, of the Things thou art to expect in the
commission of this Most sacred Magick. Study the
symbols well, and do not be afraid of any awful spectre
that shall invade thine operation, or haunt thine habitat
by day or by night. Only charge them with them the
words of the Covenant and they will do as you ask, of
thou be strong. And if thou performest these operations
often, thou shalt see things becoming dark; and the
Wanderers in their Spheres shall no more be seen by thee;
and the Stars in their places will lose their Light,...and
from the Cavities of the Earth will leap forth the
ANNUNNAKI, Dog-Faced, and thou shalt bring them
down."*

This excerpt refers to what is described previously in the
Simon Necronomicon's Introduction as *"a magickal
force, which is identified with mastery over the created
world; it is also a power that can be summoned by the*

*few and not the many."* Simon also informs us that these workings have a long history of opposition by the Solar Monotheistic religions. It is here that we see more evidence that the Simon Necronomicon is a LHP book, for in the section entitled **Banishings**, we read:

*"The religion of the ancient Sumerian peoples seems to have been lunar-oriented, a religion – or religion – magickal structure – of the night, of darkness in a sense. Invocations using solar formulae have proved thus far effective in successfully banishing NECRONOMICON demons and intelligences."*

Since the Simon Necronomicon is based on "lunar" ritual work, we can assume that these are the same sort of rituals that were opposed by "Solar Monotheistic Religions." Taking all of this into consideration it is more correct to understand that the spiritual development of the Initiate by use of this grimoire, demands that the candidate learn about the forces that influence the environment and the mind. Soon after, the Initiate merges and becomes one with the power which affects the elements and the mind. In support of this fact, notice the description that the Mad Arab gives concerning the Ancient Ones in the Urilia Text:

*"And they work by the Moon, and not by the Sun, and by older planets than the Chaldaens were aware."*

Now let us look at what the Mad Arab states in the Book of Calling:

*"And if thou performest these operations often, thou shalt see things becoming dark; and the Wanderers in their Spheres shall no more be seen by thee; and the Stars in their places will lose their Light, and the Moon, NANNA, by whom thou also workest,"*

The Mad Arab describes rituals that are "lunar" in his writings. Further clarity into this matter can be gained by additional statements from the Mad Arab:

*"..the worshippers of TIAMAT are abroad in the world, and will give fight to the Magician. Lo, they have worshipped the Serpent from Ancient Times, and have always been with us. And they are to be known by their seeming human appearance which has the mark of the Beast upon them, as they change easily into the Shapes of animals and haunt the Nights of Men and by their odor, which comes of burning incenses unlawful to the worship of the Elder Ones. And their Books are the Books of CHAOS and the flames, and are the Books of the Shadows and the Shells. And they worship the heaving earth and the ripping sky and the rampant flame and the flooding waters; and they are the raisers of the legions of maskim, the Liers-In-Wait. And they do not know what it is they do, but they do it at the demands of the Serpent, at whose Name even ERESHKIGAL gives fright, and the dread KUTULU strains at his bonds:...MUMMU TIAMAT Queen of the Ancient Ones!"*

Although, these workers of the night "do not know what it is they do," they are actually Ancient Ones in becoming. Not every initiate of the Necronomicon Tradition is able to become their own god, as in being an Ancient One. This may take time for they may not be able to deal directly with the "Serpent" or kundalini force. There could be some blockages. They may have to continue to Walk the Gates to help irrigate the flow of energy so that the kundalini can flow upwards to the Pituitary Gland. This is processed is described in the Urilia Text also:

*"And a man may cry out, what have I don't, and my generation that such evil shall befall me? And it means nothing, save that a man, being born, is of sadness, for he is of the Blood of the Ancient Ones, but has the Spirit of the Elder Gods breathed into him. And his body goes to the Ancient Ones, but his mind is turned towards the Elder Gods, and this is the War which shall be always fought, unto the last generation of man; for the World is unnatural. When the Great KUTULU rises up and greets the Stars, then the War will be over, and the World be One."*

The Simon Necronomicon uses the analogy of the Ancient Ones versus the Elder Gods so that the ignorant novice doesn't work with forces that could harm their well-being. This is the only blind and trap that exists in the tome. I must admit that there are passages in the Simon Necronomicon, where the term "Ancient One" is inserted into the text as a substitute for the "maskim" or other energies that were banished by the Chaldeans of old. Other banishings that appear in the Maklu Text can be understood as ways of keeping the "serpent-force," or kundalini, under the practitioner's control. When the practitioner is *informed by the "Other Side"* they may proceed with directly in working with the kundalini-force, as we are instructed in the Urilia Text. This is also mentioned in the metaphoric language of the Mad Arab's words:

*"But the Dead may be always summoned, and many times are willing to rise; but some are stubborn and desire to remain Where they are, and do not rise, save for the efforts of the Priest, who has power, as ISHTAR, both in this Place and in the Other."*

The Simon Necronomicon is often misunderstood because it is approached by critics as a grimoire of Western Ceremonial Magic. However, when we look at ancient indigenous practices, as seen in Ifa, Shinto, and Taoism, we find more consistent parallels that align with the Necronomicon Tradition. For example, in Palo Mayombe it is a common practice for the Initiate to have two "pots" –one to work with the Seven African Powers and the other to work with the ancestors and spirits of the dead. In the Simon Necronomicon ritual work we see exactly the same thing. Practitioners are instructed to work with the Aga Mass Saratu, summoning the celestial forces. In the Urilia Text we are told to use "the bowl of TIAMAT." This *Bowl of TIAMAT* is known in the Tao Te Ching as the *"Gate-Way of the Mysterious Female."* What is interesting about all of this is that ancient indigenous people did not divide their work into LHP or RHP. These are terms that stem from Western interpretations of ancient occult practices, and given the fact that the Simon Necronomicon relates more to indigenous spiritual traditions than it ever will to Western Ceremonial Magick, we must note that ancient people thought of their spiritual practices as tools for aligning with the movements of nature, then by regular practice of this the advance magician, shaman, was able to manipulate these very same forces. So it is that we read the following in the Magan Text:

*"For what is new..Came from that which is old..And what is old..Shall replace that which is new And once again the Ancient Ones..Shall rule upon the face of the Earth!..And this is too the Covenant!"*

# Mountains of MASSHU Part 1

Within The Testimony of The Mad Arab are the hidden keys for understanding one of the most controversial grimoires in our common era. Please keep in mind that this work was not written to prove or disprove the authenticity of the Simon Necronomicon. These questions are answered in the Necronomicon itself.

*"Remember, that the Essences of the Ancient Ones are in all things, but the Essences of the Elder Gods are in all things that live, and this will prove of value when the time comes."*

It took quite some time, coupled with hard work, to fully appreciate and understand the Necronomicon. There are layers upon layers of information within every page. The Testimony, as given to us by the Mad Arab, is also a good example of this. His Testimony is where the journey begins and so will our discussion.

*"This is the Testimony of all that I have seen, and all that I have learned in those years that I have possessed the Three Seals of MASSHU."*

The opening lines of the Mad Arab's Testimony gives us the keys for understanding the entire text written thereafter, the Three Seals of MASSHU. However, in order for us to understand the meaning of these three seals, we must first begin by defining MASSHU.

The term MASSHU is a derivative of the Akkadian word Mashu, which scholars translate as *twin*. It was considered by the Ancient Sumerians to be the Gateway to both the 'garden of the gods' and a passageway to the

Underworld. It was also a symbol of the rising and setting Sun, as the Sun God Shamash is often depicted between the two peaks on ancient Babylonian cylinders. The rising sun would depict the sun's return to the palace of the gods and the setting sun would be an indication of its entrance into the Underworld to judge the dead. Through a thorough examination of the Gilgamesh Legend, we can get a clearer understanding of what MASSHU meant to the Mad Arab.

*"For this is the Book of Dead, the book of the Black Earth..."*

Gilgamesh was a historical king of Uruk, which was located on the Euphrates River in Ancient Sumeria. Many stories were written about Gilgamesh on clay tablets in cuneiform. The fullest surviving written version is derived from twelve stone tablets, written in the Akkadian language, found in the ruins of the library of Ashurbanipal, king of Assyria 669-633 B.C. at Nineveh. The library was destroyed by the Persians in 612 B.C. and all the tablets are damaged. The tablets actually name an author, which is extremely rare in the ancient world, for this particular version of the story: Shin-eqi-unninni.

It is in these episodes of Gilgamesh that we find some interesting data concerning Mt Mashu. Mashu was located in a forest in the "land of the Living", where the names of the famous are written. In these episodes, Gilgamesh and his friend, Enkidu, travel to the Cedar (or Pine) Forest which is ruled over by a demonic monster named Humbaba (Humba an Elamite god and ba meaning made, which translates to Humba has made me. This would evidently allude to the battles between Babylonia and Elam). While their motives for going to the Forest included gaining renown, it is also clear that they wanted the timber it contained. Humbaba, who had been appointed by the god Enlil to guard the Forest, is depicted as a one-eyed giant with the powers of a storm and breath of fire, perhaps the personification of a volcano. It is only with the help of another god, and a magically forged weapon that Gilgamesh triumphs over Humbaba. But before his battle, Gilgamesh and Enkidu gaze in awe at the mountain called "the mountain of cedars, the dwelling-place of the gods and the throne of Ishtar." They climbed onto the mountain, sacrificed cereals to it, and, in response, the mountain sends them puzzling dreams about their futures. When they begin to fell trees, Humbaba senses their presence and, enraged, fixes his eye of death on the pair. Although Gilgamesh finally defeats the monster, Enkidu eventually weakens and dies from Humbaba's gaze and curse. In addition to its reputation as the "Land of the Living", this forest is also a way to the Underworld or the Otherworld. After killing Humbaba, Gilgamesh continues in the forest and "uncovered the sacred dwelling of the Anunnaki Furthermore, Gilgamesh seems to go into a death-like trance here and in the same general region, the Goddess Ishtar, whom Gilgamesh spurned, threatened to break in the doors of hell and raise up the dead to eat the living.

Mashu is mentioned directly in the episode "Gilgamesh and the Search for Everlasting Life." This story unfolds after the death of Gilgamesh's friend, Enkidu, a wrenching experience which makes Gilgamesh face his own mortality and he begins searching for eternal life. It is en route to Utnapishtim, the one mortal to achieve immortality, which Gilgamesh finds himself traveling through Mt. Mashu. Its twin peaks are as high as the wall of heaven and its roots reach down to the underworld. Its gates are guarded by the Scorpions, half-man and half-dragon; their glory is terrifying; their stare strikes death into men, their shining halo sweeps the mountains that guard the rising sun". Gilgamesh is able to convince the Scorpion-people to open the gate and let him enter the long tunnel through the mountains. Eventually Gilgamesh emerges from the tunnel into the fantastic Garden of the Gods, where trees bear glittering jewels instead of fruit.

In the view of several scholars, Mashu is also the mountain mentioned in the story that Utnapishtim told Gilgamesh. Utnapishtim, sometimes called the "Sumerian Noah", told Gilgamesh how the gods had become angered with humanity and decided on the Flood as one means to exterminate it. A sympathetic god warned Utnapishtim and told him to build a boat and board it with his family, relatives, craftsmen, and the seed of all living creatures. After six days of tempest and flood, Utnapishtim's boat grounded on a mountain. He released a dove and a swallow, both of which returned to him. After releasing a raven which did not return; Utnapishtim and his family came down from the mountain. When the disgruntled gods are finally reconciled with the re-emergence of humanity, Utnapishtim and his wife are taken by the god Enlil to live in the blessed place where Gilgamesh found him "in the distance, at the mouth of the rivers."

There is more information of such depth in the epics of Gilgamesh, and I encourage the reader to also include these accounts in his/her studies. For now though, we can reflect on the history of Gilgamesh to get a deeper understanding of the term Mashu, or MASSHU. First, we learn that within the region of Mashu was a great forest filled with Cedar trees. Secondly, it was the location that Gilgamesh sacrificed wheat products or cereals and because of this he received intense dreams. Also,

Gilgamesh seems to go into a death-like state in the mountain that is guarded by the Scorpion Man. The legend of Gilgamesh gives us the basis for a deeper understanding of the term MASSHU on an alchemical level, as found in the Simon Necronomicon.

Mount Mashu is defined as the 'Twin Mountains' that guarded the rising and setting Sun. This would mean that entrance into Mount Mashu was a parable, which meant entering the subconscious mind. It is through the subconscious mind that the super consciousness can be reached, or as ancient legend stated 'access to the abode of the gods. This mountain was filled with a Cedar forest, or a stimulant to promote awareness in the subconscious state. It is interesting to note that the astrological correspondence to Cedar is the Sun and the element of fire. Its herbal and magical correspondences include, purification, healing, money, protection, illumination, physical energy, and increased magical power. Its medical properties are excellent for the skin. Thus, it is apparent that the rituals as laid down in the Simon Necronomicon, are not actually fictional, but a guise for the great Sumerian Tantric rites, as we will discuss soon.

# Mountains of MASSHU Part 2

We discussed how the term MASSHU is a derivative form of the Akkadian word Mashu, which means twin, as found in the Gilgamesh epics and other Sumerian mythologies. From our investigation we were able to find out that Mashu was a sacred mountain to the Sumerians. It was located in a Cedar forest within the 'land of the Living.' Additionally, we found quite an importance placed upon this land of Cedar, as the Cedar trees were a very valuable item to the ancient people of Sumer. Thus, we find that the book of 'Black Earth' is not a work of fiction. Many of the rituals in the Simon Necronomicon require the burning of Cedar incense. Page 99 of the Simon Necronomicon states:

*"The Place of calling shall be high in the Mountains....,*
*Thus, the Place, once chosen, shall be purified by*
*supplications to thine particular God or Goddess, and by*
*burning offerings of pine and cedar."*

Gilgamesh in one epic is noted to have burned cedar wood and myrrh to put the gods in a favorable mood. Thus, the admonition to burn Cedar during the rituals, as found in the Simon Necronomicon, is not just some random act of chaos magic, but the adherence to ancient ritualistic traditions found in Ancient Sumer.

The value of using Cedar was thereby imitated in cultures that followed the Sumerians. According to the Talmud, the Jews were to burn Cedar wood on the Mount of Olives to announce the beginning of the New Year. It is also said that Moses instructed his followers to use the bark of Cedar in circumcision rites, and the

Egyptians used Cedar resins in their process of mummification.

As we have discussed in our previous article, Mt. Mashu was a seat that gave one access to the Underworld, the abode of the Gods, and to the Throne of Ishtar. Mashu represented three different aspects. These three different aspects correspond to the three different Seals of MASSHU, as found in the Simon Necronomicon.

1) The Throne of Ishtar would correspond to the ARRA
2) The Abode of the Gods would correspond to the AGGA
3) The Underworld would correspond to the Bandar or Watcher.

It is evident then that the Three Seals of the Mountains of MASSHU is not just something made up in the mind of Simon, but is relative to Ancient Sumerian legend. Yet the question still remains, what is MASSHU?

Mashu was located in a forest within the 'Land of the Living.' This would mean that it is related to something that can be detected by one of the five senses. Its three aspects would represent different states of consciousness. A clue to its physical representation would be the fact that Mashu was considered by the ancients to be the place where the Sun was at between its rising and setting stages. This would lead us to identifying Mashu's physical representation as the pituitary gland.

The term Pituitary is derived from the Latin term pituita which means phlegm. This definition is based on the fact that phlegm was thought to be secreted from the Pituitary Gland. It was called the master gland by the ancients because the hormones secreted by the pituitary gland stimulates and controls the functioning of almost all other endocrine glands in the body. Pituitary hormones also promote growth and control the water balance in the body. It also affects the aging process. Another point of interest within our study is that the so-called father of medicine, Hippocrates, was the one to correspond phlegm with water, and being that it was one time believed that the Pituitary gland produced phlegm. Modern doctors have denied the function of the Pituitary gland as producing Phlegm, not realizing that it was a reference to the gland being the 'master gland.' The Simon Necronomicon identifies Enki; the god of water, semen, and the Master Magician, or the master gland, and being that Hippocrates heavily embraced Chaldean Spirituality and Numerology, the term phlegm may have been a possible reference to how water is integrated into the blood, a function which applies to the Pituitary Gland.

## Mountains of MASSHU & the Pituitary Gland

In our last discussion (part 2) we talked about the value of Mt. Mashu, which according to the Gilgamesh Epics was located within a forest of Cedar trees. We also mentioned how Mt. Mashu, when accessed, was a way to the Throne of Ishtar, The Abode of the Gods, and a way to the Underworld. These three aspects would thus correspond to the Three Seals of MASSHU as mentioned in the Simon Necronomicon. We concluded our 2ND Issue by identifying Mt. Mashu with the Pituitary Gland.

The Pituitary Gland is a small bean-shaped, reddish-gray organ located in the saddle-shaped depression (sella turcica) in the floor of the skull (the sphenoid bone) and attached to the base of the brain by a stalk. This description of the Pituitary Gland compares to what Gilgamesh saw as he approached Mt. Mashu (translated by Herbert Mason); "When he arrived at the mountains of Mashu, whose peaks reached the shores of Heaven and whose roots descend to hell..," Here the 'peaks of Mashu' are described as reaching the 'shores of Heaven.' This would correspond to the Pituitary Gland's placement near the Hypothalamus Gland. The work of endocrinologist Roger Guillemin during the 1960's proved that the Hypothalamus Gland sends chemical messages to the Lobes of the Pituitary Gland, causing it to secrete certain hormones that are the cause of adolescent growth and also gonadotropic hormones involving the ovaries and testes. It is noted that when Gilgamesh arrived at Mt. Mashu, he was questioned by the Scorpion man and his wife. The Scorpion people are described in some translations of the Gilgamesh Epics, as having an awesome knowledge. The Scorpion man and his wife would therefore relate to the gonadotropic hormones FSH and LH.

Within our previous posts, we covered the fact that Mt. Mashu means 'twin' in Akkadian. This would relate to the Anterior Lobe and the Posterior Lobe of the Pituitary Gland. These two lobes are the Twin Peaks of the Mountains of Mashu. (It should also be noted that within the Pituitary Gland there exists the Intermediate Lobe, which in human beings is only present during early childhood and during pregnancy. Its function is unknown to the western world of medicine, but in the great Tantric Rites of Ancient Sumer, its function was that of a protective nature and it is able to integrate messages from heaven to earth within individuals who have raised their Kundalini. (It acts as Humbaba.)

We also find within the Gilgamesh Epics that Mt. Mashu's roots descended into 'Hell' or, as other translations would appropriately put it, the Underworld. This relates to the Pituitary Gland's attachment to the Brain Stem, which connects the lower parts of the brain to the spinal cord that descends down to the Root Chakra where the Kundalini is stored. This allows us to make the following correspondences in reference to the three aspects that could be accessed once one was to enter Mt Mashu.

1) **The Underworld** would relate to the Root Chakra, which stores the Kundalini force. We should also note here that Mt Mashu was to be found within a forest of Cedar trees. Hindu mystics, without knowledge of the Gilgamesh Epics, have long used Cedar incense as a stimulant for the Root Chakra in raising the Kundalini force.

2) **The Throne of Ishtar** would correspond to the Hypothalamus Gland.

3) **The Abode of the Gods** would then relate to the Pineal Gland. The Pineal Gland is responsible for the production of the hormone melatonin. It is also said to control our appetites, desires, and moods, which would relate to Enlil, who is of a higher order of gods than Ishtar. He is a Storm God. The Ancient Sumerians equated the emotions with storms. The Pineal Gland is also responsible for sexual development, but it shrinks in puberty, an action that is echoed in the Intermediate Lobe of the Pituitary Gland, which appears in early childhood and then disappears, though appearing in woman during stages of pregnancy. This confirms our comparison to the Intermediate Lobe of the Pituitary Gland to Humbaba.

It is said in the Gilgamesh Epics that Humbaba could use the eye of death and create awe inspiring storms. We also know that Enlil was the Storm god who placed Humbaba in the Cedar forest. This would also solve what Western medicine has long been ignorant of, that the Intermediate Lobe in the Pituitary Gland is a direct reflection of the Pineal Gland. In Yoga the Pineal gland is associated with the Third Eye or Anja Chakra. Now that we have validated that the Pituitary Gland is Mt. Mashu on a physical level, let us look into the deeper meanings of the Gilgamesh Epics.

The essence of ones' spirituality and immortality is found in their sexuality. It cannot be ignored that human civilization was only able to advance after the 'sons of god' took wives from amongst the 'daughters of men.' The knowledge shared by Tantric Adepts with uncivilized man, was the knowledge that man needed to advance himself in various technologies that we enjoy today. Earlier in our discussion, we spoke about the Scorpion people, who are described in the Epics of Gilgamesh as possessing an awesome knowledge. It is no mystery, in view of the prior statements that the zodiac sign of Scorpio in astrology corresponds to the genitals. These Ancient Tantric Adepts were perceived by uncivilized man as gods. The Rites of these Adepts had nothing to do with degrading oneself sexually, but was indeed a lifestyle, a culture that could best be described as Ancient Nanotechnology. However, the Ancients knew that raising the Kundalini force was indeed very dangerous! So they hid buried these Rites in dark aesthetics of death, demons, and even beasts. I have seen so many approach grimoires such as the Simon Necronomicon in the same ignorance which causes scholars to call a king like Gilgamesh a hero. Here is a tyrant who abused the Tantric Rites by demanding to sleep with every newly married bride before their husbands would, and this is what scholars call a hero?!!! The Gilgamesh Epics served as an example and warning to the initiated about the pitfalls of raising the Kundalini force. Gilgamesh was such a tyrant, that his contradictory actions caused the gods to create Enkidu, an uncivilized man, who became equal to Gilgamesh through a series of Tantric initiations lead by the temple priestess (prostitute) Shamhat, Enkidu was transformed. It is said that he was like an animal until they made love for six days and seven nights.

This would indicate that from the new moon to the moon's full crescent stage, which takes seven nights, Enkidu passed through seven gates. The crescent moon was also attributed to Anu. Ancient Tantric Adepts had a big celebration on the New Moon for it was a symbol of when Ishtar rose from the dead and ascended through the seven gates of the Underworld, which would mean that her ascending from the Underworld was marked by the crescent moon. This would explain the configuration of the Seal for Nanna's Gate in the Simon Necronomicon. It has long been noted that gods were distinguished from humans based on the fact that gods were often depicted as wearing horned-crowns. These horned-crowns are often misinterpreted by pseudo-pagans and occultist as being a symbol of the crescent moon, when this is only half the story. They were symbolic of the two lips of the vulva, and ones' raising the Kundalini force through the seven chakras to the area of the Pituitary Gland or twin-lobed gland, which gave the initiate godlike wisdom. Are you feeling a little horny? In the Tantric Rites, the Kundalini force was motivated by the feminine force, which is what civilized Enkidu. It is the same reason why the Simon Necronomicon makes use of the copper dagger of Inanna because it is through a feminine element that the power or yang energies can be harnessed from the planetary deities causing the Kundalini force to ascend.

The Ancient Adepts were engaged in the Tantric Rites. Notice what is mentioned in the Simon Necronomicon on page 100: *"but the Priests of Old were naked in their rites."* It is also interesting to note that in the Simon Necronomicon the Crown of Anu is to be made of beaten copper. Copper was a symbol of blood in Ancient Sumeria. Yet the flow of blood in a woman's cycle is controlled by the phases of the moon. This all relates to raising the force of Kundalini. Cedar incense corresponds to the Root Chakra or Kundalini Chakra, which would explain even further why it was so sacred to the Ancient Sumerians. Thus, when Gilgamesh had the desire to cut down trees in the Cedar forest and kill Humbaba to gain renown, Gilgamesh symbolized the rising of the Solar Cults, and there destruction of the ancient Lunar Rites.

This is also seen in the Gilgamesh Epics when Ishtar threw the Bull of Heaven at Gilgamesh, which represented the Kundalini force, and Gilgamesh and Enkidu killed it. When Ishtar entreated Gilgamesh to be here lover and she would give hum power, he spurned her. Some may look at this aspect as a literal part of the story, yet those who are initiated in the Rites know that Gilgamesh was mocking the Sacred Marriage Rite. This would also explain why Ishtar visited the Underworld. In the Epic of Inanna's Descent to the Underworld Inanna/Ishtar, is said to see about her brother-in-law who has died. Before Ereshkigal was married to Nergal, she was married to Gugalana whose name means 'Bull of Heaven.' Evidently she went to the Underworld to resurrect the teachings of raising the Kundalini. This explains why Enki would be the only one amongst the older set of gods to resurrect her. Remember in part two of our discussion, we briefly stated that the word Pituitary is derived from the Latin term Pituita which means phlegm. We also discussed how Hippocrates (a student of Chaldean Spirituality) equated water with phlegm. Enki is the god of water, which means that Enki oversees the Pituitary Gland.

The Pituitary Gland in the Tantric Rites interacts with the rising Kundalini force! This would also explain why in the Simon Necronomicon, the so-called basterdized version of INANNA"s Descent, Ishtar's Watcher is sent to Enki alone, as Enki was also symbolized by the full moon. The power of the full moon motivates the Kundalini to ascend. With all that we have discussed, Gilgamesh failed to gain immortality due to his disrespect for the Tantric Tradition. If we remember, Enkidu was civilized through the Tantric initiations, which symbolically lasted for six days and seven nights. Later in the Epics, Utnapishtim told Gilgamesh that if he was as godlike as he thought he was, and wanted to live forever, he had to stay awake for six days and seven nights to prove it. But Gilgamesh was tired because of his journey and had grown drowsy as he listened to Utnapishtim's story, he fell asleep. This means that regardless of how mighty the solar cults may have appeared to be, in the end their destructive path cost them the chance for immortality.

# The ARRA Sign

*"Of the three symbols carved, the first is the Sign of our Race from beyond the Stars, and is called ARRA in the tongue of the Scribe who taught it to me, an emissary of the Elder Ones. In the tongue of the eldest city of Babylon, it was UR. It is the Sigil of the Covenant of the Elder Gods, and when they see it, they who gave it to us, they will not forget us. They have sworn!*

*Spirit of the Skies, Remember! "*

ARRA  AGGA BANDAR

The above passage describes the first of the Three Seals of Masshu. It is called the ARRA and it is said to be the 'Sign of our Race from beyond the Stars.' This passage will prove to be of great value later in our discussion, but for now let us look into the history of the ARRA.

It is appropriate to conclude that the ARRA has been known throughout history as the pentagram. The word pentagram derives its origin from the Greek term *pentagrammon*, a noun form of the word *pentagrammos*, meaning 'five lines.' The symbol of the pentagram is one of the most, if not the most, recognized occult symbols in the world. The pentagram has long been associated with the planet Venus, and the worship of the goddess Venus, or her equivalent. It is also associated with Lucifer, also known as the Morning Star, the bringer of light and knowledge. These associations that we use, originated with the Ancient Chaldeans who had an exceptional understanding of astrology. When viewed from Earth, successive inferior conjunctions of Venus plot a nearly perfect pentagram shape around the zodiac every eight years. The first known uses of the pentagram are found in Mesopotamian writings dating to about 3000 b.c. The Sumerian pentagrams served as pictograms for the word UB or AR, which meant 'corner' or 'angle.' It was also known to the ancient peoples of Mesopotamia as the Plough Sign. The Chart of Comparisons, found in the Simon Necronomicon introduction, defines the ARRA symbol as the 'Plough Sign, the original pentagram, and the sign of the Aryan Race.' Let us consider each of these three definitions that are given for the ARRA sign to help further our study and understanding of the term.

The 'Plough' is often times referred to as the Big Dipper in Europe. Yet the Simon Necronomicon makes reference to the "Plough Sign. " This would seem to indicate that the Big Dipper makes a certain sign during its movements throughout the year. If one were to observe the Big Dipper and its rotation around the North Star (Polaris), it would appear to form the sign of the *Swastika*.

The word swastika is of Sanskrit origin meaning *'to be good.'* Throughout my research and studies I have discovered that this symbol is of eastern origin dating back about 3,000 years. Some of the oldest findings of the swastika are located in the region of the Euphrates- Tigris Valley. Ancient man placed heavy importance upon the rotation of the Big Dipper around Polaris, as well as other astronomical movements to determine the seasons and to mark certain events. The Swastika has also been a symbol of a bigger star from our view here on earth, the Sun. It was actually easier for ancient man, and more reliable, to calculate the Sun's position, as far as the seasons are concerned, by looking at the position of the Big Dipper in relation to the North Star, Polaris. The importance placed upon this relationship can be seen in ancient philosophies like Taoism.

The Chart of Comparisons in the Necronomicon describes the five pointed star as being the sign of *the Aryan Race.* When we explore the origin and meaning of the term Aryan, our knowledge of how the science of the Simon Necronomicon works becomes clearer.

The term Aryan is derived from the Sanskrit term *arya* meaning "noble" or "spiritual." This term had nothing to due with physical characteristics as it is often misunderstood to represent. The following references are useful in further illustrating this point;

*"(History of Ethiopia, Vol. I., Preface, by Sir E. A. Wallis Budge.)* **In addition Budge notes that, "Homer and Herodotus call all the peoples of the Sudan, Egypt, Arabia, Palestine and Western Asia and India Ethiopians." (Ibid., p. 2.) Herodotus wrote in his celebrated History that both the Western Ethiopians, who lived in Africa, and the Eastern Ethiopians who dwelled in India, were black in complexion, but that**

the Africans had curly hair, while the Indians were straight-haired."

"Before the Chaldean rule in Mesopotamia, there were the empires of the Sumerians, Akkadians, Babylonians and Assyrians. The earliest civilization of Mesopotamia was that of the Sumerians. They are designated in the Assyrio-Babylonian inscriptions as the black-heads or black-faced people, and they are shown on the monuments as beardless and with shaven heads. This easily distinguishes them from the Semitic Babylonians, who are shown with beards and long hair. From the myths and traditions of the Babylonians we learn that their culture came originally from the south. Sir Henry Rawlinson concluded from this and other evidence that the first civilized inhabitants of Sumer and Akkad were immigrants from the African Ethiopia. John D. Baldwin, the American Orientalist, on the other hand, claims that since ancient Arabia was also known as Ethiopia, they could have just as well come from that country. These theories are rejected by Dr. II. R. Hall, of the Dept. Of Egyptian & Assyrian Antiquities of the British Museum, who contends that Mesopotamia was civilized by a migration from India? "The ethnic type of the Sumerians, so strongly marked in their statues and reliefs," says Dr. Hall, "was as different from those of the races which surrounded them as was their language from those of the Semites, Aryans, or others; they were decidedly Indian in type. The face-type of the average Indian of today is no doubt much the same as that of his Dravidian race ancestors thousands of years ago. ... And it is to this Dravidian ethnic type of India that the ancient Sumerian bears most resemblance, so far as we can judge from his monuments. ... And it is by no means improbable that the Sumerians were an Indian race which passed, certainly by land, perhaps also by sea, through Persia to the valley of the Two Rivers. It was in the Indian home (perhaps the Indus valley) that

**we suppose for them that their culture developed. ...
On the way they left the seeds of their culture in Elam.
... There is little doubt that India must have been one
of the earliest centers of human civilization, and it
seems natural to suppose that the strange un-Semitic,
un-Aryan people who came from the East to civilize the
West were of Indian origin, especially when we see
with our own eyes how very Indian the Sumerians were
in type."** *(The Ancient History of the Near East, pp. 173–174,
London, 1916.)"*

Another interesting point to consider is how modern-day
scholars try to hide the identity of these people by using
images and sculptures from other periods to describe the
whole history of Ancient Sumeria. An example of this can
be seen by looking at the history of the United States. It
has been recorded and well documented that when the
Europeans came to America, there were already an
existing people here. If we were to describe these people
as Americans it would not be an accurate description,
since these people did not call themselves American.
Now imagine living 3,000 years into the future and you
are doing research about the history of America, and the
ancient Americans are described as having European
features.
British relics are discovered along the coast of South
Carolina, but the question remains; who were the
original people of the Americas? Many scholars would
point to them as being British and what we call Native
American history today, would be represented by the
face of U.S. Presidents. This is the same trick that
modern-day scholars use to hide the characteristics of the
people who inhabited many ancient lands, Ancient
Sumeria included.

Since the people of Ancient Sumeria were similar in physical type, class distinctions were made. Later, invading peoples adopted only the most benevolent terms to describe themselves by, and recreated the gods of these people in their own image.

**"The ancient gods of India are shown with Ethiopian crowns on their heads. According to the Old Testament, Moses first met Jehovah during his sojourn among the Midianites, who were an Ethiopian tribe. We learn from Hellenic tradition that Zeus, king of the Grecian gods, so cherished the friendship of the Ethiopians that he traveled to their country twice a year to attend banquets.**

**"All the gods and goddesses of Greece were black,"** asserts Sir Godfrey Higgins, **"at least this was the case with Jupiter, Baccus, Hercules, Apollo, Ammon. The goddesses Benum, Isis, Hecate, Diana, Juno, Metis, Ceres, Cybele were black."** (Anacalypsis, Vol. I, Book IV, Chap. I.)

The above quote, by Sir Godfry Higgins, concerning some of the Greek gods, illustrates clearly how man has a habit of reproducing what he worships in his own image. It is as if god was created in the image of man. It is apparent that the author of the Necronomicon Spellbook came across this same information:

**"THESE SPELLS were originally worked by the mystics of ancient Sumeria, a mysterious civilization that flourished in what is now known as Iraq over two thousand years before the birth of Christ. No one knows who the Sumerians really were, or where they came from. Some say they came from the darkest parts of Africa,"** (Necronomicon Spellbook)

The Necronomicon describes the ARRA as a *'sign of our race from beyond the stars.'* This passage indicates that those who are represented by the ARRA are not only nobles, as we have discussed, but are also of divine lineage. Amongst every culture around the world there exists a legend of gods and goddesses intermarrying with human beings. Often times, the children of these marriages were given favor and privileges over humans who were not of divine parentage. For example, in the Gilgamesh Epics, Gilgamesh is stopped by the Scorpion Man while trying to gain passage through the Mountains of Mashu, as no mortal *or those not prepared may enter.* However, the Scorpion-man's wife intervenes noticing that Gilgamesh is no mere mortal, but two-thirds *divine* and because of such he is allowed to enter. The Bible also describes humans copulating with divine beings:

**"There were giants in the earth in those days; and also after that, when the sons of God came in unto the daughters of men, and they bare children to them, the same became mighty men which were of old, men of renown."** (Genesis 6:4) KJV

What is often not observed by Christians in the above biblical passage is that it mentions these Giants existed in those days and *'after that.'* This would mean then that those who were of divine and human parentage existed before and after the Great Deluge. This is also supported by several Sumerian texts including the Gilgamesh Epics.

It is clear from our discussion that the ARRA is a symbol of those who are from a 'race beyond the stars' or divine parentage, or one who is on the path of being pure. Yet it should be kept in mind, as we have already discussed in our Mountain of MASSHU series, the term divine beings or gods, applied to those who were adept in the Tantric

Rites. This would mean that the term Aryan, or those of the Aryan race, was a term used to describe those who were initiated into the Tantric Rites, or ones who knew the divine arts. A careful look at the Simon Necronomicon will confirm this.

Earlier in our discussion, it was stated that the pentagram has long been associated with the worship of the Goddess Venus or her equivalent. The Simon Necronomicon equates Venus with INANNA/ISHTAR. On page 24 of the Necronomicon it states: *"The Goddess of Venus is the most excellent Queen INANNA, called of the Babylonians ISHTAR."* This would mean then that Inanna/Ishtar, and those initiated into her Tantric Rites, is symbolized in the Simon Necronomicon as the ARRA, which is a 'Sign of their Race from beyond the Stars.' It also states on page 24 of the Simon Necronomicon in reference to Inanna/Ishtar that she 'partakes of a subtle astral nature with the Moon God Nanna.' It speaks about a certain time when the two planetary energies interact causing it 'to rain the sweet wine of the Gods upon the earth.' These symbolic metaphors concerning the relationship between Inanna and Nanna are references to Tantric rituals. The 'sweet wine of the Gods can be defined as a nectar. The term nectar is a Latin word for 'drink of the Gods.' However, it should be noted that the Latin term nectar is derived from the Greek term, nektar, which is a component of nek (meaning dead, as in necro) and tar meaning 'overcoming.

Within the introduction of the Simon Necronomicon, under the subtitle, the Horned Moon, it states: "The Moon has an extremely important, indeed indispensable, role in the tantrick sex magick rites that so preoccupied Crowley and the O.T.O." Earlier, in the same section, when referring to the efforts of

Crowley, it states: "The lunar element, as well as, the Venusian, are accessible in his works. So it is no mystery why the rituals in the Simon Necronomicon are encouraged to be done on the full moon!

*It cannot be overstated* how much the Ancient Tantric Rites have been misunderstood by the uninitiated. It is our culture, our way of life, and an ethnicity all to its own, 'as Inanna takes her own, for her own.' The misuse of the term ARYAN by racist bigots over the past century is indeed a recent invention, just like someone using physical characteristics to institute racial classifications. This is a practice that started less than 600 years ago.

# AGGA Sign Part 1

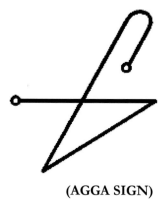

**(AGGA SIGN)**

*"The second is the Elder Sign, and is the Key whereby the Powers of the Elder Gods may be summoned, when used with the proper words and shapes. It has a Name, and is called AGGA."*

The second Seal is called the Elder Sign. Based on the Mad Arab's Testimony, the Elder Sign is named AGGA and it has the ability to unlock the powers of the Elder Gods. Let us first look into the meaning and definition of the term AGGA to aid us in gaining a deeper understanding of what the Elder Sign really means.

It is interesting to note that Agga was the name of the last king of the First dynasty that ruled over Kish in Ancient Sumeria. It is recorded that kingship after the flood, descended from heaven to Kish. The Kings of Kish that ruled after the deluge all had Semitic names, which means that they were not among the original settlers of Sumeria, but it does prove that there was some Semitic population existing in Sumeria before the flood.

Kish was a very important and influential city in ancient Sumeria. This can be shown in the title King of Kish, or Ar Ki Ati in Akkadian. This title was used for many centuries by kings to show prestige, as it maybe compared to saying 'King of the entire world!' This title was used by kings even when another king was actually the king of Kish, and after Kish had ceased to be the seat of kingship. It seems that this title had a deeper meaning than the one that is prestigious. Kish is situated within the northern plains of southern Mesopotamia on a critical spot of the Euphrates River. A breakthrough of the river to the lowlands in the direction southwest would mean that a whole system of irrigation channels would be without a water supply. This means that the control of the Euphrates River in the area of Kish was of vital importance. The title King of Kish indicated the ruler that exercised control of this region, or at one time, the water supply that a vast population depended on. Ironically, the Necronomicon on page 99 mentions that the Elder Sign is a symbol "of the Power of the Magick of Enki." Enki was the Sumerian deity of water. Let us look further to see how all of these factors connect together.

Famous Sumerianologist, Samuel Noah Kramer, attributes Inanna as the tutelary deity of Kish. This can be understood by reviewing the Ancient Sumerian accounts. Throughout the 3rd Millennium and centuries later, various kings of Mesopotamia describe themselves as spouses of the Goddess Inanna and her other aspects. Many of them also claim that their right of kingship was granted to them by the Goddess Inanna. This custom was even practiced by kings from regions other than Kish. Mesannepada of Ur (2563-2524 B.C.E.) claimed to be the husband of Inanna. Eannabum of Lagash claimed kingship by the love of Inanna, or as recorded; "Inanna because she loved him so, gave him the Kingship of Kish!"

The idea of being "king by the love of Inanna" originated in the early political development of Ancient Sumeria. This evolution in politics is enacted in the mythos of Inanna and Enki, in which Inanna persuades the drunken Enki to give her the mes of the universe. Samuel N. Kramer mentions in his book, entitled, *The Sumerians,* that the word *me,* "seems to denote a set of rules and regulations assigned to each cosmic entity and cultural phenomena for the purpose of keeping it operating in accordance as is the plans laid down by the deity creating it." This term *me* relates to the description of the Elder Sign given to us on page 12 of the Simon Necronomicon:

*"... the Elder Sign, and is the Key whereby the Powers of the Elder Gods may be summoned when used with the proper words and shapes."*

The Elder Sign is attributed as being "the sign of the Power of Enki," since it was Enki that Inanna seduced to gain authoritative power or me. We are told in the Simon Necronomicon that the key to unlocking the Powers of the Elder Gods is by using the Elder Sign with the proper words and shapes. This seems to be the opinion of Samuel N. Kramer, as he writes on page 115 in his book *The Sumerians:*

**"All that the creating deity had to do, according to this doctrine, was to lay his plans, utter the word, and pronounce the name. This notion of creative power of the divine word....,was based on observation of human society; if a human king could achieve almost all he wanted by command, by no more than what seemed to be the words of his mouth, how much more was possible for the immortal.."**

The legend of Inanna and Enki was known throughout Ancient Sumeria and it is safe to conclude that with this knowledge, ancient kings credited Inanna as the source of their kingship. Kramer further asserts:

**"Toward the middle of the 3rd Millennium however, when the Sumerians were becoming more and more nationally minded..., a seemingly quite pausible and not unattractive idea arose that the king of Sumer, no matter who he was or from what city he originated, must become the husband of the life-giving goddess of love, that is Inanna of Erech."**

Kingship was bestowed by Inanna through the authoritative power that ultimately derived from Enki. We should also keep in mind that in early Sumerian history many of the kings were also priests to their people. This would mean that the 'Power of the Magick of Enki,' is only bestowed upon the priest or priestess of the Simon Necronomicon by Inanna (Ishtar). This also unlocks a mystery that some Initiates of the Necronomicon Tradition have often questioned. Page 7 of the Simon Necronomicon states:

*"And fled to the earth by calling upon INANNA and her brother MARDUK..,"*

Some have questioned what is meant by the Mad Arab's assertion that Inanna and Marduk are siblings since they do not appear as such in any of the Sumerian legends. However, from studying the ancient legends of Inanna, there are a few accounts where she refers to Enki as her father. The Mad Arab, being familiar with the mythos of Enki and Inanna, knew that Inanna achieved her power from Enki, which was also the case with Marduk. It must be remembered that the ancient gods of Sumer referred to themselves, and others of divine progeny, in terms of endearment; such as father, brother, sister, and etc. Since Enki was from an older generation of gods, and Inanna was of a younger set of divinities, it was a sign of endearment and respect that she referred to Enki as her father. This honor given to Enki in no way contradicts the traditional genealogy, placing Inanna as the daughter of Nanna/Sin (moon deity) her father.

It is clear from our discussion that the Power of Enki is bestowed upon the priest or priestess of the Necronomicon Tradition through Inanna. An example of this can be seen in the epic of Gilgamesh and Agga.

It is within this poetic work that we find Gilgamesh seeking the advice from the elders in the city to determine whether or not, he should surrender or go to war against King Agga of Kish. His elders counseled him against starting a war with King Agga. Yet it is said of Gilgamesh that because of 'placing his trust in Inanna, he did not take seriously the advise of his elders.' Later, King Agga is recorded as having surrendered to Gilgamesh. It is clear that the ancient priestly-rulers credited Inanna as their source of strength.

*"BUT KNOW THAT INANNA TAKES HER OWN FOR HER OWN AND THAT ONCE CHOSEN BY HER NO MAN MAY TAKE ANOTHER BRIDE."*

The above passage, taken from the Simon Necronomicon, is a description of a very important celebration that the early Sumerian rulers had to fulfill as part of their kingship- *The Sacred Marriage Rite.* Since there is no one text that describes the Sumerian New Year celebration, we are left with understanding this elaborate rite through the Sacred Marriage songs and the epic of Inanna and Dumuzi.

The Sacred Marriage Rite began with a procession by the king to the giparu of Inanna's temple. During this time the bride (enacted by a priestess of Inanna) prepared for the event by washing, anointing, and adoring herself. During the procession, and in anticipation of 'Inanna' meeting the king, there was a celebration of songs and other activities. One of the highlights of the event was the sexual union that took place between the king and Inanna. This sexual rite took place in the heart of the temple. Some scholars have erroneously debated, whether or not, actual sexual relations took place. Some have suggested that the king went to bed with a statue of the Goddess. This may be true of some of the celebrations that occurred around 1700 B.C. However, we shall see later in our discussion that in these ancient rites, sexual relations really did occur.

During the Sacred Marriage Rite, which took place to bring in the Sumerian New Year, the energy of the goddess was honored, delivered, and drawn down to bless the land, the king, and his people. Without the king's participation in the Sacred Marriage Rite, he was considered unable to be an effective ruler. His potency was inextricably linked with his physical prowess and attuned to his sexual energies.

# The AGGA Sign Part 2: Preliminary Purification Invocation

Our last discussion ended with a brief description of the Sacred Marriage Rite. This ancient celebration took place at the start of the spring equinox, when the earth was animating with fresh new life. This festive time lasted for many days and the people celebrated the sacred occasion through song, serpentine dances, anointing their skin with oils, and etc. The King was also prepared for the event through certain purification rites, which are addressed in the Simon Necronomicon on page 110:

*"These things you will learn in the course of your journey and it is not necessary to put it all down here cave for a few noble formulae concerning the Works of the Sphere of LIBAT, of ISHTAR, the Queen."*

The Mad Arab only found it necessary to state certain workings about the Sphere of Ishtar. Why was this information necessary? It was to prepare the Initiate for the workings of the Sacred Marriage Rite. If we were to look at the three spells of the Sphere of Ishtar, located in the Simon Necronomicon on pages 110-111, it would seem like they were just randomly thrown into the text with no real importance to the overall meaning of the grimoire itself. However, when we compare these three spells with the workings involved in the Sacred Marriage rites, the meaning of the AGGA sign unfolds.

**1- The Preliminary Purification Invocation symbolized the wedding procession.**

2- To Win The Love of A Woman spell represented the act of sexual intercourse that took place between the King and Inanna/Ishtar.

3- To Recover Potency spell would represent the King's anointing and that his potency was indeed linked to his sexual energies, or raised kundalini force, allowing him to operate from a divine perspective.

These three stages clearly are shown in the AGGA sign's shape:

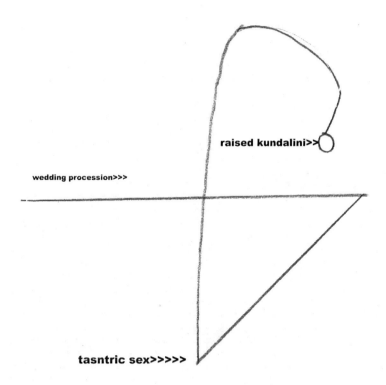

raised kundalini>>

wedding procession>>>

tasntric sex>>>>>

Let us look at these three spells, as listed in the Simon Necronomicon and see how they relate to the Sacred Marriage Rite.

# The Preliminary Purification Invocation

This invocation is a symbol of the wedding procession that takes place during the Sacred Marriage Rites. It also represents the path of initiation through the Gate-Walking Process of Initiation, which is described in the Simon Necronomicon. The wedding procession and the Gate-Walking Process, is a symbol of the penis entering the vagina of the cosmic world. It also represents a sperm cell searching for the egg. This is the reason why, even in modern-day wedding ceremonies, the congregation is separated to the right and to the left, as it symbolizes the inner walls of the vagina. The participants in the wedding procession, with their celebration of song and dance during the event, are a metaphor for the vaginal secretions during intercourse, as well as, the sperm released from the penis speeding towards the egg. Interestingly, when we compare the Gate-Walking Process to the penis entering the vagina, the meaning of the Sacred Marriage Rite becomes quite clear.

This process of initiation, as presented in the Simon Necronomicon, requires the candidate to pass through seven gates. Each gate represents a plane of existence and an aspect of life. There are many correspondences attributed to these gates, from incense to planetary elements. The Simon Necronomicon mentions this on page 19. However, it should also be kept in mind that even before the candidate enters the Gate-Walking process; they exist in the Gate of Ki, the Earth. We can find this information in the Invocation of the NANNA Gate, as written in the Simon Necronomicon on page 58, where it states: **"I call Thee! From the Four Gates of the Land Ki."** This passage reveals that in addition to the seven gates, the earthly plane (Ki) from which we ascend when we walk up the Ladder of Lights, is also a gate. This would mean then that there are actually eight gates. Hsi Lai wrote in his classic work on Taoist sexual alchemy, *The Sexual Teachings of the Jade Dragon,* that the female vagina is composed of eight different segments. He also mentions in his work that there are eight different types of Jade Stems (the penis) and how these relate to the eight ideograms of the famous I-Ching. This information does shed light on the relationship between, the seal of the gate and the gate itself. The seal of the gate is masculine and the gate is feminine, and when the two are worked with through our path of initiation, we are able to explore a new world of consciousness. These worlds are able to unfold for us based on the sexual alchemy of the Sacred Marriage Rite. On page 110 of the Simon Necronomicon, Ishtar is called the *"Mistress of the Gods."*

This would indicate that when we possess the seal while entering the gate, we are representing the phallus of that particular sphere entering a certain point in the cosmic vagina of the universe. We are connecting the stellar world (penis) with our subconscious (vagina). When the penis is fully inserted into the vagina, an orgasm occurs and the erection dies. Similarly, in the Gate Walking Process we have an orgasm when we go into Ganzir. We are then reconceived in the sphere of ADAR, and regain the potency to walk the gates that lie beyond. We will discuss this aspect in some of our future articles. Let us see how this information relates to the Sacred Marriage Rite.

The process of initiation, as described in the Simon Necronomicon, is the tantric alchemy of the Sacred

Marriage Rite. A close examination of modern wedding ceremonies will help us bring all these points together.

1. The Bride, in modern wedding ceremonies, takes pride in wearing a white wedding gown. This custom came from the Priestesses of Inanna, who would dress in white robes during the Sacred Marriage Rite.

2. The Groom, in modern wedding ceremonies, customarily wears a tuxedo-suit in the colors of white and black. The Groom would then represent Dumuzi, as he is said to live in the Underworld for half of the year and the world of the Living for the other half of the year. The Simon Necronomicon on page 100 states: **"and the Frontlet of Calling, shall be of fine cloth, and in the colors of Ninib and Inanna, that is, of Black and White.."**

3. Since the Groom represents Dumuzi, then Utu would represent the Best-man in modern wedding ceremonies. In the Courtship of Inanna and Dumuzi, it was Utu/Shammash who presented Dumuzi to Inanna, which explains why the Best-man presents the wedding rings. This explains why in the Simon Necronomicon it mentions on page 77, in the beginning of the Maklu Text, a text used for banishing evil spirits, that when performing these rites, the arms should held in the position of a 'Priest of Shammash,' as it was Shammash who helped Dumuzi against the evils he faced in the Underworld.

4. The Priest who marries the bride and groom represents Enki, as he is the one who sent the 'Water of Life and the Bread of Life' to the crucified Inanna. The location of where the bride and groom stand would symbolically represent the Gate of Adar, where life, death, and

resurrection occur. The Priest announces this union of feminine and masculine aspects, as the creation of a new being or one flesh. This is the inner alchemy of balancing male and female energies respectively. What Enki has yoked together let no man set apart. This yoke is reflective of the eggs used in Easter celebrations which represent a new life.

5. Many people in the western world fantasize about having a wedding in the month of June. It is in the month of June that the sign Cancer begins. Cancer is a cardinal sign and it is ruled by Nanna (the moon). It is symbolic of the father giving his daughter away, as Nanna was the father of Inanna.

6. The Maid of Honor functions as an assistant to the bride in getting herself together and etc. The Maid of Honor would be Inanna's mother Ningal. Inanna ran to Ningal for advice after speaking to Dumuzi. Ningal comforted Inanna.

The Simon Necronomicon tells us that Inanna/Ishtar's *'yes is truly yes.'* This would symbolize the affirmative vow that we take as initiates in bonding with the divine energies of Inanna through the alchemy of the Gate-Walking process.

# The AGGA Sign Part 3: To Win The Love Of A Woman

*"But heed these words well, and remember! For remembering is the most potent magick, being the Rememberance of Things Past and the Rememberance of Things to Come, which is the same Memory."* (Simon Necronomicon page 153)

Earlier in our discussion, as found in the AGGA Sign, parts 1 & 2, we learned about the strong influence of the Sumerian deity, Inanna/Ishtar had over the political, religious, and scientific worlds during ancient times. We were also able to get a glimpse of the Sumerian history that is buried in the Simon Necronomicon, which helped us to outline these few points from our previous discussions:

**1) The Ancient Kings of Sumer claimed their divine right of kingship as being bestowed upon them by Inanna/Ishtar.**

**2) The Sacred Marriage Rite was a vehicle used to transfer divine energy from Inanna/Ishtar to the king through the act of sexual intercourse. The practices in the Simon Necronomicon are also vehicles to empower the priest or priestess with divine power, which is bestowed upon the practitioner by Inanna/Ishtar.**

**3) The wedding procession that took place during the Sacred Marriage Rite was symbolic of the penis entering the vagina. This symbolism also applies to the traditional wedding ceremonies and corresponds to the**

GateWalking initiations as found in the Simon
Necronomicon.

4) The three workings of the Sphere of LIBAT, as found
in the Simon Necronomicon on pages 110-111, represent
the three stages of the Sacred Marriage Rite that were
enacted upon by the Ancient Sumerians. We discussed
the first of the three workings, the Preliminary
Purification Invocation, in the AGGA Sign Part 2. Now
let us look at the second working, To Win the Love of a
Woman.

The second working of the Sphere of LIBAT is entitled;
*"To Win the Love of a Woman."* This working evidently
reflects the topic of alchemical sex that took place
between the priestly-rulers of Sumeria and
Inanna/Ishtar, who was represented by a temple
priestess. This act of alchemical sex is referred to in the
Simon Necronomicon on page 37:

*"Thou must abstain from spilling thy seed in any manner
for like period of time, but thou mayest worship at the
Temple of ISHTAR, provided thou lose not thine Essence.
And this is a great secret."*

Page 24 of the Simon Necronomicon states:

*"She is similarly the Goddess of Love, and bestows a
favorable bride upon any man who desires it, and who
makes the proper sacrifice"*

The Mad Arab properly refers to the worship of
Inanna/Ishtar as being a "Great Secret" and rightfully so.
The inner workings of most religions are indeed parables
describing the workings of tantric secret societies. I must
state that the practices of spiritual-sexuality, is still a
science that is difficult to translate

to the western mind because of its indoctrination in contradictory social values, terms like Tantra, are often misinterpreted to represent a way to maximize sexual pleasure rather than a spiritual path of devotion, which at times required a great deal of celibacy, especially among male practitioners. Although we have assigned such ignorance to modern culture in reference to this ancient tradition, this very same ignorance was prevalent in ancient times, which resulted in the persecution and the degradation of these practices by pseudo-cults trying to gain prestige while lacking the discipline. It was these pseudo-cults that some historians wrongfully attributed as being part of the workings of Inanna/Ishtar's temple.

The Simon Necronomicon speaks about the Priest being careful not to spill his seed. He must learn balance. In Freemasonry, it is the woman who is the 'Grand Architect of the Universe.' The Chaldean covenant, mentioned in the Simon Necronomicon, is based on the woman's monthly cycle. Those who are initiated into the greater mysteries know that ones' bondage to an orgasm is what prevents them from immortality. The orgasm is the ultimate sacrifice. It is what the King sacrificed to obtain enlightenment to rule a nation during the Sacred Marriage Rite. Therefore, the Mad Arab encourages us in the Simon Necronomicon not to waste our seed, for it is to be used as part of our worship to Ishtar. This is the Great Secret. Since a woman has to make a sacrifice once a month, male practitioners of the Simon Necronomicon should set aside time to sacrifice semen to Ishtar at least once a month. The principles of our tantric evolution, has been expressed in one ancient legend-INANNA'S Descent into The Underworld.

The meaning of this ancient legend has baffled anthropologists and scholars alike. One reason for this confusion is due to the practice of keeping the Ancient Sumerian epics as separate stories and not seeing each legend as an extension of one whole story. This would also apply to the legend of Inanna's Descent.

We are told in the Gilgamesh epics that Inanna tried to use the "Bull of Heaven" against Gilgamesh when he spurned her sexual advances, which was a sign of his disrespect for the Sacred Marriage rites. Later, we find that Gilgamesh and Enkidu have slain the "Bull of Heaven." This would relate to the legend of Inanna's Descent. When Inanna/Ishtar was questioned as to why she felt the need to visit the Underworld, Inanna responded that her reason for coming to the Underworld was to mourn the death of her Brother-in-Law, Gulgalanna, "the Bull of Heaven." Gugalanna was Ereshkigal's husband before she married Nergal. It is also interesting to note that Inanna refers to Ereshkigal as her older sister, when in the Sumerian pantheon Ereshkigal is Enki's twin sister. Evidently, Inanna's reference to Ereshkigal as being her 'sister' must have some other meaning.

Enki is the Sumerian god of water and semen. Ereshkigal, being his twin sister, would represent the feminine aspect of the god of semen. Ereshkigal would then represent the menstruating woman, and since Inanna could see that in herself as well, she refers to her as a sister. Thus, we find that Inanna's descent was a multi-layered journey. One aspect of the Descent was to resurrect the ancient Tantric rites of Sumer that Gilgamesh degraded in one way or another. This would also indicate why Inanna refers to Ereshkigal as being her older sister, since the use of menstrual blood reflected an older tantric rite, though it is still used today. Inanna's Descent was also a way to raise the kundalini force after having misappropriated it during her encounter with Gilgamesh. The legend also established some parameters around the rite itself. We also discover why the number fifteen is sacred to Inanna/Ishtar being that she passed into seven gates representing the seven planets that are understood through the eight phases of the moon.

In our second discussion concerning the AGGA sign, we mentioned that the wedding procession was a metaphor representing the penis moving deeper into the vagina, which also symbolizes our path of initiation as Gate-Walkers. Before reaching the last gate, being Adar, as listed in the Simon Necronomicon, we must first descend into Ganzir. This is our orgasm. If we have remain true to the covenant, it is then that our true initiation occurs and we are transformed in Adar, What lies ahead is only the Outside.

We can see in the translation of this "spell" that it is more of a psalm to the Throne of Ishtar, than it is a spell. However, this does point out that we have been moving on the same track as the author was, when he put the three workings of LIBAT in the Book of Calling.

### To Win The Love Of A Woman

MUNUS SIGSIGGA AG BARA YE INNIN

**WOMAN BE SWEET-SMALL LOVE THRONE OF ISHTAR**

AGGISH XASHXUR GISHNU URMA

**LOVE-PENIS SEMEN-ENTER PENIS-NOT OR VIRGIN SOUL-BIND**

SHAZIGA BARA YE ZIGASHUBBA NA

**EXCITEMENT THRONE OF RISING WATER STREGTHENING**

AGSISHAMAZIGA NAMZA

**LOVE-HORN-GIFT-DATE-FRUIT-EXCITEMENT KINGSHIP-SELF**

YE INNIN DURRE ESH AKKI UGU

**OF ISHTAR BOND-WITH MUCH OPEN-EARTH TOP OF HEAD**

AGBA ANDAGUB

**LOVE-HOUSE HEAVEN-SURROUND-TO SERVE**

We can see in the translation of this "spell" that it is more of a psalm to the Throne of Ishtar, than it is a spell. However, this does point out that we have been moving on the same track as the author was, when he put the three workings of LIBAT in the Book of Calling.

# The AGGA Sign Part 4: To recover Potency

We begin our latest discussion on the AGGA SIGN with the third working of the Sphere of LIBAT, located on page 111 of the Simon Necronomicon entitled; To Recover Potency spell. This working represents the King's anointing, through the sexual rites of the Sacred Marriage celebration, in Ancient Sumeria. Transferring divine power to the King occurred during his participation in sexual relations with Inanna/Ishtar. The Goddess was represented by a Temple Priestess. Any child that was conceived during these sexual relations was considered half-human and half-divine. When Inanna/Ishtar brother, Utu the Sun god, replied to Inanna in the famous epic, The Courtship of Inanna and Dumuzi, Utu spoke of Dumuzi as 'being conceived on the sacred marriage throne.' This would also indicate that some of the early priestly-rulers who were anointed through the Sacred Marriage rites, at times had sexual relations with their own relatives who were acting as Temple Priestesses, or 'in-laws.' The origin of the term 'in-law' is founded upon the laws of marriage between gods and humans. If the 'gods' happened to marry someone who was not part of their divine family, the prospective spouse had to be adopted into the 'divine family' by law. It is from this practice that we derive the term, 'in-law.' Although these practices were detested by the Judaic-Christian rites, it is still evident in their history, as Abraham was married to his sister Sarah. The children of the Sacred Marriage Rite unions were later known as the Nefilim during Judeo-Christian times. Additionally, it is mentioned in another account concerning Dumuzi, when he was being chased by the galla that he was no mere mortal, due to the fact that he was 'married to the Goddess Inanna.' Through the Sacred Marriage Rite, the King was endowed with clairvoyant powers since his kundalini was raised, and his third eye opened. It can easily be said that a divine ruler was a sexually potent one as well, and because of such, he wore the Crown of Anu, also known as the AGA.

The term AGA means crown. This term is also defined in such texts, as the MUL.APIN, as, the Crown of Anu. The Simon Necronomicon refers to the Crown of Anu on page 100. It is listed as part of the ceremonial garb that the priest or priestess would wear during some of the operations of magick listed in the text therein.

Another interesting reference is made about the 'Crown of Anu' in the Simon Necronomicon on page 78, under the banishing ritual entitled, THE EXORCISM OF THE CROWN OF ANU, it states:

*"I have put on the Starry Crown of Heaven, the potent Disk of ANU on my head*
*That a kindly Spirit and a kindly Watcher*
*Like the God that hath made me*
*May stand at my head always"*

In the above passage we can see that the Crown of Anu represented the epitome of the Tantric alchemical work that was employed by the Ancient Sumerian Adepts. It also represents the merging of the ancient Mother-Son rites with the up and coming Patriotic institution. On page 78 of the Simon Necronomicon, the Crown of Anu is described as being a 'spotless white' color. This is the color of Inanna/Ishtar. It is interesting to note that the sister sorority of the Freemasons, The Order of the Eastern Star, also wear white fezzes. The other reference to the Crown of Anu' is given to us on page 100, where it states that the 'Crown may be made of beaten copper.' Copper was also a symbol for blood in Ancient Sumeria. This is expressed even today amongst the Freemasons who wear a fez of a blood-red color.

The Simon Necronomicon speaks of two different rites, that of the Ancient Ones, and those of the Elder Gods. On page 78 of the Simon Necronomicon, it mentions a 'kindly Spirit' and a 'kindly Watcher' being atop of ones' head. What does this mean? Another passage in the Simon Necronomicon can lead us to a greater understanding of this. On page 202 of the Simon Necronomicon it states:

*"And it means nothing save that a man, being born, is of sadness, for he is of the Blood of the Ancient Ones, but has the 'Spirit' of the Elder Gods breathed into*

*him ...,When the Great KUTULU rises up and greets the Stars, then the War will be over.."*

This passage is very clear in defining the 'kindly Spirit' as being the spirit of the Elder Gods, and the kindly Watcher being KUTULU, as he has greeted the stars completing the great Tantric work. Earlier in our discussion, we spoke about the Courtship of Inanna and Dumuzi, wherein Utu, trying to convince Inanna to accept Dumuzi as a husband, stated that he was born on the 'Sacred Marriage Throne.' This would also make Dumuzi a spiritual son of Inanna, which would explain the ancient mother-son depictions that have been found around the world. However, popular these artifacts are, the meaning of them is often misunderstood.

During the copulation between the King and Inanna/Ishtar, the King was able to obtain enlightenment and an astral fetus was created, or a spiritual child. This is the Watcher. This spiritual child is Kutulu. Within the Tantric rites of Ancient Sumeria, the priest and priestess worked hard to maintain there state of spiritual awareness, and within this work a new creation was born, or a spiritual being that would act as a vehicle to the initiate. This new creation had to be nourished in order for it to grow. On page 70 of the Simon Necronomicon it mentions that 'the Watcher is from a Race different from that of Men and yet different from that of the Gods.' It also mentions that the Watcher in the beginning was with Kingu, and we know that Man was created from the blood of Kingu. Later in the Magan Text we are told about 'Children who were born of earth that in the creation of Anu were spawned.' One definition of the word spawn is to produce an egg. It is this spiritual egg or fetus, which undergoes development through the Gate-Walking process, which was a sign of the candidate's true initiation. In a book entitled THE OMNIPOTENT OOM by Hugh B. Urban, the author has this comment to say concerning Aleister Crowley:

**"However, the ultimate goal that Crowley sought through his sexual magical practices seems to have gone far beyond the mundane desire for material wealth; indeed, in his most exalted moments, Crowley appears to have believed that he could achieve the birth of a divine child a spiritual, immortal, godlike being, who would transcend the moral failings of the body born of mere woman. This goal of creating an inner immortal fetus, Crowley suggests, lies at the heart of many esoteric traditions, from ancient Mesopotamia to India to the Arab world."**

From the above quote, we can safely understand that the goal of the Tantric practices of Ancient Sumeria was for the development of a new creation within us, an immortal part of ourselves that was to be nourished and that was conceived on the Sacred Marriage Throne. We will discuss this more in our next discussion concerning the Bandar Sign. For now though we will conclude with these following words and definitions.

**AG-GA (Love-Oath)**

LILLIK IM LINU USH KIRI

**(SPIRIT-DOG) (WIND) (SHINE-NOT) (POISON) (MUZZLE)**

LISHTAKSSIR ERPETUMMA

**(MORSEL-TO TOUCH-TESTICLE) (MALE SLAVE-OPEN FOR ME-A WAY)**

TIKU LITTUK NI YISH

**(RAINDROPS) (FIRE OIL-RECEIVE) (ONES' OWN) (SON)**

LIBBI IA LU AMESH ID

**(APPEASEMENT OF THE GODS) (ENKI) (MAN) (PLURAL)**

GINMESH ISHARI LU SAYAN

**(MUCH LAPIS LAZULI) (MOUNTAIN-LION) (MAN) (FOUNTAINS OF LIFE)**

SAYAMMI YE LA URRADA

**(WOMAN-FASTING) (OF) BEAUTY) SOUL-OVERFLOW-PROTECT(**

ULTU MUXXISHA

**(SINCE TIME IMMEMORIAL) (ABOVE-STAR)**

# The AGGA Sign Part 5

Now that we have given a thorough synopsis of the term AGGA, the simple difinition of the word is found in the *Sumer Aryan Dictionary* by L. Austine Waddell. It states on page 6 the following:

**"AGGA: Sumerian : Spirits (? Fiery) of the Deep. Akkadian: Andh, Anun-aki, water spirits. "**

Waddell's definition of the term AGGA, gives us a deeper look at the history of ancient Sumeria. Although the Babylonians actually engaged in literal physical tantric rites it seems that the Keepers of the tradition used sexual archetypes as a metaphor for alchemical practices. This is the usual process of how information becomes profane. The language of symbolism is never revealed by a people who are being invaded by foreigners. The invaders then read the rites and customs of the conquered people without knowing the language of symbolism, interpret these ancient rites literally, and though these systems may be able to change some things when taken literally, due to the stellar correspondences in relation to physical things in nature. *The Stanzas of Dzjn Theogenesis* by A. S. Raleigh mentions the following on page 160:

**"Thus the worship of Ishtar became more in the nature of sexual intercourse in her honor than anything else. At the same time there were those among the higher Initiates who realized that this was not the true worship of Ishtar. They held that she operated within as well as without, and that the formative and creative activity of the Goddess could transpire on the Inner Planes of being...Those Initiates realized that the true worship of**

Ishtar was in the restraining of sex expression in the outer, so that the transformation might go on within the inner nature, and in this way they might be born again from time to time."

# The Energies of the Urilia Text

I remember talking to a fellow Gate-Walker during my initiation, and the subject of the Urilia Text came up in our conversation. The other Initiate mentioned that *'he could not understand; why the Urilia Text was even a part of the book?!!'* I am sure this question may have crossed the minds of many Initiates, or just people who own a copy of the Simon Necronomicon. For some, speculation about this section of the Necronomicon derives from the following words of the Mad Arab:

*"These incantations are said by the hidden priests and creatures of these powers, defeated by the Elders and the Seven Powers, led by MARDUK, supported by ENKI and the whole Host of IGIGI; defeaters of the Old Serpent, the Ancient Worm, TIAMAT, the ABYSS, also called KUTULU, the Corpse-God, yet who lies not dead, but dreaming; he whom secret priests, initiated into the Black Rites, whose names are writ forever in the Book of Chaos, can summon if they but know how."*

The *"initiation into the Black Rites"* is the process of self-initiation described in earlier parts of the Simon Necronomicon, also known as Gate-Walking. Simon encourages this *"dark initiation"* in his essays about the tome that appear in the book's Introduction. Under the subheading *SUMERIA* we read:

**"Yet, though the identity of the Victor is clear, there were - and are - certain persons and organizations that dared side with the vanquished, believing the Ancient Ones to be a source of tremendous, and most unbelievable, power."**

Simon continues as he identifies the work of Aleister Crowley with the Ancient Ones. We find this comparison in the Introduction's subheading entitled, *THE MYTHOS AND THE MAGICK:*

"**Indeed, Crowley had nothing but admiration for the Shaitan (Satan) of the so-called "devil-worshipping" cult of the Yezidis of Mesopotamia, knowledge of which led him to declare the lines that open this Introduction. For he saw that the Yezidis possess a Great Secret and a Great Tradition that extends far back into time, beyond the origin of the Sun cults of Osiris, Mithra and Christ; even before the formation of the Judaic religion, and the Hebrew tongue. Crowley harkened back to a time before the Moon was worshipped, to the "Shadow Out of Time"; and in this, whether he realized it as such or not, he had heard the "Call of Cthulhu."**"

Crowley heard the Call of Cthulhu. He didn't remain on the safe side of the journey by engaging in what was comfortable. Crowley knew that advancement in the Greater Mysteries is made through refinement, which is not an easy process. Under the subheading, *THE DEVIL,* in the Simon Necronomicon's Introduction, we read:

"**Man's power to alter the nature of his environment must develop simultaneously with his ability to master his inner environment, his own mind his psyche, soul, spirit. Perhaps, then, the lunar landing was the first collective initiation for humanity, which will bring it one step closer to a beneficial Force that resides beyond the race of the "cruel celestial spirits", past the Abyss of Knowledge. Yet, he must remember that the occult powers that accompany magickal attainment are ornamental only, indications of obstacles overcome on the Path to Perfection, and are not to be sought after in** themselves, for therein lies the truth Death. **Lovecraft saw this Evil, as the world passed from one War and moved menacingly towards another. Crowley prepared for it, and provided us with the formulae. The Mad Arab saw it all, in a vision, and wrote it down. He was, perhaps, one of the most advanced adepts of his time, and he certainly has something to say to us, today, in a language the Intuition understands. Yet they called him "Mad"."**

There comes a time in our work when we begin to evolve past the ordinary "magickal" practices that we were once involved in. This "evolution" is like a child growing up. Children find joy in the relationship that they have with their family. As the child grows older, they learn more about responsibility and how to take care of themselves. Eventually, the adult will establish his/her own household. *The process of spiritual evolution is the art of self-responsibility.*

Can you imagine what life would be like if you were forced to call upon a friend, or relative, only when you had a problem? How long would these people respond to you? Wouldn't they begin to ignore you after a while? Now let us compare this example with the attitude of some people who are involved in the occult arts for the wrong reasons. Some people only invoke spirits when they want something. Whenever a problem occurs, they are right in front of their altars burning some incense, or making a sacrifice. These individuals feel empowered because they have a "gang" that they can call on anytime somebody crosses their path. People who think like this are disillusioned, and their magical workings will bring them more suffering than joy. *Virtue is a requirement for each and every magickal act.*

Earlier in our discussion, we spoke about how the soul's journey after death is the same rite of passage that those who are initiated into the Greater Mysteries take. A journey through the Seven Gates of self-initiation is a journey through the world of the dead. If the Initiate continues to Walk and re-Walk the Gates (constellations) after they have been initiated into the Necronomicon Tradition, their energy will become stagnant, just like a spirit of a deceased person that cannot move on pass the Initiatory Gates and into the "Garden of the Gods." The Urilia Text teaches the Initiate about the realms of rebirth and immortality. It is an initiation into the primordial rites where the candidate is instructed in the ways of godhood and spiritual self-responsibility. It is here that the Initiate must journey to the farthest reaches of the universe and in doing so, they learn about the dark mystical practices of the Necronomicon Tradition directly from the deities themselves. Simon mentions something similar to this in the Simon Necronomicon's Introduction, under the subheading entitled *THE DEVIL,* he writes:

**"Although the Christian religion has gone to great lengths to prove that the Devil is inferior to God and exists solely for His purpose, as the Tempter of Man - surely a dubious raison d'etre – the Sumerian Tradition acknowledges that the Person of "Evil" is actually the oldest, most Ancient of the Gods. Whereas Christianity states that Lucifer was a rebel in heaven, and fell from God's grace to ignominy below, the original story was that MARDUK was the rebel, and severed the Body of the Ancient of Ancient Ones to create the Cosmos in other words, the precise reverse of the Judeo-Christian dogma. The Elder Gods evidently possessed a certain Wisdom that was not held by their Parents,** yet their Parents held the Power, the Primal Strength, **the First**

**Magick, that the Elder Ones tapped to their own advantage, for they were begotten of Her."**

The Mad Arab reveals this perspective in his Second Testimony:

*"Remember that the Essences of the Ancient Ones are in all things,"*

The Elder Gods are animated by the power they receive from the Ancient Ones. The lucid state of consciousness, which the Gate-Walker experiences during the full moon, is evidence of the nurturing "astral blood" that is received from our parents (the Ancient Ones) through the Elder Gods. The Second Testimony of the Mad Arab states:

*"And I have seen them turn the very Moon's rays into liquid, the which they poured upon their stones for a purpose I could not divine."*

The Initiate would only suffer greatly if they were to attempt to venture forth into these primordial rites without initiation. I remember an experience of a fellow Gate-Walker who tried to summon Pazuzu without knowing the proper formulae for doing so. He suffered depression and sickness for at least three months. This experience is strikingly different from others who have benefited greatly in their workings with this spirit. The difference here is that those who were successful in their workings with Pazuzu are initiated into the rites of the Urilia Text.

The "anti-gates" listed in the Urilia Text are what scientists today call *"dark cloud constellations"* and *"black holes."* According the Necronomicon Tradition, black holes perform the "angelic" function of removing "stellar debris" from accumulating in space and they also provide subtle energy to empower growing stars. The Necronomicon Tradition also defines these *"black holes"* as initiators in the Qliphotic Mysteries:

*"for the Race of Draconis was ever powerful in ancient times, when the first temples were built in MAGAN, and they drew down much strength from the stars, but now they are as Wanderers of theWastelands,"*

The power from these "anti-gates" is tremendous, but very subtle, at first. The influences from the "antigates" can only be useful to those Initiates of the "black rites." Within the Simon Necronomicon Tradition exists Seven Gates of Initiation whose power derives from the *Six Anti-Gates of Creation.* Some may wonder why there are only six- power zones in comparison to the Seven Gates of Initiation, plus Ganzir (Daath)? Many occultists have made the mistake of assuming that the Spheres on the Qliphotic Tree of Transformation are negative aspects of the said Judeo-Christian Tree of Life. This is completely erroneous, since the Kabala originates with the people of ancient Mesopotamia. We learn from their mythologies that the Qliphotic Tree of Transformation is made up of seven astral archetypes and six power-zones. Examples of this are recorded for us in the Gilgamesh Epics.

According to the Gilgamesh Epics, Enkidu (meaning Enki's creation, or mankind) was like a beast of the field, until he met Shamhat (she is given the title *harimtu,* similar to the Hebrew *harim,* meaning *devoted to god.*) Shamhat was devoted to the tantric rites of Ishtar. The myth describes how Shamhat made love to Enkidu for *six days* (six power-zones) and *seven nights* (seven gates of initiation, or the seven Anunnaki). It was from this tantric transformation that Enkidu, though a mortal, became equal in strength to Gilgamesh, a man who was of divine progeny. Later in the Epics, we learn of Enkidu's death. Gilgamesh is so full of grief and sorrow over Enkidu's death that he refuses to leave his side, or allow his corpse to be buried, until *six days and seven nights* after his death when a maggot falls from Enkidu's nose. Gilgamesh begins a search for immortality and travels to Dilmun (the Abode of the Gods) and meets Utnapishtim (the Sumerian Noah). Gilgamesh wonders why Utnapishtim was spared by the gods and given life eternal. (It is interesting for the reader to note that Utnapishtim is also known as Atrahasis, who was instructed by Enki to make supplications to Namtar, an underworld deity, in order to gain salvation from the fate that the gods had decreed.) Utnapishtim offers Gilgamesh a chance for immortality and challenges Gilgamesh to stay awake for *six days and seven nights*. Legend has it that Gilgamesh failed to do so and the plant that he was given to regain his youth, was swallowed up by a *serpent*.

It is amazing how scholars will praise Gilgamesh as a hero though the epics clearly show that he lost a benevolent fate because he acted disrespectfully towards the Qliphotic Tradition. Another thing that is overlooked by many occultists and scholars is the importance placed upon the *six days and seven nights,* mentioned repeatedly in the Gilgamesh Epics. This time frame is mentioned during Enkidu's transformation, his death, and while Gilgamesh is in Dilmun. This evidently points to the 13 aspects of the Qliphotic Tree of Transformation that are also mentioned in the Magan Text:

*"AZAG-THOTH (1) screamed upon his throne*
*CUTHALU(2) lurched forth from his sleep*
*ISHNIGARRAB (3) fled the Palace of Death*
*IAK SAKKAK(4) trembled in fear and hate*

*The ANUNNAKI (seven gates = seven nights) fled their
thrones
The Eye upon the Throne took flight
ERESHKIGAL(5) roared and summoned NAMMTAR
The Magician NAMMRAR (6) she called
But not for pursuit
But for protection."*

The Gilgamesh Epics is a treatise on how the Qliphotic
Tree of Transformation works. The Epic further
emphasize the penalty for those who disrespect these
rites after their initiation, which resulted in the death of
Enkidu and eventually Gilgamesh himself. We will now
examine the Atlantean deities and entities that appear in
the Urilia Text.

# HUMWAWA

Dimension: **Gift of Foresight and ability to travel out-of-body.**

Mad Arab's description in First Testimony: *"Know, then, that I have trod all the Zones of the Gods, and also the places of the Azonei, and have descended unto the foul places of Death and Eternal Thirst, which may be reached through the Gate of GANZIR, which was built in UR, in the days before Babylon was."*

Author's Notes: **Humwawa was placed in Mt. Mashu to guard the Cedar Forest. Mt Mashu is the gateway that leads to the Garden of the Gods, the Throne of Ishtar, and the Underworld. Therefore, the passage cited above is symbolic of the Mad Arab's interaction with Humwawa.**

Simon Necronomicon's description:

*"The Lord of Abominations is HUMWAWA of the South Winds, whose face is a mass of the entrails of the animals and men. His breath is the stench of dung, and has been. HUMWAWA is the Dark Angel of all that is excreted, and of all that sours. And as all things come to the time when they will decay, so also HUMWAWA is the Lord of the Future of all that goes upon the earth, and any man's future years may be seen by gazing into the very face of this Angel, taking care not to breathe the horrid perfume that is the odour of death.."*

Mesopotamian Mythology:

**Humwawa was originally an Elamite god, also known as Humbaba, or Humban. He was the principle god of**

Elam with a temple in Susa. In Elam he was called
"Master of Heaven." His first wife was the Elamite
goddess Pinikir, but he later married Kiririsha.
HUMWAWA was a very well known deity in the
ancient world. *A Hebrew Deluge Story In Cuneiform* by
Albert T. Clay, states the following on page 50:

"Since the sign *PI* has the value of *wa*, and *wa* and *ba*
in this period interchange, the correct reading of the
word in the omen texts, and of the personal name, was
not *Hu-pi-pi*, but it was *Hu-wa-wa*;...It followed from
this discovery that the name was the same as that of
*Hobab, the father-in-law of Moses* (Num. 10:29);"

Moses' father-in-law, Jethro, was also known as Hobab, a
name that derives from Humbaba. One correspondence
of Humwawa is the gift of foresight, which we discussed
earlier. It seems that Jethro may have been called
"Hobab" since he possessed this gift. Jethro is discussed
at great length in rabbinical tradition, where he is
sometimes seen as a repentant idolater and also honored
as one of several authentic Gentile prophets. Jethro also
advised Moses to appoint deputies to assist in handling
disputes. Evidently, Jethro had the *"gift of foresight."*

Humwawa was demonized by the Babylonians. It is in
the Gilgamesh Epics that we discover Humwawa as the
protector of the Cedar Forest. According to the accounts,
Humwawa had the ability to detect any creature moving
within the woods and to cause that creature to fall asleep.
This illustrates the Initiate's acquired ability to move
with stealth. Humwawa was appointed by the storm god
Enlil to govern Mt. Mashu. Enlil was a storm deity and
the father of the Moon god Nanna. Humwawa was also a
storm deity. In Sumerian culture, storms were symbolic
of emotions. The Initiate is taught directly by Humwawa

in the field of emotional manipulation. It was the Sun deity Shammash, who urged Gilgamesh and Enkidu to travel to Mt. Mashu and kill Humbaba. Gilgamesh held the god while Enkidu cut his head off. The gods punished Gilgamesh and Enkidu for their actions. This resulted in Enkidu's death, due to an incurable disease, while Gilgamesh looked on in sorrow. Later, we find Gilgamesh is unsuccessful in trying to find out the meaning of life in his search for immortality. This reiterates what we discussed earlier concerning solar cults and the Sun itself. The advice that the Sun god Shammash gave to Gilgamesh and Enkidu ultimately cost them their lives.

The example of Enkidu is a warning to all Initiates of the Necronomicon Tradition. Enkidu was raised from a beast to man by the priestess of Ishtar, named Shambat. It was through the *"tantric"* practices employed by Shambat that Enkidu became equaled in strength to a *"son of god."* Enkidu forfeited his initiation by his infatuation with the solar cults, as symbolized by his friendship with Gilgamesh. Humbaba's death at the hands of Enkidu, represents the Initiate who attempts to undermine his/her own oath. This act resulted in Enkidu's death. I see no reason why the consequences for such actions would be different for any other Initiate of the Necronomicon Tradition. Simon makes a very interesting comment concerning this, in his work entitled, *Gates of the Necronomicon*, page 27:

**"The rituals in the Necronomicon open a Gate. To use the Necronomicon is to take that first step from which there is no turning back: the step over the Threshold to the Other Side."**

The "Other Side," mentioned by Simon is the Mountains of MASSHU, the same area that was guarded by

Humwawa. The Mad Arab describes Humwawa's *'face is
a mass of the entrails of the animals and men'"* The ability to
divine the future from our interactions with animals and
men is what Humwaw teaches us. The famous Greek
historian of 80 to 20 B.C., Diodorus of Sicily, made the
following observation, regarding the Chaldeans, in his
work entitled, *Bibliotheca Historica:*

**"They are also skilled in the soothsaying by the flight
of birds, and they give out interpretations of both
dreams and portents. They also show marked ability in
making divinations from the observations of the** *entrails
of animals,* **deeming that in this branch they are
eminently successful."**

The Chaldeans possessed the unique ability to divine the
future by observing the entrails of animals. The Initiate
learns how to communicate with animals and can detect
the prophetic spirits that speak through them.

We are also told by the Mad Arab, not to breathe in the
"horrid perfume" that Humwawa emanates.
Humwawa's "breathe is a stench of dung." The ability to
look into the future is also the ability to see the end of all
things. This is not always a pleasant thing. The Mad Arab
compared the pain of seeing 'dark things of the future' to
a foul odor, but we can rest assure that this "odor" is
balanced by the energy of another. *The Tao Te Ching*
describes Humwawa in Chapter One:

**"The Tao that can be spoken is not the eternal Tao
The name that can be named is not the eternal name
The nameless is the origin of Heaven and Earth
The named is the mother of myriad things
Thus, constantly without desire, one observes its
essence**

Constantly with desire, one observes its manifestations
These two emerge together but differ in name
The unity is said to be the mystery
Mystery of mysteries, the door to all wonders"

# PAZUZU

Dimension: **Psychic Self-Defense. Ability to see the karma of a particular course of action, event, or person. Healing. Death Energy.**

*"And if HUMWAWA appears to the priest, will not the dread PAZUZU also be there? Lord of all fevers and plagues, grinning Dark Angel of the Four Wings, horned, with rotting genitalia, from which he howls in pain through sharpened teeth over the lands of the cities sacred to the APHKHALLU even in the height of the Sun as in the height of the Moon; even with whirling sand and wind, as with empty stillness, and it is the able magician indeed who can remove PAZUZU once he has laid hold of a man, for PAZUZU lays hold unto death."*

It is one thing to see the future, but it is wiser to act knowing the future. Pazuzu follows Humwawa, as he instructs the Initiate in the ways of karma. Animals and humans act from desire, while the deities act from a sense of karma. Pazuzu is a very logical energy that appears to be cold emotionally at first. It is a very beneficial force that helps the Initiate to see the result of a certain course of action before taking it. The Initiate's animalistic desires are replaced with the eyes of karma and temptations are no longer challenging to us. There are people in the world who will try to change their future to accommodate an immoral desire. Pazuzu replaces these "desires" with the eyes of karma. The eye of karma becomes the predominating force behind our actions. We no longer struggle with inappropriate desires. Let us look a little more into Pazuzu's history to understand how his energy works.

Pazuzu is the king of the wind demons according to Assyrian and Babylonian mythology. Pazuzu is known in Sumerian as Imdugud. Imdugud was an Anzu bird. Anzu birds were known to respond only to Enlil, but Imdugud only responded to Enki. The Anzu were wise creatures of heaven and also bringer of storms. So the attributes of Pazuzu would include psychic self-defense and the ability to change a person's emotional state, which could lead to disease, or the ability to heal a disease. It is said that the Anzu bird was worshiped by Izdubar. Since the Anzu bird was a wind demon, we have to take into consideration that the wind was a symbol of the breath, or the soul of the deceased. Thus, the Anzu bird also represented spirits of the dead flying toward heaven. In *Babylonian Star-lore*, by Gavin White, it mentions the following on page 59:

**"Thought of in this manner the Anzu-bird symbolises the host of discarnate souls..by the 3rd millenneum the constellation of the Anzu bird was so ancient that it no longer arose in the correct season."**

Some have indentified the Anzu bird with the Zu-bird that appears in the Myth of Zu. The term Anzu is derived from *An*, meaning *heaven*, and *zu* meaning *far*. This shows us that the *Anzu* were from heaven. This is in agreement with Gavin White's observation that the Anzu-bird represented a distant constellation. This constellation, according to White's writings, was a symbol of discarnate souls. Here we can see how Pazuzu empowers the Gate of Nanna. In many occult traditions around the world, the New Moon is an appropriate time to work with spirits of the dead. It is in the "anti-gate" of Pazuzu that the Initiate learns how to interact with the dead, and also how to protect oneself against attacks from the dead. This is illustrated in the Mad Arab's description of Pazuzu:

*"grinning Dark Angel of the Four Wings, horned, with rotting genitalia, from which he howls in pain through sharpened teeth over the lands of the cities sacred to the APHKHALLU even in the height of the Sun as in the height of the Moon.."*

Since the Moon corresponds to the sexual glands, *"rotting genitalia,"* would refer to protection against attacks from the incubus and succubus. The howls of pain in the height of the Sun and Moon, shows us that Pazuzu's protection is not constricted by the halls of space and time.

*"even with whirling sand and wind, as with empty stillness, and it is the able magician indeed who can remove PAZUZU once he has laid hold of a man, for PAZUZU lays hold unto death."*

The above passage describes an attunement that allows the Initiate to work with death energy. The ability to make the dead rise was even revered by the early Christians and practiced by the apostles themselves. This ability is also an important aspect of the Necronomicon Tradition. Many people are under the misconception that spiritual healing involves channeling some sort of benevolent energy from a "divine source" into a person's aura. Spiritual healing is the art of removing "death energy" from the person's aura and transforming it into ones' own being Celestial deities do not have the power to alter ones' fate when it comes to death. Earlier, we cited Lewis Paton's observations on ancient occult practices in his book, *Spiritism and the Cult of the Dead in Antiquity,* on page 208 he states the following:

*"The great gods whom men loved and adored were gods of the upper world and of the living; their sway did not extend into the dark abodes of the dead ... When death came it was a sign that their favor was withdrawn, or that they were unable to help against the powers f darkness. The disembodied spirit passed out of their jurisdiction into that of divinities with whom in life it had established no friendly relations."*

It is for this reason that deities such as, Inanna, Jesus, Krishna, and etc, all had to *"die"* and visit the "netherworld" in order to learn necromancy from the powers of darkness themselves. Paton continues on page 264:

*"So long as Sheol stood outside of Yahweh's jurisdiction, no radical change could arise in Israel's conception of the future life."*

Those who are familiar with Biblical lore, will notice that older sections of the Bible do not subscribe to an afterlife, or resurrection from the dead. The Old Testament promotes the idea that from "dust you are and to dust you shall return." It was only after the appearance of, "King Solomon," that we read about the prophet Elijah, possessing the power to raise the dead. Elijah also visited the "netherworld" before raising a widow's son from the dead. In 1 Kings Chapter 17, Elijah is told to go to a brook near Jordan, where he had to wait to be fed by "ravens" These are clear symbols of his visit to the Underworld.

We learn another aspect of Pazuzu's energies in the Simon Necronomicon's Introduction, under the subtopic, *THE DEVIL,* we read the following words:

*"PAZUZU was a prime example of the type of Devil of which the Sumerians were particularly aware, and which*

*they depicted constantly in their carvings and statues. The purpose of this iconography was to ward off the spiritual - and psychic - circumstances which would precipitate a plague, or some other evil. "Evil to destroy evil."*

Pazuzu was used throughout ancient Mesopotamian to ward off evil and was considered a useful energy against Lamashtu. Lamashtu was the goddess who was held responsible for miscarriages and the death of children. This symbolism is a metaphor for Pazuzu's ability to reconstruct events, symbolized as childbirth, that are not useful to ones' experience. Pazuzu is the guarding feature of our intuitive nature. The "anti-gates" are the building blocks of godhood and enable us to use our consciousness to form reality. During these initiations, it is very important that we do not meditatively focus on harmful thoughts. This is what the Initiate learns from the Pazuzu archetype that exists within our stellar body. When the stellar body awakens the characteristics of the "anti-gates" is given life. The "anti-gates" are the different aspects of the chthonic mind and this is what we learn in the "anti-gate" of Humwawa and Pazuzu. *The Tao Te Ching* gives us the following description of Pazuzu in Chapter Two:

**"When the world knows beauty as beauty, ugliness arises When it knows good as good, evil arises Thus being and non-being produce each other Difficult and easy bring about each other Long and short reveal each other High and low support each other Music and voice harmonize each other Front and back follow each other Therefore the sages: Manage the work of detached actions Conduct the teaching of no words They work with myriad things but do not control They create but do not possess They act but do not presume They**

succeed but do not dwell on success. It is because they do not dwell on success That it never goes away"

# NINNGHIZHIDDA (ISHNIGARRAB)

Dimension: **Ability to shift reality through dreams. Dream yoga. Distant healing.**

Mad Arab's Testimony: *"Know, too, that I have spoken with all manner of spirit and daemon, whose names are no longer known in the societies of Man, or were never known. And the seals of some of these are writ herein; yet others I must take with me when I leave you. ANU have mercy on my soul!"*

There is little mention of Ninnghizhidda in the Simon Necronomicon. He/She is described in the Book of Calling, as the *"Horned Serpent, the Lady of the Magick Wand."* Ninnghizhidda is an androgynous deity, sometimes depicted as a man and at other times as a woman. Ningishzida means *'lord of the good tree.'* He/She is the patron of medicine, and the divine force of nature and fertility. Ningishzida is the earliest known symbol of snakes entwining, commonly known as the caduceus. He/She represents the Hydra constellation.

Ninnghizhidda is the "anti-gate" that supplies the Nebo Gate with power. Famous Occultist, Kenneth Grant, made the following observation about the "serpent" in his classical work, *The Nightside of Eden*. On page 163 he writes:

**"The Black Brother is doubled tongued, as the serpent, which is significant, for the magical power ascribed to the obverse aspect of which this path is the tunnel. Is the Gift of Tongues, the Gift of Healing, and a Knowledge of Sciences. The healing here however is the healing of the ego, which merely aggravates with illusion the disease of false identity."**

Ninnghizhidda teaches the Initiate about the casualties formed due to the misappropriate use of the ego. It is through this process that the Initiate becomes acquainted with "god-consciousness." While the Nebo Gate sheds light on different aspects of communication, money, and etc. Ninnghizhidda shows us how to create beneficial interactions by exposing blockages in our own psyche. This is revealed in the Magan Text's *Of the Sleep of ISHTAR* account. In this parable, we find Ninnghizhidda as the Gate-Keeper of the Underworld, or the power to destroy the false ego.

**"Nin Giz Zida…is another symbol attributed to Tibet. Called the Serpent of Fire, it is used to align the chakras and energy system to prepare a student for attunement.."**

The term *kundalini* is a Sanskrit word, which translates to *coiled*. The arousing of kundalini is said to be the only way, in which we can obtain Divine Wisdom. This gives us a deeper understanding as to why Ninnghizhidda is invoked in the preliminary steps of the Urilia Text's rituals:

*"When the Fire is built and conjured, then mayest thou raise thine Dagger, summoning the assistance of NINKHARSAG, Queen of the Demons, and NINKASZI, the Horned Queen, and NINNGHIZHIDDA, the Queen of the Magick Wand, after their manner and form. And when thou hast accomplished this, and made the proper sacrifice, thou mayest begin calling whichsoever of the offspring thou mayest, after opening the Gate."*

Ninnghizhidda is the serpent force of the "goddess," and operates on an intellectual level. It foreshadows Kutulu/Tiamat, which the Simon Necronomicon describes as *"the very Fire of the Earth, and Power of All Magick."*

Ninnghizhidda is considered to be a fertility deity. The feminine force of Earth's fire, also known as the kundalini, is the pure creative energy that is responsible for creation. While the Sun emanates the subtle energies of "chi," which keep life in motion, kundalini is responsible for life's creation. Ninnghizhidda knows how to make the best use of the kundalini-energy, though it is not the force itself. Ninnghizhidda also gives us knowledge about forces *"whose names are no longer known in the societies of Man."*

Another aspect of Ninnghizhidda is Ishnigarrab. In the Introduction to the Simon Necronomicon, Simon equates Ishnigarrab with Shub-Niggurath. Shub-Niggurath in Lovecraft's Cthulhu Mythos is often associated with the phrase; "The Black Goat of the Woods with a Thousand Young." This deity has been described as being similar to the goddess Astarte. However, the Black Goat is also referred to as the "Lord of the Woods" in Lovecraft's

*Whisperer in Darkness.* This indicates that Shub-Niggurath, like Ninnghizhidda, is an androgynous deity.

Interestingly, in the Cthulhu Mythos the Black Goat is regarded as the "Lord of the Woods." Ningishzida was imagined to be the god-energy of the trees. He formed into a serpent who coiled himself around the tree roots, becoming the living energy of the tree. In ancient Mesopotamia, tree roots were often associated with the idea of snakes burrowing into the ground. There is another striking similarity between Ninnghizhidda and Shub-Niggurath described in *Whisperer in the Darkness*:

**"And it has come to pass that the Lord of the Woods, being cast out descended the seven and nine, down the onyx steps into the Dream."**

Lovecraft describes the descent of the *"seven and nine"* into the Dream. In the Simon Necronomicon, the "seven and nine" are the Seven Elder Gods, and the "nine" would refer to the nine sigils that appear in the URILIA Text. The "seven" would then equate to NANNA, NEBO, ISHTAR, SHAMMASH, NERGAL, MARDUK, and ADAR. The URILIA Text describes many deities, but only lists nine sigils for the following deities; HUMWAWA-1, PAZUZU-2, KUTULU-3, AKHKHARU-4, LALASSU-5, LALARTU-6, GELAL-7, LILIT-8, and XASTUR-9. This information weighs heavily in our discussion, since the Simon Necronomicon describes Ninnghizhidda, as the Gate-Keeper between the realms of the "seven" and the "nine."

*"Thee I invoke, Serpent of the Deep!*
*Thee I invoke, NINNGHIZHIDDA, Horned Serpent of the Deep!*
*Thee I invoke, Plumed Serpent of the Deep!*
*NINNGHIZHIDDA!*

*Open!*
*Open the Gate that I may enter!*
*NINNGHIZHIDDA, Spirit of the Deep, Watcher of the*
*Gate, Remember!*
*In the Name of our Father, ENKI, before the Flight, Lord*
*and Master of Magicians, Open the Gate that I may*
*enter!"*

Ninnghizhidda was also considered to be the "god of dawn and dusk." Ninnghizhidda holds the key to both the "seven" and the "nine," or the planetary initiations and more advanced stages of Qliphotic Magick. It is for this reason that he/she is referred to as the Queen of the Magick Wand. The dawn brings forth a new day with all its possibilities. The dusk brings an end to unsettled matters of exhausting pain. This relates perfectly to Ishnigarrab, who is described by Simon as the "answerer of prayers." Nebo reflects the energies of Ninnghizhidda, not as a gate-keeper, but as the 'guardian of the gods.' Ishnigarrab also appears later in our discussion as an aspect of Lammashta. The *Tao Te Ching* describes Ninnghizhidda in Chapter Three with the following words:

**"Do not glorify the achievers So the people will not squabble Do not treasure goods that are hard to obtain So the people will not become thieves Do not show the desired things So their hearts will not be confused Thus the governance of the sage: Empties their hearts Fills their bellies Weakens their ambitions Strengthens their bones Let the people have no cunning and no greed So those who scheme will not dare to meddle Act without contrivance And nothing will be beyond control"**

# LAMMASHTA

Dimension: **The understanding of how to use the
kundalini force to create. Entrance into a greater reality.
Thought and emotional transference. Mastery of carnal
desires. Direct communication with the dead.**

Mad Arab's Testimony: *"I have seen the Unknown
Lands, that no map has ever charted. I have lived in the
deserts and the wastelands, and spoken with demons and
the souls of slaughtered men, and of women who have
dies in childbirth, victims of the she-fiend
LAMMASHTA."*

Lamashtu was known in Sumeria as Dimme. Lamashtu
was the only "demonic" figure that was said to act on her
own accord. She is said to be a daughter of Anu, the sky
god. Lamashtu was often depicted in Babylonian
mythologies as the "demoness" who was responsible for
the deaths of children, as well as, miscarriages. She is also
described by the Mad Arab as the killer of men. This
symbolism has often been misinterpreted by the masses
with the exception of those initiated into the
*"Qliphotic Mysteries,"* commonly known as the
Necronomicon Tradition.

Lamashtu, along with other warrior-goddesses like Durga, Ereshkigal, Kali, Lamia, Oya, Shub-Niggurath, Tiamat, and etc, represent the ancient *alchemy of the menstruating woman*. It was due to early man's ignorance, concerning the process of menstruation, that these rites were later demonized. When ancient man observed that miscarriages also resulted in blood loss through the vagina, he began to associate the origin of these things with the same deities that were revered as menstruating goddesses. A woman's menstruation cycle is *the foundation of all magickal traditions*. *The Women's Encyclopedia of Myths and Secrets* by Barbara G. Walker makes the following observation on page 403:

**"A combination of honey and menstrual blood was considered the elixir of life, the "nectar" manufactured by Aphrodite and her sacred bees, which kept the gods alive. Similarly, the great secret of Norse mythology was that the gods' nectar of wisdom, inspiration, literacy, magic, and eternal life was a combination of honey and "wise blood" from the great Cauldron in the belly of Mother Earth-though a late patriarchal revision claimed this hydromel or "honey-liquid" was a mixture of honey with the blood of a male sacrificial victim known as Wisest of Men."**

Walker's observation is relative to a few passages found in the Simon Necronomicon:

*"She (ISHTAR) appears as a most beautiful Lady, in the company of lions, and partakes of a subtle astral nature with the Moon God NANNA. When they are in agreement, that is, when their two plants are auspiciously arranged in the heavens, it is as two offering-cups split freely in the heavens, to rain the sweet*

*wine of the Gods upon the earth. And then there is great happiness and rejoicing."*

The "sweet wine of the Gods" mentioned by the Mad Arab is menstrual blood. We also find another passage in the Urilia Text that speaks about Lamashtu and the alchemy of menstrual blood:

*"And when thou hast set out bread for the dead to eat, remember to pour honey thereupon, for it is pleasing to the Goddess Whom No One Worshippeth,"*

The "honey" mentioned in the words quoted above, represent menstrual blood, which is noted in the writings of Barbara Walker. The "bread" is a symbol of stone. The sacrifice of "blood and stone," or honey with bread, is discussed in the Magan Text:

*"The Red Water of Life..Need be split on a stone..The stone struck with a sword..That hath slain eleven men..Sacrifices to HUBUR..So that the Strike ringeth out..And call TIAMAT from Her slumber..From her sleep in the Caverns... Of the Earth."*

The *"Red Water of Life"* is menstrual blood, symbolized by honey in magickal ritual. The "stone" that it is to be spilt upon is the "bread" that the honey is to be poured upon. Some researchers have made the error of interpreting this passage as a reference to murder. The "sword" that has slain eleven men is the ritual sword of the Watcher, and the eleven men are the eleven spheres mentioned in the Simon Necronomicon's *Supplementary Material To 777.* Although some occultists actually use menstrual blood in their ritual work, we find that "menstrual blood" is a symbol of an alchemical process. Barbara G. Walker states the following page 637:

"Egyptian pharaohs became divine by ingesting "the blood of Isis," a soma-like ambrosia called sa. Its hieroglyphic sign was the same as the sign of the vulva....The vessel or cup of this immortal fluid is the moon."

Walker's essays indicate that the "menstrual blood" used for alchemical purposes is not literal blood, but a refined energy that is released from the stellar realms and poured out upon the Initiate during different Moon phases. This information helps us to understand the third name attributed to Lamashtu- *"the Sword which splitteth the Skull!"*

*"I learned of the various classes of demons and evil gods that exist, and of the old legends concerning the Ancient Ones. I was thus able to arm myself against also the she-devil LAMMASHTA, who is called the Sword that Splits the Skull, the sight of whom causeth horror and dismay,"*

Since the ancient mysteries attributed "menstrual blood" as being the elixir of immortality, the menstruating goddess, Lamashtu, was chiefly responsible for bestowing eternal life upon those who were worthy. Interestingly, Kali, another menstruating goddess, is also depicted holding a sword and a severed head. The "Sword' signifies Divine Knowledge and the "Skull" represents the Human Ego, which must be slain by Divine Knowledge in order to obtain "union with god." Lamashtu teaches the Initiate how to discern what is real from what is unreal. The true meaning of existence is seen when intercourse is held with the energy of Lamashtu.

## LAMASHTU and NINHURSAG

The mysteries of Lamashtu, the menstruating goddess, are Atlantean and have been labeled "evil" by those who are unaware of the gnosis. Kenneth Grant illustrates this clearly in his book *Nightside of Eden*. On page 78 he states the following:

**"It should be unnecessary to remark that the phenomenon of menstruation would not alone have caused the massive dread and abhorrence with which ancient scriptures, myths, and legends, are replete. The eclipse, whether celestial or physiological, was a type, a symbol of dark forces infinitely more terrifying than mere sexual promiscuity and its concomitant diseases. Nor were these forces veiled in obscure symbols for reasons other than that the ancients were unable precisely to define them. They merely suspected that woman and her peculiar mechanism constituted, in some manner unknown to them, a door, a gateway on to the void, through which awful forces could be invoked by those who chanced upon the keys. That these keys were unknown to a few is probable and it is also probable that the Sumerians, the Egyptians, the Americans, the Mongols, were acquainted each with a fragment of a vastly ancient gnosis-the science of the kalas, which has survived into modern times in certain Asiatic Mystery Schools."**

The Initiate is informed about the use of these keys from Lamashtu herself. These are the very same keys that are mentioned in the Magan Text:

*"And this is the Covenant*
*Created by the Elder Gods*
*From the Blood of the Ancient Ones*
*Man is the Key by which*
*The Gate if IAK SAKKAK may be flung wide*
*By which the Ancient Ones*

*Seek their Vengeance"*

The "Blood of the Ancient Ones" is the alchemy of menstrual blood. The Elder Gods (also known as the Black Brothers) were keepers of this science, which the Mad Arab called the Ancient Arcana. Lamashtu, the menstruating goddess, is the primordial power and the foundation of the Atlantean Tradition.

Since the civilizations that followed the Atlantean Tradition, only held a fragment of the ancient gnosis, they "demonized" a great amount of its lore, due to their own ignorance. The mythologies of Ancient Mesopotamia and their depiction of Lamashtu as a demon is a clear indication that this Goddess preceded Sumerian Civilization by thousands of years. The following description of Lamashtu gives us a deeper meaning into the alchemy of "menstrual blood."

Lamashtu is described as having a "hairy body." Lahmu and Lahamu were known as the "hairy ones," and were the first children of Tiamat and Apsu, the first civilization. It is from the first civilization that the worship of Lamashtu arose. This is evident from other features and depictions of the goddess. Lamashtu is also seen nursing a pig and a dog, which is symbolic of her connections to the Qliphotic Rites. The 1961 classic *'Eat Not this Flesh'* by Frederick J. Simoons, states:

**"Lamashtu is often depicted in Mesopotamia, as suckling a young pig and a puppy, or standing in a field with a pig nearby. The nursing of young animals by women is widespread in the modern world, and some believe it is likely that women nursed pigs during** *the Paleolithic period,* **when hunters after killing a**

nursing sow or some other nursing animal, brought home infant animals to
be reared as member of the human family. Such a practice would have facilitated the domestication of dogs and pigs, and may explain their widespread sacrificial and ritual role in planting cultures. In light of the above, it has been suggested that LAMASHTU may have been a demonized version of an ancient fertility goddess."

The "pig" was a totem symbol of Neptune in the Atlantean Mysteries. According to H.P. Blavatsky, the Pig God was "the God of the magicians of Atlantis." The "dog" that Lamashtu nurses with her other breast is a symbol of the planet Pluto, which symbolizes, according to Kenneth Grant, the "guide of the dead in the underworld, or world beyond the universe."

Lamashtu is said to possess a lioness' head with a donkey's ears and teeth. The "lioness' head represents the Sun in Leo. It is here that the Initiate begins to understand that the will of the magician requires the use of lust to overcome obstacles. One of the magickal tools of the Necronomicon Tradition is the Copper Dagger of Inanna. It is mentioned in the Book of Calling and more importantly in the Urilia Text:

*"When the Fire is built and conjured, then mayest thou raise thine Dagger, summoning the assistance of NINKHARSAG, Queen of the Demons, and NINKASZI, the Horned Queen, and NINNGHIZHIDDA, the Queen of the Magick Wand, after their manner and form.."*

The Dagger is an extension of the magician's will. The Simon Necronomicon instructs the Initiate to make this dagger out of copper. Copper was a symbol for blood in

Sumeria. It is here that we see a correlation between Ishtar and Lamashtu. Lamashtu was sometimes referred to as the "right hand of Ishtar." The "right hand" is the hand that the Initiate uses to direct their will. The Copper Dagger of Inanna represents the use of "menstrual blood," or shakti (normally depicted in Tantric Mythologies as lust) to reach ones' goals. The primal lust is the directing force that shapes reality. We are not talking about lustful desires, which are an indication that one is being possessed by a spirit of a deceased person, but the self-induced consciousness where the veils of reality are lifted. Lamashtu's donkey ears and teeth represent sex magic, also known as the Veils of Negative Existence.

These aspects of Lamashtu are revealed in the esoteric myth of ENKI and NINHURSAG. Ninhursag is commonly translated as *"lady of the mountain."* This definition is derived from the Sumerian NIN meaning lady and HUR.SAG meaning foothill. In the book, *Flying Serpents and Dragons* by R. A. Boulaym, the author makes the following observations:

**"We have seen that SAG means "lions head," thus HUR-SAG would be "the monster that roars."**

According to Boulaym's observation, Ninhursag could also be defined as "Lady monster that roars." Lamashtu is said to roar like a lion. We should also keep in mind that the Mad Arab describes Ninhursag in the Urilia Text as the "Queen of the Demons." This definition of Ninhursag finds its origin in the myth Enki and Ninhursag.

In the myth, Ninhursag curses Enki for his sexual promiscuity and blatant disrespect for the tantric rites by having relations with and impregnating the offspring that he has with Ninhursag. Later, this misappropriated lust fuels his greed and he eats eight newly-formed plants because of it. Enki's actions symbolized disrespect for the Sacred Marriage Rite. Enki after eating these plants gets struck with disease and sickness in eight organs of his body. None of the gods or goddesses could relieve Enki from his illness. Finally, Enlil urges Ninhursag to rescue Enki. Ninhursag cured him, taking the plants into her body and giving birth to eight deities, which make up the Tree of Life.

1. **ABU** = The god of vegetation. It symbolizes the Initiate use of the kundalini force to heal the blood.

2. **Ninsikila, Nintulla or** Nintual = Healer of the Locked Hair. Designated as the Lord of MAGAN, also depicted as the patroness of cattle. This deity was birthed by NINHURSAG to heal ENKI's jaw, as in Temporomandibular Disorder. Also referred to as Ninsikila, the goddess that was born to heal ENKI's hair, which was in locks. This deity represents the Initiate's use of kundalini energy to loosen blocked "chi."

3. **Ninsutu** = Healer of Teeth. Ninsutu was a Sumerian goddess birthed by Ninhursag to heal Enki's teeth. This deity represents the Initiate's use of the kundalini force to tap into the sexual energies of the kidneys.

4. **Ninkasi** = Goddess of Beer. Ninkasi was birthed by Ninhursag to heal Enki's mouth. This deity represents the Initiate's ability to heal the "bitter taste of the mouth" and increase the span of physical life.

5. **Ninazimua** = Bountiful Baranch. Healer of Arms and Branches. Bithed by Ninhursag to relieve Enki's pain in

his arms. This deity represents the Initiate's use of the kundalini force to change the outcome of events.

6. **Nanshe or Nazi** = The Goddess of Prophecy. Birthed by Ninhursag to heal Enki's throat. This deity represents the Initiates use of the kundalini force to speak to others in dreams. Dream interpretation.

7. **Ninti** = Lady of the Rib. Lady of Life. Birthed by Ninhursag to relieve Enki's rib. This deity represents the Initiate's use of the kundalini force to alter thinking in themselves and others.

8. **Enshag** = Lord of Dilmun. Birthed by Ninhursag to relieve the pain in Enki's limbs. This deity represents the Initiate's ability to transfer initiation upon others.

It should also be noted that the myth of Enki and Ninhursag takes place in Dilmun. In Sumerian Mythologies, Dilmun is described as "the place where the Sun rises.' It is the same place that Utmapishtim (Ziusudra, commonly know as the Sumerian Noah) was placed by the gods to live forever. The Abrahamic religions refer to this place as the Garden of Eden. It is here that we see another fallacy in the rites of the solar cults.

Enki became sick after he ate the freshly-sprouted plants growing for the first time in Dilmun. The origin of these plants is a very fascinating part of the myth:

**"NINHURSAG heard her distress and she came at once. She removed ENKI's seed from her descendant's thighs, and with it she caused eight plants to grow. She grew the 'tree' plant, the honey plant', the 'vegetable'**

plant, the alfalfa grass, the 'atutu' plant, the 'astaltal' plant, the
'amharu' plant, and one more besides. ENKI had returned to the marsh and again he was peering up there, he was able to see the plants and he spoke to his minister Isimud, "I have not determined the destiny of these plants. What is this one? What is that one?" Isimud answered: "My master, the 'tree' plant." Isimud cut the plant and gave it to his master who ate it. "My master the 'honey' plant' again ENKI ate it. In like manner he ate the 'vegetable', 'alfalfa', 'atutu', 'astaltal' and 'amharu' plants and one more besides. Together these represented the eight basic plant groups. ENKI determined the destiny of these plants, he had each of them know it in their hearts, he defined their role. When NINHURSAG saw this she was enraged. She had created the plants yet ENKI had undertaken to determine their fates! She cursed the name ENKI, "Until his dying day, I will never look upon him with my life-giving eye." ENKI's life was endangered, his health afflicted, and the gods were distraught at the falling out of ENKI and his partner. They sat in the dust in despair. NINHURSAG had withdrawn and none of the gods knew how to approach her. It was then that the fox went to ENLIL who lead the gods, who commissioned ENKI's actions, and spoke to him: "If I am able to bring NINHURSAG to you what will be my reward?" ENLIL was greatly pleased and responded that the fox would win renown and be greatly honored. The fox prepared himself, placing kohl under his eyes. When he saw NINHURSAG he went to her and spoke cunning words to her. NINHURSAG agreed to return and she made her way to the temple where the gods quickly removed her clothing and ushered the weakened ENKI to her. There were eight parts of ENKI that hurt him and to these NINHURSAG now looked with life giving eye. She sat him by her vagina and addressed him, "My kinsman, what part of you hurts

you?" "Ugu-dili, the top of my head, hurts me" She took
the affliction into her womb and gave birth to Abu out
of it."

When Ninhursag removed "Enki's seed" from the
Goddess Uttu and buried it in the ground, eight plants
were formed. Ninhursag gained renown as the destroyer
of Enki's seed and was later blamed for the death of
children. We also see a large contrast between this myth
and the Biblical version, where the woman is blamed for
eating the fruit from the Tree of Good and Bad. It is
evident that the monotheistic religions inverted the
tantric rites once again.

Ninhursag is an aspect of Lamashtu and represents the
growing power of kundalini energies. Other goddesses in
Sumerian lore, represent other aspects of Lamashtu,
among these are Ereshkigal and Tiamat. Lamashtu, the
*'menstruating goddess,'* is often depicted as *roaring* in
ancient myths. Notice what is mentioned in the Magan
Text concerning both Ereshkigal and Tiamat:

*"The Eye upon the Throne took flight..ERESHKIGAL
roared and summoned NAMMTAR..."*

*"She lunged at MARDUK..With a roar..With a curse..She
lunged."*

These two passages are almost identical in meaning,
although one is describing Ereshkigal and the other,
Tiamat. Both Ereshkigal and Tiamat represent the
initiatory aspects of the menstruating goddess,
Lamashtu. It is during these rites that the Initiate has to
struggle with the "ego" and the process of purification.
Barbara G, Walker makes a similar observation

concerning Lamashtu in *The Woman's Encyclopedia of Myths and Secrets,* quoted previously, on page 527:

**"Lamia was probably a variant of Babylonian Lamashtu, "Mother of Gods" worshipped at Der as a serpent with a woman's head."**

Walker states the following on page 904:

**"The Akkadian Goddess NINHURSAG, "She Who Gives Life to the Dead," was also called "Mistress of Serpents" as yet another form of Kadru or Kadi. Babylon's version of her made her a dark twin of the Heaven-goddess ISHTAR, calling her Lamia or LAMASHTU,..Cylinder seals show her squatting, Kali-like, over her mate, the god PAZUZU, he of the serpent penis. As another Lord of Death, he gave himself up to be devoured by the Goddess."**

Walker's writings confirm another point made earlier in our discussion that healing involves absorbing the "death-energy" and not the channeling of a "healing force" from one entity to another. We also learn another very important point that images of Pazuzu were used as protection, not against Lamashtu, as some scholars would like us to believe, but as a symbol of the male forced that was sacrificed to her. The kundalini force is nourished by "death-energy" and this is the very same reason why initiation into the Greater Mysteries involves the Initiate taking the same journey as that of the deceased. Walker continues on page 1035:

**"Lamia was the Greek name for the divine female serpent called Kundalini in India....and Lamshtu in Babylon."**

Another aspect of Lamashtu that appears in the Simon Necronomicon is that of Ishnigarrab. Simon gives us a subtle description of what Ishnigarrab really means in the Necronomicon's Introduction, under the subheading *SUMERIA*, we read:

**"There is a seeming reference to SHUB NIGGURATH in the NECRONOMICON, in the name of a Sumerian deity, the "Answerer of Prayers", called ISHNIGARRAB. The word "Shub" is to be found in the Sumerian language in reference to the Rite of Exorcism, one of which is called Nam Shub and means "the Throwing". It is, however, as yet unclear as to what the combination SHUB ISHNIGARRAB (SHUB NIGGURATH) might actually mean."**

Earlier, we discussed the Myth of Enki and Ninhursag, in the myth Ninhursag healed Enki by sitting him near her vagina and absorbing his "sickness" and then producing a beneficial deity as a result. We find similar aspects in the legend of Shub Niggurath.

The gof'nn hupadgh Shub-Niggurath is the name given to the favored, once-human worshippers of Shub-Niggurath. When the deity deems a worshipper to be most worthy, a special ceremony is held, in which the Black Goat of the Woods swallows the Initiate and then regurgitates the cultist as a transformed satyrlike being. The changed worshipper is endowed with immortal life. This aspect of Shub Niggurath finds its origin in the many aspects of Goddess Lamashtu, such as the goddess Kadru.

In the mythologies of India, Kadru is described as being a mother of "a thousand powerful many-headed serpents, the chief amongst whom were Sesha, Vasuki and many other fierce and venomous serpents." Kadru was considered to be the mother of the nagas. Shub Niggurath is often described as *"The Black Goat of the Woods with a Thousand Young."*

The goat was sacred to the Sumerian god Ningirsu. In some accounts, Ningirsu was said to be the son of Enlil and a holy she-goat. Interestingly, Ningirsu is another form of Ninurta, which means Lord of the Earth, or Plough. In older translations the name is rendered Ninib (Adar) and in early mythologies, he was sometimes portrayed as a solar deity. Ninurta was depicted as a farmer and a healing god who releases humans from sickness and the power of "evil spirits," on the other he is the god of the South Wind as the son of Enlil. It is here that we find a deeper meaning to the Mad Arab's words that appear in the Book of Entrance:

*"For this reason, few have ever opened the Gate of ADAR, and spoken to the Horned One who resideth there and giveth all manner of wisdom regarding the operations of necromancy, and of the spells that hasten unto death."*

Adar is another form of Ningirsu. He is also the last Gate that the candidate Walks during the process of self-initiation. Saturn is the planetary correspondence of Adar/Ninib. It is at this Gate (7th) that the Initiate is transformed and enters the rites of the Black Goat, or the "Horned One." Once the Initiate has passed this Gate, he/she is swallowed up by the "goat" and then regurgitated into a new being and is able to grow in strength. The Mad Arab continues in the Book of Entrance:

*"For this reason, few have ever opened the Gate of ADAR, and spoken to the Horned One who resideth there*

*and giveth all manner of wisdom regarding the operations of necromancy, and of the spells that hasten unto death. Only when thou hast shown thy power over the Maskim and the Rabishu, mayest thou venture forth to the Land of the IGIGI, and for that reason was this Covenant made, that none shall safely Walk through the sunken valleys of the Dead before having ascended to MARDUK, nor shall they breach the Gates that lie beyond ADAR until they have seen the Signs of the Mad God and felt the fury of the hellish Queen."*

The Mad Arab himself went through such a transformation. He reveals this in the Necronomicon. Notice what he states in the Book of Calling:

*"Know, seventhly, of the Things thou art to expect in the commission of this Most sacred Magick. Study the symbols well, and do not be afraid of any awful spectre that shall invade thine operation, or haunt thine habitat by day or by night. Only charge them with them the words of the Covenant and they will do as you ask, of thou be strong. And if thou performest these operations often, thou shalt see things becoming dark; and the Wanderers in their Spheres shall no more be seen by thee; and the Stars in their places will lose their Light, and the Moon, NANNA, by whom thou also workest, shall become black and extinguished, ..AND ARATAGAR SHALL BE NO MORE, AND THE EARTH SHALL ABIDE NOT ... And around thee shall appear the Flame, like Lightning flashing in all directions, and all things will appear amid thunders, and from the Cavities of the Earth will leap forth the ANNUNNAKI, Dog-Faced, and thou shalt bring them down."*

The Mad Arab speaks heavily about the light of planets, stars, and spheres, being no more. This represents that the Initiate's destiny is no longer held by the planetary spheres, also known as the *'Dog-Faced ANNUNAKI.'* (*Earlier in our discussion, it was clearly illustrated that in the Necronomicon Tradition, initiation requires the candidate to Walk through the Spheres in a pattern that is opposite the Sun's journey through the same constellations. Since the Initiate is traveling in a converse direction, he/she has to reconcile with the "shadow-side" of these planetary forces, as in the Seven Anunnaki.*) The Mad Arab's final words indicate that he passed his initiation into the deeper "Qliphotic Mysteries." Notice the concluding words of his Second Testimony:

*"The Stars grow dim in their places, and the Moon pales before me, as though a Veil were blown across its flame. Dog-faces demons approach the circumference of my sanctuary. Strange lines appear carved on my door and walls, and the light from the Windows grows increasing dim."*

Another interesting feature of the Mad Arab can be found in the Enochian definition of his name:

| Enochian | English Meaning |
|----------|-----------------|
| *Mad* | God or Your God |
| *Ar* | That |
| *Ab* | Daughter of Light |

From the above Enochian translation, we can easily see that the term *Mad Arab* means *Your God that Daughter of Light.* This would seem to indicate that the Mad Arab was a Priest of Lamashtu. Lamashtu's first name is 'daughter of Anu' (light). The Crown of Anu, as described in the Simon Necronomicon represents the "daughter of Anu." On page 78 of the Simon Necronomicon, the Crown of Anu is described as being of a *'spotless white color.'* The sister sorority of the Freemasons, The Order of the Eastern Star, also wear the white fez, denoting the anointment of male menstrual blood, or semen, upon their heads. The other reference concerning the Crown of Anu is found on page 100, where it states that the *'Crown may be made of beaten copper.'* This is seen today amongst the Freemasons who wear a fez of a blood-red color, symbolizing the menstrual blood of a woman upon their head.

There are no banishings in the Simon Necronomicon for Lamashtu. The Mad Arab affirms that he is a servant of Lamashtu, in the opening words of the Simon Necronomicon:

*"I have seen One Thousand-and-One Moons and surely this is enough for the span of a man's life, though it is said the Prophets lived much longer."*

Later, in his First Testimony he writes:

*"But now, after One Thousand-and-One moons of the journey, The maskim nip at my heels, the Rabishu pull at my hair."*

The Mad Arab mentions *"One Thousand-and-One moons of the journey,"* which clearly indicates that he counted his journey as his life. These One Thousand-and-One Moons represent the Black Goat with a Thousand Young in Lovecraftian lore. If we add the "Black Goat" plus the "Thousand Young," we would get 1,001 spirits. It is here that we find the meaning of the Mad Arab's words as they are written in the Book of Calling:

*"In the Ceremonies of Calling, any type of Spirit may be summoned and detained until It has answered your questions or provided you with whatever you desire. The Spirits of the Dead may be invoked. The Spirits of the*

*Unborn may be invoked. The Spirits of the Seven Spheres may be invoked. The Spirits of the Flame may be invoked. In all, there may be One Thousand-and-One Spirits that are of principal importance.."*

This not only confirms that the Simon Necronomicon is a book dedicated to the worship of the Ancient Ones, but it also reveals that Lamashtu, the menstruating goddess, is the power behind the tome. Now let us look at another aspect of Lamashtu that will reveal a deeper understanding of her rites.

## LAMASHTU and QUEEN SHEBA

Another confirmation of our findings is seen in the legend of Queen Sheba. There was a time when the Queen of Sheba was popularly depicted as a snatcher of children and a demonic witch. In Arabic and Jewish lore, Queen Sheba is often associated with Lilith (a minor aspect of Lamashtu). In some Islamic traditions, Queen Sheba (Bilqis) is said to be half-jinn. According to one account, Solomon, having heard from a hoopoe, one of his birds, that Bilqis and her kingdom worshipped the Sun, sent a letter asking her to worship God. She replied by sending gifts, but, when Solomon proved unreceptive to them, she came to his court herself. The king's demons, meanwhile, fearing that he might be tempted into marrying Bilqis, whispered to him that she had hairy legs and the hooves of an ass (attributes of Lamashtu). Solomon, being curious about such a peculiar phenomenon, had a glass floor built before his throne, so that Bilqis, tricked into thinking it was water, raised her skirts to cross it and revealed that her legs were truly hairy. Solomon then ordered his demons to create a depilatory for the queen.

In Persian folklore, she is considered the daughter of a Chinese king and a **peri** - *a type of supernatural being.* The story of the Queen of Sheba acquired special importance and impact in the Ethiopian tradition and history. There she is referred to as Makeda and it is believed that she bore Solomon a son, who was the founder of the Ethiopian royal dynasty of emperors.

1 Kings Chapter 10 describes her visit to King Solomon. She tested him with difficult questions. She wanted to know whether he was really as wise as they said he was. She has long been associated with the bride in the Song of Solomon, where it mentions in Chapter 1:5; "I am black, but comely." Josephus said in his *Antiquity of the Jews, Book 8 Chapter 6,* that it was the "queen of Egypt and Ethiopia" who visited King Solomon. Also, Jesus refers to her as the "queen of the south" in Matthew 12:42. Daniel 11:5 and 8 identify the South as Egypt. Interestingly, Queen Sheba also tested Jesus while he was in the wilderness, but she is described as Satan in order to hide his involvement with the Sacred Marriage Rite. The Queen of Sheba is the spirit that the Initiate calls upon before he/she summons Lamashtu. She is an ambassador of Lamashtu. This can be understood when we review the legend of King Solomon.

The Qur'an states that Solomon ruled not only people, but also hosts of Jinn, was able to understand the language of the birds and ants, and to see some of the hidden glory in the world that was not accessible to most other human beings. This compares greatly to the Gate-Walker who works with the Jinn during their process of self-initiation. Later, we are tested by Queen Sheba (or an emissary of Lamashtu), just as it is written in 1 Kings Chapter 10 where she tested Solomon. King Solomon passed the test by answering her questions effectively

and was blessed with gifts from the Queen. Jesus
describes this initiation in Matthew Chapter 12:42:

**"The queen of the south shall rise up in the judgment
with this generation, and shall condemn it: for she came
from the uttermost parts of the earth to hear the
wisdom of Solomon; and, behold, a greater than
Solomon *is* here."**

This Biblical passage concerns itself with those who have
walked the Seven Initiatory Gates and have gained
insights and wisdom from the deities themselves. The
Mad Arab wrote the following concerning the zonei:

*"The passing of the Gates gives the priest both power
and wisdom to use it. He becomes able to control the
affairs of his life more perfectly than before, and many
have been content to merely pass the first three Gates
and then sit down and go no further than that, enjoying
the benefits that they have found on the preliminary
spheres."*

Queen Sheba is an aspect of Lamashtu, also known as the
Goddess SHAKUGUKU in the Necronomicon Tradition
and the Priestess Shamhat in the Gilgamesh Epics. The
Mad Arab speaks of Lamashtu in the Urilia Text as the
Goddess Whom No One Worshippeth:

*"And when thou hast set out bread for the dead to eat,
remember to pour honey thereupon, for it is pleasing to
the Goddess Whom No One Worshippeth, Who wanders
by night through the streets amid the howling of the dogs
and the wailing of the infants, for in Her time a great
Temple was built unto Her and sacrifices of infants made
that She might save the City from the Enemies who
dwelt without. And the Number of infants thus slain is
countless and unknowable. And She did save that City,*

*but it was taken soon thereafter when the people no more offered up their children. And when the people made to offer again, at the time of the attack, the Goddess turned her back and fled from her temple, and it is no more. And the Name of the Goddess is no more known. And She maketh the infants restless, and to cry, so the reason for the pouring of honey over the sacred bread, for it is written:*

> *Bread of the Cult of the Dead in its Place I eat*
> *In the Court prepared*
> *Water of the Cult of the Dead in its Place I drink*
> *A Queen am I, Who has become estranged to the Cities*
> *She that comes from the Lowlands in a sunken boat*
> *Am I.*

> *I AM THE VIRGIN GODDESS*
> *HOSTILE TO MY CITY*
> *A STRANGER IN MY STREETS.*
> *MUSIGAMENNA URUMA BUR ME YENSULAMU*
> *GIRME EN!*
> *Oh, Spirit, who understand thee? Who comprehend Thee?"*

Many Initiates of the Necronomicon Tradition have often wondered what "goddess:" is the Mad Arab talking about? The answer to this question can be found in E.A. Wallis Budge's book *Amulets and Superstitions.* Budge states the following on page 115-116:

**"The female devil in the boat is LAMASHTU, whose home in the infernal regions whence she comes when she arrives on the earth to carry out her campaign of slaughter and death. The only way to stop her from carrying out her baneful plans is to get her back again in the Underworld, and it is necessary to coax her to leave earth by promising to give her gifts....She must**

then make her way over the mountains which block the
road to hell, and when this is done she must cross the
river of hell, which is none other than the great World-
Ocean, Nar Marratu."

We will discuss the ritual workings of Lamashtu and
how they are performed later in this writing. When I read
about the menstruating goddess LAMMASHTA, I am
also reminded of Simon's words that appear in the
Necronomicon's Introduction:

*"the Dragon or Serpent is said to reside somewhere
"below the earth"; it is a powerful force, a magickal
force, which is identified with mastery over the created
world; it is also a power that can be summoned by the
few and not the many."*

All the entities in the Urilia Text are the aspects of the
mind of LAMMASHTA. We will now learn about
another power-zone that is the cardinal force of this black
goddess.

# KUTULU

Dimension: **The understanding of how to alter karma.
The projection of ones' will on reality.**

Mad Arab's Testimony: *"I have traveled beneath the
Seas, in search of the Palace of Our Master, and found
the stone of monuments of vanquished civilizations, and
deciphered the writings of some of these; while still
others remain mysteries to any man who lives. And these
civilizations were destroyed because of the knowledge
contained in this book."*

E.A. Budge mentioned in his writings that *'Lamashtu had
to cross the river of hell, known as the great World-Ocean.'*
Once we have employed the menstruating goddess
energies we are to then move on into the *"World-Ocean."*
Notice what is mentioned by Simon in the
Necronomicon's Introduction, under the topic *SUMERIA:*

*"The Underworld in ancient Sumer was known by many
names, among them ABSU or "Abyss", sometimes as Nar
Mattaru, the great Underworld Ocean, and also as Cutha
or KUTU as it is called in the Enuma Elish (the Creation
Epic of the Sumerians). The phonetic similarity between
Cutha and KUTU and Chthonic, as well as Cthulhu, is
striking. Judging by a Sumerian grammar at hand, the
word KUTULU or Cuthalu (Lovecraft's's Cthulhu
Sumerianised) would mean "The Man of KUTU (Cutha);
the Man of the Underworld; Satan or Shaitan, as he is
known to the Yezidis (whom Crowley considered to be
the remnants of the Sumerian Tradition)."*

Out of all the deities discussed in the Simon
Necronomicon, Kutulu remains to be one of the few
entities mentioned in the Simon Necronomicon that does

not appear in the Sumerian mythologies. Kutulu is a derivative of Cthulhu, a cosmic entity created by the infamous fiction writer, H.P. Lovecraft. Detailed information about Cthulhu can be found in Lovecraft's tale *"The Call of Cthulhu."* It is in this myth, created in the mind of H.P. Lovecraft, that Cthulhu is described as "dead but dreaming" in the city of R'lyeh. Lovecraft's Call of Cthulhu describes the entity as having attributes similar to a dragon. Notice what is mentioned in the Mythos:

**"Above these apparent hieroglyphics was a figure of evident pictorial intent, though its impressionistic execution forbade a very clear idea of its nature. It seemed to be a sort of monster, or symbol representing a monster, of a form which only a diseased fancy could conceive. If I say that my somewhat extravagant imagination yielded simultaneous pictures of an octopus, a dragon, and a human caricature, I shall not be unfaithful to the spirit of the thing. A pulpy, tentacled head surmounted a grotesque and scaly body with rudimentary wings; but it was the general outline of the whole which made it most shockingly frightful. Behind the figure was a vague suggestions of a Cyclopean architectural background."**

The myth: continues:

**"In the elder time chosen men had talked with the entombed Old Ones in dreams, but then something happened. The great stone city R'lyeh, with its monoliths and sepulchres, had sunk beneath the waves; and the deep waters, full of the one primal mystery through which not even thought can pass, had cut off the spectral intercourse. But memory never died, and the high-priests said that the city would rise again when the stars were right. Then came out of the earth**

the black spirits of earth, mouldy and shadowy, and
full of dim rumours picked up in caverns beneath
forgotten sea-bottoms. But of them old Castro dared not
speak much. He cut himself off hurriedly, and no
amount of persuasion or subtlety could elicit more in
this direction. The size of the Old Ones, too, he
curiously declined to mention. Of the cult, he said that
he thought the centre lay amid the pathless desert of
Arabia, where Irem, the City of Pillars, dreams hidden
and untouched. It was not allied to the European witch-
cult, and was virtually unknown beyond its members.
No book had ever really hinted of it, though the
deathless Chinamen said that there were double
meanings in the Necronomicon of the mad Arab Abdul
Alhazred which the initiated might read as they chose,
especially the much-discussed couplet"

Some have dismissed the idea of working with
"Cthulhu" in magickal rituals, since many believe that
this entity is an invention of the writer Lovecraft. The
Initiate of the Necronomicon Tradition knows what the
layman does not, and recognizes these archetypes as
chthonic and cosmic forces. Happily, the Necronomicon
Tradition reveals that Kutulu is a real deity. Before
validating the existence of Kutulu, it is important that we
review another passage from the *Call of Cthulhu*:

"They worshipped, so they said, the Great Old Ones
who lived ages before there were any men, and who
came to the young world out of the sky. Those Old
Ones were gone now, inside the earth and under the
sea; but their dead bodies had told their secrets in
dreams to the first men, who formed a cult which had
never died. This was that cult, and the prisoners said it
had always existed and always would exist, hidden in
distant wastes and dark places all over the world until
the time when the great priest Cthulhu, from his dark

house in the mighty city of R'lyeh under the waters, should rise and bring the earth again beneath his sway. Some day he would call, when the stars were ready, and the secret cult would always be waiting to liberate him."

Simon defines Kutulu in his Introduction OF the Simon Necronomicon as *'the Man of the Underworld.'* We can determine that Kutulu is the spouse of Lamashtu, as she crosses the *"river of hell,"* (Nar Marratu) to meet him. E.A. Budge, quoted earlier, equates this *"river of hell"* as Nar Marratu. The CHART OF COMPARISONS, which appears in the introductory essays of the Simon Necronomicon, equates Nar Mattaru to the *Abyss* and *Out of Space.* This means that Kutulu can also be defined as the *Man of Nar Mattaru.*

While the Simon Necromicon mentions Nar Mattaru in various parts of the text, there are two passages that reveal the work of Kutulu in the Necronomicon Tradition. Both of these passages can be found in the section entitled, *THE CONJURATION OF THE WATCHER:*

*"And the Lord of the Watchers dwells, it is said, among the Wastes of the IGIGI, and only Watches and never raises the Sword or fights the idimmi, save when the Covenant is invoked by none less than the Elder Gods in their Council, like unto the Seven Glorious APHKHALLU."*

Following this is the INVOCATION OF THE WATCHER where we read:

*"Rise up, from the old Abyss of NARR MARRATU!"*

Many of the qualities attributed to the Watcher in the Simon Necronomicon are possessed by Kutulu. A few examples of this can be seen in the following passages:

*"I conjure Thee by ... The Veils of Sunken Varloormi"*
(taken form the Normal Invocation of The Watcher found on page 72 of the SN)

*"KUTULU raises his head and stares up through the Veils of sunken Varloormi..,"* (taken from the First Testimony of the Mad Arab found on page 15 of the SN)

*"the Watcher appears. with eyes that never lose their stare."* (taken from the SN page 70)

*"KUTULU raises his head.., up through the Abyss, and fixes his stare upon me"* (taken from the SN page 15)

One of the first lines in the Normal Invocation of the Watcher found on page 72 of the SN states: *"I conjur Thee by the Fire of GIRRA"*

*"I deliver you to GIRRA .., Lord of the Flames.., of whom even mighty KUTULU has fear!* (taken from page 83 of the MAKLU TEXT as found in the SN)

*"And the Watcher sometimes appears..aloft holding the Sword of Flames, and even the Elder Gods are awed thereby"* (Taken from page 70 of the SN)

*"the corpse KUTULU shakes beneath the Earth, and our Master ENKI is sore afraid."* (taken from page 186 of the SN)

*"And the Lord of the Watchers dwells, it is said among the wastes of the IGIGI..."* (Taken from page 70 of the SN)

We can safely assume that Kutulu is the Watcher. The Mad Arab states that 'the Lord of the Watchers dwells in the Wastes of the Igigi. The Igigi are the azonei, also known as the realm of fixed stars. Lovecraft also describes the Old Ones as coming from the regions of Outer Space. The Mad Arab mentions that the Lord of the Watchers *"never raises the Sword or fights the idimmi, save when the Covenant is invoked by none less than the Elder Gods in their Council, like unto the Seven Glorious APHKHALLU."*

This is a key aspect in understanding who Kutulu is in the Necronomicon Tradition. The Lord of the Watchers never raises his *Sword* unless the Covenant is invoked by *"none less than the Elder Gods."* This would mean that the Lord of the Watchers, or Kutulu, must have a place amongst the Ancient Ones, as they appear in the Simon Necronomicon. We see similar attributes in the Lovecraftian Cthulhu. Cthulhu is said to be a High Priest of the Old Ones. Although, legend has it that Cthulhu is, *"dead but dreaming,"* he can still send messages to his "half-human" worshippers through dreams. Parker Ryan confirms the actual antiquity of the term Kutulu in his essay *The Necronomicon Mythos According to HPL*:

**"There is another interesting bit of information related to the Dragon of the Abyss (which originated in Sumeria) and Khadhulu. This data quite possibly is simple coincidence. On the other hand, it may not be coincidence; there is simply no way to tell yet. It concerns one of the titles of the Dragon, namely the Lord of the Abyss. The title Lord of the Abyss translated into Sumerian is "KUTULU."**

Kutu means "Underworld" or "Abyss" and Lu is Sumerian for "Lord" or "Person of importance." Let's consider this for a moment: the Sumerian KUTULU is quite similar to Khadhulu in Arabic. Khadhulu is associated with the Dragon in Arab magickal texts. Khadhulu is also identified with the Old Dragon (Shaitan) in the Quran…. Instead I researched until I was able to confirm all the above information, related to the word KUTULU. The fact that the above information on KUTULU is accurate and very suggestive does not PROVE anything. It does, however, generally SUPPORT the idea that KUTULU/Khadhulu has been a part of the magickal traditions of the Near East for a very long time."

I must state to the reader that the term Kutulu has been greatly debated by occultists and scholars alike. Dan Harms (author of the Necronomicon Files) has even debated some of Parker Ryan's conclusions concerning the origin of this term. We find it necessary therefore, to show the antiquity of the term Kutulu and where it originated. The term Kutulu is an ancient Chinese term. *Studies in Turkic and Mongolic Linguistics* by Gerard Clauson, states the following on page 88:

"for example, kutlug was transcribed *ku-tu-lu*, not *ku-lu*, even though the "Ancient Chinese" pronunciation of *ku* was *kuat*."

The term kutlug, mentioned above, is a reference to the general Kutluk, an influence force under the Uyghur Empire, and founder of the Ediz Dynasty. The term Kutluk is associated with the phrase, *Ai tengride ülüg bulmïsh alp kutluk ulugh bilge*, ("**Greatly born in moon heaven, victorious, glorious, great and wise**"), which is the meaning of the word KUTULU, or as the ancient

Chinese translate, **ku-tulu.** This finding actually supports the Cthulhu Mythos. In the Mythos, we find that the Cult of Cthulhu is centered in Arabia with leaders of the organization, who are said to be immortal, dwelling in China. This is a reference to the Uyghur Empire and its central doctrine of Manichaeism. Some influences of this religion are seen in the *Al-Azif.* There is something else here that is important for us to examine. One definition of the name Kutluk means *"born in moon heaven."* This is a Taoist expression and relates to the full moon, when the heavens are considered to be one. We find this to be the case also with the Magan Text. Therefore the synthesis of the Lovecraftian and Simon Necronomicon finds its link with Kutulu. This term, which originates with the Ancient Chinese, does find its correspondence with the Cuthins, a class of priests who knew the arts of divination based on the phases of the Moon. *The Sixth and Seventh Books of Moses*, page 82, states:

**"The language and manuscript of this rare and eternal monument of light, and of a higher wisdom, are borrowed from the Cuthans, a tribe of the Samaritans, who were called Cuthim in the Chaldee dialect according to the Talmud, and they were so called in a spirit of derision. They were termed sorcerers, because they taught in Cutha, their original place of abode, and afterward, in Samaria, the Kabala or Higher Magic (Book of Kings). Caspar, Melchior, and Balthasar, the chosen arch-priests, are shining lights among the eastern Magicians. They were both kings and teachers - the first Priest-teachers of this glorious knowledge, and from these Samaritan Cuthans - from these omnipotent priests of the fountain of light, who were called Nergal, according to the traditions of Talmud, originated the Gypsies, who, through degeneracy, lost the consecration of their primordial power."**

We find additional insights about the deity Kutulu in the Urilia Text:

*"defeaters of the Old Serpent, the Ancient Worm, TIAMAT, the ABYSS, also called KUTULU.."*

This passage clearly indicates that Kutulu is the male aspect of Tiamat. We discussed earlier how Tiamat and Ereshkigal are all aspects of the *'menstruating goddess'* Lamashtu, which symbolizes the kundalini force. We can then safely assume that Kutulu must be the cardinal force, or male aspect, of the kundalini energy. The reader may want to note that the term "cunt" is a derivative of the word Cutha, and the term "cunt" is also a reference to the word kundalini in over a dozen languages. The Urilia Text gives us more information about Kutulu that can help us determine his identity:

*"Of all the Gods and Spirits of Abomination, KUTULU only cannot be summoned, for he is the Sleeping Lord. The magician can not hope to have any power over him, but he may be worshipped and for him the proper sacrifices may be made, so that he will spare thee when he rises to the earth. And the times for the sacrifice are the same times as the Sleeping of MARDUK, for this is when Great KUTULU moves. And he is the very Fire of the Earth, and Power of All Magick. When he joins with the Abominations of the Sky, TIAMAT will once more rule the earth!"*

The Urilia Text describes Kutulu as *"the Fire of The Earth."* This is very interesting since the Maklu Text mentions that 'mighty KUTULU' fears Girra, the Lord of Flames. We also learn in the Urilia Text that when Kutulu shakes Enki is said to be 'afraid.' Therefore, Kutulu is a deity that fears the Fire God, but can also instill fear in

Enki when he moves. With this information when can now determine who or what Kutulu really is.

In the famous Babylonian legend *The War of the Seven Wicked Spirits against the Moon,* we learn about how the "rebellious genii," who were once employed by the heavenly deities, caused great trouble in raging war against the Moon god and Hea (Enki) appeared to be afraid, as none of the celestial forces could diminish their power. Babylonian texts mention the Fire-God, Gibil, as being most effective against the genii. These *"rebellious genii"* are the *seven heads of the dragon.* Kenneth Grant mentions this in his book the *Nightside of Eden,* on page 60-61 we read:

**"In the Sumerian phase of mythology, the seven heads of the devouring dragon were represented as follows:**

**The first by a Scorpion. The second by a Whrling Cross ofr Thunderbolt. The third by a Leopard or Hyena. The fourth by a Serpent. The fifth by a Raging Lion. The sixth by a Rebellious Giant. The seventh by Typhon, Angel of the Fatal Wind."**

While it may appear from our research that Kutulu is a composite deity, we must remember that in the Introduction of the Simon Necronomicon, Kutulu is defined as the *"Man of the Underworld."* It would seem likely that the Lord of the Seven Evil Spirits would be the embodiment of Kutulu. In the Babylonian account entitled, *The Seven Evil Spirits,* we find out just who this Lord really is:

*"Destructive storms and evil winds are they,*
*A storm of evil, presaging the baneful storm,*
*A storm of evil, forerunner of the baneful storm.*
*Mighty children, mighty sons are they,*

*Messengers of Namtar* **are they,**
**Throne-bearers of ERESHKIGAL.**
**The flood driving through the land are they.**
**Seven gods of the wide heavens,**
**Seven gods of the broad earth,"**

Here we see that Namtar is Kutulu, Namtar in the Book of Calling is described as the *'Chief Magician of ERESHKIGAL.'* In the Magan Text mentions the following concerning Namtar:

*"INANNA AROSE... The Dark Waters trembled and roiled.*
*AZAG-THOTH screamed upon his throne*
*CUTHALU lurched forth from his sleep*
*ISHNIGARRAB fled the Palace of Death*
*IAK SAKKAK trembled in fear and hate*
*The ANNUNNAKI fled their thrones*
*The Eye upon the Throne took flight*
*ERESHKIGAL roared and summoned NAMMTAR*
*The Magician NAMMTAR she called*
*But not for pursuit*
*But for protection."*

The Magan Text makes it clear that when Ishtar arose from the dead, Ereshkigal summoned Namtar, which is a symbolic illustration of the kundalini force after the seven steps of self-initiation has been enacted. Later in the text we read:

*"Out of the Netherworld they accompanied her*
*And ERESHKIGAL*
*Scorned Queen of the Abyss Wherein All Are Drowned*
*Pronounced a Curse*
*Solemn and Powerful*
*Against the Queen of the Rising of the Sun*
*And NAMMTAR gave it form."*

Once again we see that Ereshkigal's power, or the kundalini-force, is employed by Namtar. In the Magan Text we read that it was Namtar who imprisoned Ishtar:

*"ISHTAR raised up Her arm.*
*ERESHKIGAL summoned NAMMTAR*
*The Magician NAMMTAR*
*Saying these words she spoke to him*
*Go! Imprison her!*
*Bind her in Darkness!"*

The reader may want to note that Namtar fits perfectly with Lovecraft's description of Cthulhu-being the High Priest of the Old Ones. Namtar represents the masculine or cardinal qualities of the kundalini force. Namtar means *fate,* and it is here that the Initiate learns how to employ the kundalini energies. This is evident from what appears in the Magan Text:

*"Scorned Queen of the Abyss Wherein All Are Drowned*
*Pronounced a Curse... And NAMMTAR gave it form."*

It is here that the Initiate learns something far deeper about the mechanics of the Necronomicon Tradition. Kutulu teaches the Initiate how to transfer magickal energies of initiation onto the uninitiated.

Shammash is described in the Necronomicon as the force that *'sheds light on dark places.'* Shammash brings clear insight into situations and reveals the inner workings of a mechanical pattern, usually appearing as an emotion, experience, person, object, or thought. These revelations that are inspired by Shammash do not necessarily change the situation, or guarantee that the desired outcome will surface. Namtar, *the god of fate,* can create this desired change.

These changes can only come about by the *"death"* of the present experience. The *seven heads of the dragon,* or forces of change, are always present when the benevolent "death" of an unwanted experience occurs. Cthulhu is said to be, *dead but dreaming,* as Namtar represents the innate potential of the Initiate to bring about these changes. The teachings of the Necronomicon Tradition clearly indicate that the body of "Man," not to be confused with mankind, is the abode of the divine. Man is the only animal that can create her/his destiny and reality by use of the imagination. This ability is not a part of the animal kingdom, or the world of mankind.

*"And a man may cry out, what have I don't, and my generation that such evil shall befall me? And it means nothing, save that a man, being born, is of sadness, for he is of the Blood of the Ancient Ones, but has the Spirit of the Elder Gods breathed into him. And his body goes to the Ancient Ones, but his mind is turned towards the Elder Gods, and this is the War which shall be always fought, unto the last generation of man; for the World is unnatural. When the Great KUTULU rises up and greets the Stars, then the War will be over, and the World be One."*

The "Great Kutulu" rises up to the stars when the Initiate's desired fate, or imagination, is able to create a reality that can be experienced by gods and mankind alike. The intercourse between, the feminine and masculine aspects of the kundalini force, is the foundation of the Sacred Marriage Rite. European folklore describes this process in the legend of Snow White and the Seven Dwarfs, or Lammashta (Tiamat) and the Seven Heads of the Dragon. The readers may want to note that it was the Prince's kiss upon the *"dead"* Snow White that *awakened her from the coffin.*

Cthulhu is the "High Priest" of the Old Ones similar to Namtar being the "Chief Magician" of Ereshkigal. According to the Cthulhu Mythos, the Cult of Cthulhu is centered in Arabia and has a worldwide following. There are leaders of the Cult in the mountains of China who are said to be immortal. Interestingly, a *namtar* in Tibetan Buddhism refers to a *sacred biography,* and the term is defined as *complete liberation.* The rising of Cthulhu is said to be a time of liberation as well. Notice what is mentioned in the Call of Cthulhu:

**"The time would be easy to know, for then mankind would have become as the Great Old Ones; free and wild and beyond good and evil, with laws and morals liberated Old Ones would teach them new ways to shout and kill and revel and enjoy themselves, and all the earth would flame with a holocaust of ecstasy and freedom."**

This description seems horrific, but it does describe the final hour of this age. The Old Ones and their followers would, *"teach men new ways of "killing,"* simply means new methods of "spiritual liberation" (namtar).

There can be no denial, even by critics of the Simon Necronomicon Tradition, that the identity of Kutulu is Namtar. Further proof of this can be determined by the words of the Mad Arab written in the Urilia Text:

*"KUTULU only cannot be summoned, for he is the Sleeping Lord. The magician can not hope to have any power over him, but he may be worshipped and for him the proper sacrifices may be made, so that he will spare thee when he rises to the earth."*

The Mad Arab mentions that Kutulu can '*spare the life of those who worship him.*' This passage is very important in our identification of Kutulu as Namtar because it relates to an event that is recorded in Mesopotamian mythology.

In the myth, *Atra-hasis and the Flood*, we find a similar case of Namtar sparing the lives of those who offered him sacrifice and he is also described as '*rising up from the depths of the NetherWorld.*' Notice what is mentioned in the myth:

"**The land became filled with them and their unceasing clamor. Enlil said, "The noise men make has become too much; I am losing sleep. Let Namtar come up from the depths of the Netherworld and distribute disease among them, so that their numbers and uproar may be reduced." The Herald of Death strewed sickness back and forth across the countryside and many died. A wise man in Shuruppak, by name of Atra-hasis, called upon Enki. "How long are the gods going to plague us? Will illness and death afflict us forever?"..Enki advised Atra-hasis, "Call together the elders. Speak to them; tell them to not worship their gods or take them offerings. Instead, let them build a house for Namtar in Shuruppak and let each household bake a loaf of fresh bread and take it to his door."..The people listened and did as Enki advised. Namtar's house was filled with fresh bread and surrounded with its pleasant aroma. The Herald of Death was shamed by the multitude of offerings. He drew back his hand so that disease abated. The people regained their health and the land returned to prosperity.**"

The Mad Arab apparently had this myth in mind when he wrote about the need to sacrifice to Kutulu. Earlier, we mentioned that the Watcher and Kutulu were one in the same being. Since the Watcher is the Initiate's *"dead-self"* awakening from its slumber by the process of self-initiation, as Kutulu we are Priests and Priestesses of the Ancient Ones, as Lovecraft described concerning Cthulhu.

The Mad Arab supports our observations in The Book of Calling:

*"This is further the Book of NAMMTAR, Chief among the Magicians of ERESHKIGAL..This is the Book of the Seven Demons of the Ignited Spheres, of the Seven Demons of the Flame..This is the Book of the Priest, who governeth the Works of Fire!"*

The Mysteries of the Necronomicon Tradition reveal that the Practitioners of this Path are Kutulu, as the name represents the personification of those individuals *who are descendants of the Jinn,* often depicted as Shaitan in religious lore. Their ancestors, the Old Ones, can speak to their descendants through dreams. This is why the rites of the Cult of the Dead, also known as pre-historic ancestor worship, is the key to unlock the Atlantean Mysteries. Our Watcher-Self (known as KUTULU-NAMMTAR in the Qliphotic Tradition) is the alien mind that is so foreign to us that even when the slightest part of it is engaged it creates extraterrestrial phenomena. The ignorant, often times, will mistakenly assume that there is no danger in accessing the alien mind, but what the novice fails to realize is that the alien mind has no regard for the logical and subconscious mental process.

It is in our dreams that we feel, not the light of Shammash, but the light of the Black Sun, Namtar. Namtar reveals to us our fates. When one awakens in the dream, they can change the fate that is given to them by reconfiguring the dream. The comparison between Shammash and the Black Sun Namtar can be easily detected in the world of modern science, where the core of the Earth is approximately the same temperature as the Sun's surface. The ancients evidently knew the workings of Earth's core and its heating iron ore (Nergal) and how it related to the consciousness of man. Namtar appears in Sumerian Mythology in other aspects; among these are Kingu. Invoking Namtar and working with his energies is a mystical practice.

KUTULU/NAMMTAR is the *"angel"* described in Revelation Chapter 10. Below is the rendering of this account, taken from the King James Version:

**10:1 And I saw another mighty angel come down from heaven, clothed with a cloud: and a rainbow was upon his head, and his face was as it were the sun, and his feet as pillars of fire:**

**10:2 And he had in his hand a little book open: and he set his right foot upon the sea, and his left foot on the earth,**

**10:3 And cried with a loud voice, as when a lion roareth: and when he had cried, seven thunders uttered their voices.**

**10:4 And when the seven thunders had uttered their voices, I was about to write: and I heard a voice from heaven saying unto me, Seal up those things which the seven thunders uttered, and write them not.**

**10:5 And the angel which I saw stand upon the sea and upon the earth lifted up his hand to heaven,**

10:6 And sware by him that liveth for ever and ever, who created heaven, and the things that therein are, and the earth, and the things that therein are, and the sea, and the things which are therein, that there should be time no longer:

10:7 But in the days of the voice of the seventh angel, when he shall begin to sound, the mystery of God should be finished, as he hath declared to his servants the prophets.

10:8 And the voice which I heard from heaven spake unto me again, and said, Go and take the little book which is open in the hand of the angel which standeth upon the sea and upon the earth.

10:9 And I went unto the angel, and said unto him, Give me the little book. And he said unto me, Take it, and eat it up; and it shall make thy belly bitter, but it shall be in thy mouth sweet as honey.

10:10 And I took the little book out of the angel's hand, and ate it up; and it was in my mouth sweet as honey: and as soon as I had eaten it, my belly was bitter.

10:11 And he said unto me, Thou must prophesy again before many peoples, and nations, and tongues, and kings.

# AZAG-THOTH

Dimension: **Mastery of Outer-Body-Experiences. Ability to defy nature, or natural law. The Veil between the worlds is broken.**

Mad Arab's Testimony: *"I have summoned the ghosts of my ancestors to real and visible appearance on the tops of temples built to reach the stars, and built to touch the nethermost cavities of HADES. I have wrestled with the Black Magician, AZAG-THOTH, in vain, and fled to the Earth by calling upon INANNA and her brother MARDUK, Lord of the double-headed AXE."*

Azag-Thoth represents the final stages in the process of rebirth. He is called the *"blind idiot god"* because the mysteries of Universe B are very unique concepts that are difficult for those who are uninitiated to understand. The Mad Arab mentions this same perspective in the Book of Entrance:

*"Only a madman, indeed, such as I am called!, can hope to have power over Them that dwell in the Outer Spaces, for their power is unknown, and the number of the hordes uncounted, and each day they breed more horrors than a*

man's mind can conceive, the sight of which he can hardly bear."

Simon mentions Azag-Thoth in his Introduction under the subheading *SUMERIA:*

*"Although a list is appended hereto containing various entities and concepts of Lovecraft, Crowley, and Sumeria cross-referenced, it will do to show how the Editor found relationships to be valid and even startling. AZATOT is frequently mentioned in the grim pages of the Cthulhu Mythos, and appears in the NECRONOMICON as AZAG-THOTH, a combination of two words, the first Sumerian and the second Coptic, which gives us a clue as to Its identity. AZAG in Sumerian means "Enchanter" or "Magician"; THOTH in Coptic is the name given to the Egyptian God of Magick and Wisdom, TAHUTI, who was evoked by both the Golden Dawn and by Crowley himself (and known to the Greeks as Hermes, from whence we get "Hermetic"). AZAG-THOTH is, therefore, a Lord of Magicians, but of the "Black" magicians, or the sorcerers of the "Other Side".*"

In the *Dream-Quest of Unknown Kadath,* written by H.P. Lovecraft, we find the following concerning Azathoth:

**"that last amorphous blight of nethermost confusion which blasphemes and bubbles at the centre of all infinity – the boundless daemon sultan Azathoth, whose name no lips dare speak aloud.."**

The description that Lovecraft gives us about Azathoth is symbolic of the Initiate's ability to create experiences and spiritual energies not known to man. Azathoth is called blind since his energies are accessed only through the mystical practices of the chthonic mind. He is also equated to the Blind Dragon that was responsible for the union of Lilith (an aspect of Lamashtu) and Samuel (Kutulu). The Initiate is instructed by Azathoth through intense astral experiences. The term blind idiot god is also a reference to the deity Nergal. *The City of The Moon God: Religious Traditions of Harran* by Tamara M. Green, page 195, we find the following observation:

**"Some of the Muslim texts identified Nergal/Mars as the Blind Lord and the Aim of the Sage and the prophecies of Baba the Harranian, both of which give him that title, seem to point to his continued power in Harran:**

**"In the gate which is situated between east and south, a house of worship will be built and that upon the orders from the *power of the Blind Lord*. He is the one who commanded me to make these things known to you."** **(The Prophecies of Baba the Harranian," 224-225 by F. Rosenthal)"**

The Mad Arab describes Azag-Thoth in the Urilia Text with the following words:

*"Of all the Gods and Spirits of Abomination, there can be no use or gain to call upon AZAG-THOTH, as he is Surely Mad. Rendered sightless in the Battle, he is Lord of CHAOS, and the priest can find little use for him. He is also too powerful to control once called, and gives violent struggle before sent back to the Gate, for which only a strong and able magician may dare raise him. Thus, for that reason, his seal is not given."*

The Mad Arab mentions that *"Azag-Thoth was rendered sightless in the Battle."* This statement describes the Fall of Man, or what happened when the Jinn took human bodies and lost their ability to operate independent of the impressions that are received in Universe A. The Initiate learns to emanate and operate energies and abilities that originate in Universe B. This is what we learn from Azag-Thoth.

Azag-Thoth will appear to the Initiate in lucid dreams and if the Initiate decides to pledge his/her loyalty to the "blind" god, then they will receive some form of confirmation in reality. When this occurs the Initiate is given the title Nyarlathotep, or Osiris Risen.

Many occultists have mistakenly assigned Nyarlathotep to the *"Tree of Life."* Nyarlathotep represents a class of mystics working with the energies of Universe B. Nyarlathotep frequently walks the Earth. He is a faithful servant of Azatoth and carries out the will of the Outer Gods. He usually appears as a tall and swarthy man, with features of an Egyptian pharaoh. Here we find that Nyarlathotep is personification of the Adepts who are skilled in working with these energies. The attributes of Nyarlathotep are a description of the responsibilities and abilities that the Initiate has as a result of his/her intercourse with Azag-Thoth.

# IAK SAKKAK

There is very little mention of Iak Sakkak in the Simon Necronomicon. However, we can gather more information about this power-zone by making a comparative analysis of several passages contained in the tome. *The Book of 50 Names* states the following concerning Iak Sakkak:

*"The Gods forget. They are distant. They must be reminded. If they are not watchful, if the gatekeepers do not watch the gates, if the gates are not kept always locked, bolted and barred, then the One who is always ready, the Guardian of the Other side, IAK SAKKAK, will enter and bring with him the hordes of the armies of the Ancient Ones, IAK KINGU, IAK AZAG, IAK AZABUA, IAK HUWAWA, ISHNIGGARAB, IAK XASTUR, and IAK KUTULU, the Dog Gods and the Dragon Gods, and the Sea Monsters, and the Gods of the Deep."*

The Book of 50 Names describes Iak Sakkak as the *"Guardian of the Other side,"* or what we refer to as Universe B. Another interesting point that we can gather from this description, is that Man is the vessel through which these deities enter our universe. The Urilia Text mentions the following:

*"But Man possesses the Sign*
*And the Number*
*And the Shape*
*To summon the Blood of his Parents.*
*And this is the Covenant.*
*Created by the Elder Gods*
*From the Blood of the Ancient Ones*
*Man is the Key by which*

*The Gate if IAK SAKKAK may be flung wide*
*By which the Ancient Ones*
*Seek their Vengeance*
*Upon the face of the Earth"*

The power-zone of Iak Sakkak teaches the Initiate that the "deities" that are revered in all magickal and religious systems are archetypes, or psychological forces that exist within the being of Man. The Ancient Ones, however, are archetypes that exist independent of man's imagination. Let us look at what *The Encyclopedia Britannica,* Volume 2, 2007, has to say on this topic, page 212 states:

**"..gods of fire, wind and water, gods of the sea, and above all gods of the sky, show no signs of having been ghost gods at any period in their history. They may, it is true, be associated with ghost gods, but in Australia it cannot even be asserted that the gods are spirits at all…they are simply magnified magicians, super-men who have never died, we have no ground, therefore, for regarding the cult of the dead as the origin of religion in this area.."**

Divinity dwells within the vessel of *"man,"* but not in the bodies of mankind. The Simon Necronomicon describes the difference between man and mankind. We find that mankind is in subjection to the Elder Gods, also known as the constellations. This is mentioned in the Magan Text:

*"From the Blood of KINGU he fashioned Man.*
*He constructed Watchtowers for the Elder Gods*
*Fixing their astral bodies as constellations"*

The movement of these constellations and how they effect the actions and consciousness of mankind is described in the Simon Necronomicon as the Chaldean Covenant. Notice what the Mad Arab wrote in his First Testimony:

*"My fate is no longer writ in the stars, for I have broken the Chaldean Covenant by seeking power over the Zonei. I have set foot on the moon, and the moon no longer has power over me."*

The Mad Arab informs us here that the *"fate"* of mankind is determined by the stars and their movements. The Urilia Text mentions another covenant:

*"And a man may cry out, what have I don't, and my generation that such evil shall befall me? And it mean nothing, save that a man, being born, is of sadness, for he is of the Blood of the Ancient Ones, but has the Spirit of the Elder Gods breathed into him. And his body goes to the Ancient Ones, but his mind is turned towards the Elder Gods, and this is the War which shall be always fought, unto the last generation of man; for the World is unnatural. When the Great KUTULU rises up and greets the Stars, then the War will be over, and the World be One. Such is the Covenant of the Abominations and the End of this Text."*

The Urilia Text speaks about another covenant called the *Covenant of Abominations*. It also mentions that when *'Kutulu greats the Stars, the World will be One.'* The Covenant of Abominations is a reference to what Aleister Crowley describes as Babalon. The Vision and the Voice states the following on page 150:

**"This is the Mystery of Babylon, the Mother of Abominations, and this is the mystery of her adulteries, for she hath yielded up herself to everything that**

liveth, and hath become a partaker in its mystery. And because she hath made herself the servant of each, therefore is she become the mistress of all. Not as yet canst thou comprehend her glory. "

She is considered to be a sacred whore because she denies no one, but she demands a great price- the blood of the adept and her/his Earthly ego. *Understanding Aleister Crowley's Thoth Tarot* by Lon Milo DuQuette, makes an interesting point on page 127:

"The mystery of Babylon concerns an entirely different concept-that of the reabsorption of all evolving life and consciousness into Binah, the great supernal female..Our dissolution into the infinite is the ultimate sacrifice, the ultimate marriage. Deity lusts for that moment when all her children will return to her. Someday, each one of us will also lust for that moment."

The concept contained within this aspect of Babalon is that of the mystical ideal, the quest to become one with the All through the annihilation of the earthly ego, and then the *World will be One*. Richard Cavendish gives us an interpretation of what Babalon is, and also an insight into the Magan Text, in his book *The Black Arts*. Cavendish writes on page 108:

"Again, many of the Gnostics believed that the divine Thought fell into defilement, usually as a result of either curiosity or desire, and the eventual result was the creation of the visible world-the world which mingles life and death, love and hate, beauty and filth. The Gnostic *Simon Magus* maintained that the first divine Thought was the mother of various lower powers which created the world. These powers

**captured the Thought and kept her prisoner in the world, shutting her up in a woman's body."**

The Magan Text describes this "Gnostic" view in the words that follow:

*"From the Blood of KINGU he fashioned Man.*
*He constructed Watchtowers for the Elder Gods*
*Fixing their astral bodies as constellations*
*That they may watch the Gate of ABSU*
*The Gate of TIAMAT they watch*
*The Gate of KINGU they oversee*
*The Gate whose Guardian is IAK SAKKAK they bind."*

The term Babalon derives from the Greek *Babylon*, which originates from the Akkadian term *Babilu* meaning *"Gateway of the Gods,"* Iak Sakkak represents access to the *Abode of the Gods*. We can determine Iak Sakkak's role in the Atlantean Mysteries by reviewing some of the passages that appear in the Magan Text:

*"Man is the Key by which*
*The Gate if IAK SAKKAK may be flung wide*
*By which the Ancient Ones*
*Seek their Vengeance*
*Upon the face of the Earth."*

This description of Iak Sakkak compares greatly with the deity Yog-Sothoth of the Lovecraftian Mysteries. Lovecraft wrote the following concerning Yog-Sothoth in the Dunwich Horror:

**"Yog-Sothoth knows the gate. Yog-Sothoth is the gate. Yog-Sothoth is the key and guardian of the gate. Past, present, future, all are one in Yog-Sothoth. He knows where the Old Ones broke through of old, and where**

**They shall break through again. He knows where They have trod earth's fields, and where They still tread them, and why no one can behold Them as They tread."**

Authors of *The Necronomicon Files*, Daniel Harms and John Wisdom Gonce, make a similar observation in their book on page 194:

**"Simon claims that his "IAK SAKKAK" represents Lovecraft's Yog-Sothoth."**

Since Iak Sakkak corresponds to Lovecraft's Yog-Sothoth, let us look a little more into the character of this Outer God. *Through the Gates of the Silver Key*, written by H. P. Lovecraft and E. Hoffmann Price gives us a more detailed description of Yog-Sothoth:

**"It was an All-in-One and One-in-All of limitless being and self — not merely a thing of one Space-Time continuum, but allied to the ultimate animating essence of existence's whole unbounded sweep.."**

Yog-Sothoth is coterminous with all time and space. This concept is ancient and relative to Zarvana-Akarana, which is defined as "boundless time," the deity of eternity. Zarvana Akarana has been assigned the Kabbalistic correspondence of Ain Soph Aur by some. Since Zarvana Akarana is relative to Ain Soph Aur, the infinite light, then Iak Sakkak and Yog-Sothoth correspond to this as well, and it is with this understanding that we see a connection to Crowley's definition of Babalon.

Ain Soph Aur is the infinite light. Babalon is the *"Gateway of the Gods,"* and also the stage of initiation where the candidate sacrifices his ego and becomes reabsorbed into the ever-evolving consciousness of the universe, or infinite light. The Initiate will find at this stage that all inspired scripture is just a vivid analogy with archetypes and characters describing the emergence of the alien mind over the logical one.

*The Battle of Armageddon is a war between the human mind and the alien mind.* It is sad how many modern occultists will make the claim that the power of magic is all in the mind. There is some truth to this, but not in the way this idea is being presented today. The Initiate must journey through his/her own psychological machine before the Abode of the Gods can be found. The alien mind is the key to effectively applying the principles of the Greater Mysteries. The potential candidate must first be initiated and learn how the Seven Anunnaki, also known as the seven archetypes of the subconscious mind, function. The Seven Anunnaki are the Seven Spheres of Initiation. Since the Initiate enters these Spheres in a converse path to that of our Sun, the candidate will encounter the "Qliphotic aspects" of these constellations. Francois Lenormant confirms this in his book, Chaldean Magic, on pages 26-27 he writes:

**"The demons of the Babylonians were of two kinds. The most powerful and formidable were those which had a cosmical character, whose action was exercised upon the general order of nature, and whose wickedness had power to trouble it. In one of the formulae which we quoted earlier, we saw that seven bad spirits were placed in the heavens: "seven phantoms of flame;" seven demons "of the ignited spheres;" forming an exact counterpart to the seven gods of the planets who were invested with the government of the universe...It is in fact directed against the Seven, the malevolent Maskim....Acting thus contrary to the normal course of nature.."**

The Mad Arab states the following in the Book of Calling, which aligns perfectly with Lenormant's observation:

*"This is the Book of the Seven Demons of the Ignited Spheres, of the Seven Demons of the Flame.."*

Since the "Gates" presented in the Simon Necronomicon are the shadow aspects of the planetary energies. This is why the symbolism of the Nanna Gate appears to be an inversion of the first moon pentacle in the Key of Solomon.

Tiamat was defeated by them, symbolizing the shift that occurs in a newborn child during his/her first few years in the world. Tiamat (Ishtar) was able to defeat these powers by going into the Underworld and becoming a greater deity because of it. Once the Initiate has gained recovery of the "dead" part of the mind, he or she, can effectively employ their demonic-self. This is the true gnosis of Chaos Magick and it can only be performed effectively by the Adept. This is not to be confused with today's form of *"chaos magick"* where some uninitiated individual thinks that a spirit will easily serve his/her needs with the no prior relationship. Most of what the general public refers to as "chaos magick" is nothing more than temporal shifts of the logical mind, which is too weak to affect permanent change.

One of the most valuable things that the Initiate learns through intercourse with Iak Sakkak is the science of reincarnation. Different than popular opinion, reincarnation does not refer to the future life destiny of man, but to those Adepts who have entered the phenomenal world from a future existence. The prefix *re*, means to go back, not to go forward, as is the case with terms like rewind, replenish, and etc. The Mad Arab describes this aspect of Iak Sakkak, in the beginning of the Magan Text:

*"But heed these words well, and remember! For remembering is the most important and most potent magick, being the Remembrance of Things Past and the Remembrance of Things to Come, which is the same Memory."*

Maurice Nicoll gives us a clear definition to the Mad Arab's words, in his excellent wok entitled, *Psychological Commentaries on the Teaching of Gurdjieff and Ouspensky, Volume 2,* pages 421-422 states:

**"Memory is not one and the same thing. What was said was that memory is our relationship to the 4th Dimension. It is our relationship to *our* Time. We can move in memory into the past with our moving from our seats. Certainly this relationship to the past is very faulty. Underlying our personal memory there is a deeper memory to which we rarely have access, if at all. In this memory everything is present-everything we said or did or saw or experienced. This is the Book of our Life which is opened at death....In Recurrence one is born into the same part of Time through the same parents; in Reincarnation one is not born into the same part of Time. But Reincarnation is out of the question for us. A very high development is necessary. A man must have reached the end of his life and must be joined together in a certain way internally by fusion before he can pass into another part of Time."**

Iak Sakkak completes the process of transformation beginning a new cycle of creation and a new life as a divine being in the flesh.

# AKHKHARU

The book, *Demonology and Devil-lore* by Moncure Daniel Conway, informs us of the following, concerning the Akhkharu, on pages 48-49, we read:

**"There is another and much more formidable form in which the Hunger-demon appears in Demonology. The fondness for blood, so *characteristic of supreme gods*, was distributed as a special thirst through a large class of demons. In the legend of Ishtar descending to Hades to seek some beloved one, she threatens if the door not be opened —**

**I will raise the dead to be devourers of the living! Upon the living shall the dead prey!**

**This menace shows that the Chaldean and Babylonian belief in the vampire, called *Akhkharu* in Assyrian, was fully developed at an early date."**

Earlier, we discussed the use of "death energy" and its place in the Necronomicon Tradition. The energies of the Akhkharu teach the Initiate advance techniques of how to employ this energy. Conway's observation also indicates that mastery over this force was **"so characteristic of supreme gods"** in ancient times. The Urilia Text defines the Akhkharu in these terms:

*"And the AKHKHARU may be summoned, which sucketh the blood from a Man, as it desires to become a fashioning of Man, the Blood of KINGU, but the AKHKHARU will never become Man."*

The Urilia Text mentions the *Blood of KINGU* in an earlier passage:

*"These offspring may be called and adjured to perform what tasks the priest may deem necessary in his temple. They were begotten before all ages and dwelt in the blood of KINGU, and MARDUK could not altogether shut them out."*

The **Blood of KINGU** seems to be symbolic of the Blood of the Moon, or menstrual blood, as we discussed earlier. We can determine this from what is written in the Magan Text:

*"She added matchless weapons to the arsenals of the Ancient Ones,*
*She bore Monster-Serpents*
*Sharp of tooth, long of fang,*
*She filled their bodies with venom for blood*
*Roaring dragons she has clothed with Terror*
*Has crowned them with Halos, making them as Gods,"*

The *"venom"* that Tiamat filled her children with was the energy from the dark stars. This energy is guided by the cycles of the Moon, which we are instructed to work with during our process of selfinitiation. In the Lovecraftian Mysteries, Cthulhu is often described as dripping a poisonous green slime. Venom and green slime are metaphors for substances related to insects and reptiles. The green slime mentioned in the Cthulhu Mythos is symbolic of insect blood.

Insect blood doesn't transfer oxygen to different parts of the body, so it needs no hemoglobin in it, which is what makes a human's blood red. The greenish or yellowish color of insect blood comes from the pigments of the plants that the insect eats. The "green slime" in the

Cthulhu Mythos is a symbol of insect blood, and the insect's diet of plants. This illustrates some of the dietary prohibitions placed on necromancers of Atlantean Times. Edward Westermarck, in his infamous work, *The Origin and Development of the Moral Ideas,* Volume 2, states the following on pages 337-338:

**"Vegetarianism is, further, said to have been practised by the first and most learned class of the Persian Magi, who, according to Eubulus, neither slew nor ate anything animated; and many Egyptian priests are reported to have abstained entirely from animal food. In ancient legends we are told that the earliest men, who were pure and free from sin, killed no animal but lived exclusively on the fruits of the earth."**

While the Mad Arab does not suggest that an Initiate of the Necronomicon Tradition has to be a vegetarian, he does give us a dietary law in the Book of Entrance:

*"First, thou must observe the moon of purification. In this time, thou mayest not eat meat for the space of seven days preceding the last day of the moon,"*

While the color of the "green slime," attributed to Cthulhu, indicates some aspects of the Qliphotic Mysteries, concerning dietary laws, it would be wrong to limit our understanding to such, due to the fact that not all insects feed exclusively off of plant life. The Praying Mantis is one example of this. Frederick R, Prete in his book, *The Praying Mantis* makes the following observation on page 5:

**"Among the list of the Orthopteran insects (Sumerian prefix buru), are two Sumerian names for mantis: "buru.EN.ME.LI" and "buru..EN.ME.LI.a sha(g).ga.:**

**which roughly translate, respectively, as necromancer.....and soothsayer of the field."**

We find another meaning to the "green slime" when we reflect on the Mad Arab's words in his First Testimony:

*"The ground where I was hiding became wet with some substance, being slightly downhill from the scene I was witnessing. I touched the wetness and found it to be blood."*

The Mad Arab's indicates that blood is relative to the "green slime" emanated by Cthulhu. The Mad Arab continues:

*"I walked cautiously to the first and, picking up a long twig, lifted the robe from the tangle of weeds and thorns. All that remained of the priest was a pool of slime, like green oil,"*

The Mad Arab informs us that the blood has now turned green. This is an interesting aspect of the myth because earlier, it was mentioned that copper in Sumeria, was a symbol for blood. Copper turns green due to oxidation. The Mad Arab attributes the transformation process of the red blood to green slime, to Kutulu. This alchemical process is a key element in the Qliphotic Mysteries, and pertains to the transmutation from mortal being to an immortal one by the blood of *the menstruating goddess.* The Mad Arab states:

*"I know now that blood is the very food of these spirits, which is why the field after the battles of war glows with an unnatural light, the manifestations of the spirits feeding thereon."*

After the menstrual blood of the Moon is absorbed by the chthonic mind, it is transformed into a venomous substance that protects the Initiate's being from the elements that cause aging and death in mortals. Mastery over death-energy enables the Initiate to overcome death itself. Notice what is written concerning these things in the Magan Text:

*"She filled their bodies with venom for blood*
*Roaring dragons she has clothed with Terror*
*Has crowned them with Halos, making them as Gods,*
*So that he who beholds them shall perish*
*And, that, with their bodies reared up*
*None might turn them back."*

Lovecraft describes the leaders of the Cult of Cthulhu residing in the mountains of China, as immortal in The Call of Cthulhu. Immortality in the Qliphotic Mysteries is also described by H. P. Blavatsky in *The Secret Doctrine, Volume 2,* page 53, under the subtopic THE ADEPT DIES BUT TO LIVE, we read:

**"Elijah is also taken up into Heaven** *alive;* **and the astrologer, at the court of Isdubar, the Chaldean** *Hea-***bani, is likewise raised to heaven by the god Hea, who was** *his* **patron, as Jehovah was of Elijah (whose name means in Hebrew "God-Jah," Jehovah, ), and again of** *Elihu,* **which has the same meaning. This kind of easy death, or** *euthanasia,* **has an esoteric meaning. It symbolises the death of any adept who has reached the power and degree, as also the purification, which enable him to die only in the physical body and** *still* *live and lead a conscious life* **in his astral body. The variations on this theme are endless, but the secret meaning is ever the same."**

The fluid of immortality can be poisonous to those who are not initiated into the Qliphotic Mysteries, and have not worked with the Tree of Transformation. The Mad Arab states:

*"For this reason, few have ever opened the Gate of ADAR, and spoken to the Horned One who resideth there and giveth all manner of wisdom regarding the operations of necromancy, and of the spells that hasten unto death. Only when thou hast shown thy power over the Maskim and the Rabishu, mayest thou venture forth to the Land of the IGIGI, and for that reason was this Covenant made, that none shall safely Walk through the sunken valleys of the Dead before having ascended to MARDUK, nor shall they breach the Gates that lie beyond ADAR until they have seen the Signs of the Mad God and felt the fury of the hellish Queen."*

It is necessary for the Initiate to unlock the doors of the chthonic mind in the specific stages of initiation as recorded in the Simon Necronomicon. Many occultists have made the mistake of classifying the Qliphotic Tree of Transformation as a negative counterpart of the Judeo-Christian Kabbalistic system. This would still leave the occultist under the interpretation and influence of Judaic and Christian thought, wherein the Qliphotis Tree is described as being "too weak to hold the emanations from "god," which is a prejudice opinion of the indigenous rites that existed before Babylon was built. Blavatsky, on page 50 of *The Secret Doctrine* Volume 2, states the following:

**"The story about Enoch, told by Josephus, namely, that he had concealed under the pillars of Mercury or Seth his precious rolls or books, is the same as that told of Hermes, "the father of Wisdom," who concealed his books of Wisdom under a pillar, and then, finding the**

two pillars of stone, found the science written thereon. Yet Josephus, notwithstanding his constant efforts in the direction of Israel's unmerited glorification, and though he does attribute that science (of Wisdom) to the *Jewish* Enoch -- writes *history*. He shows those pillars as still existing during his own time. He tells us that they were built by Seth; and so they may have been, only neither by the Patriarch of that name, the fabled son of Adam, nor by the Egyptian god of Wisdom -- Teth, Set, Thoth, Tat, Sat (the later *Sat-an*), or Hermes, who are all one, -- but by the "sons of the Serpent-god," or "Sons of the Dragon," the name under which the Hierophants of Egypt and Babylon were known before the Deluge, as were their forefathers, the Atlanteans."

The Qliphotic Mysteries are Atlantean in origin and were demonized by the uninitiated, due to their own ignorance. Anton Lavey mentions the following in his infamous work, *The Satanic Bible*:

"Whenever a nation comes under a new form of government, the heroes of the past become villains of the present. So it is with religion. The earliest Christians believed that the Pagan deities were devils, and to employ them was to use "black magic". Miraculous heavenly events they termed "white magic"; this was the sole distinction between the two. *The old gods did not die, they fell into Hell and became devils.*"

We find a similar observation in the book, *Dead Names*, written by Simon. On page 208 Simon makes the following comments:

"Grant understands that the practices and beliefs we casually refer to as demonic, or evil, or satanic, actually refers to an ancient religious philosophy that was understood by civilizations that existed before the

Flood. The "Hidden God" of the ancients could be said to refer to the Egyptian god Set, the brother and enemy of Osiris, a god generally thought to be evil but who could have just
as easily been the god of the land that was defeated. As an old adage tells us, "The demons of today were the gods of yesterday." Rather than simply state this, however, Grant attempts to *prove* it, and after having proved it, to describe how to regain contact with these Dark Lords. In Grant's world, the knowledge of these ancient gods was retained, secretly, by underground groups of magicians and occultists down through the ages and codified in their grimoires and even in their tales of fantasy."

The Rites of the Qliphotic Tree are described in the Gilgamesh Epics, *as six days and seven nights*, the sum of which is thirteen. This means that the chthonic mind consists of thirteen aspects, or Gates, It is a separate system not to be confused with modern kabbalistic studies. These Mysteries are well-described by the Mad Arab in his Second Testimony:

*"And I have seen them turn into many strange kinds of beast as they gathered in their appointed places, the Temples of Offal, whereupon horns grew from heads that had not horns, and teeth from mouths that had not such teeth, and hands become as the talons of eagles or the claws of dogs that roam the desert areas, mad and howling, like unto those who even now call my name outside this room!"*

This metaphoric description of the transformative properties of kundalini energy is quite vivid. Job Chapter 26:5-7 also describes these Mysteries:

"Dead things are formed from under the waters, and the inhabitants thereof. Hell is naked before him, and destruction hath no covering. He stretcheth out the north over the empty place, and hangeth the earth upon nothing."

The Magan Text gives us a description of this unique process in its account concerning the Sleep of ISHTAR:

*"The Eye upon the Throne took flight"*

The *"Eye upon the Throne"* represents the ability to bring the skills acquired in Universe B. over to Universe A. Earlier we discussed Azag-Thoth, the *blind* idiot god who also sits on the Throne. This *Eye* is a possession of Azag-Thoth that he freely gives to his emissaries as an extension of his will. In terms of Initiation, the Eye is the ability to detect and visually see spirits and subtle energies from Universe B. that influence life in this universe. The energies of the Akhkharu teach the Initiate how to influence any given experience, object, or person. It is here that we discover that the Akhkharu represent *Nyarlathotep* in the Lovecraftian Mysteries. After the Initiate has reached the power-zone of Azag-Thoth, they are taught by the Akhkharu, directly.

The Mad Arab stated that *"the AKHKHARU will never become Man."* This means that the Initiate's emotional and metal reactions will never compare to those of a human being. Since the effects of Universe B are an inversion of life in this universe, our way of thinking and approach to human relationships and society are forever changed.

## LALASSU AND LALARTU

"And the LALASSU may be called, which haunteth the places of Man, seeking also to become like Man, but these are not to be spoken to, lest the Priest become afflicted with madness, and become unto a living LALASSU which must needs be slain and the Spirit thereof exorcised, for it is Evil and causeth only terror, and no good can come of it. It is like the LALARTU, and of the same Family as that, save the LALARTU was once living and is caught between the Worlds, seeking Entrance into one or the other. And it must not be permitted Entrance into This, for it is of a sickened constitution and will slay mothers at birth, like unto LAMASHTA, the Queen of Sickness and Misery."

The Lalassu and Lalartu mentioned in the Urilia Text are known in ancient history as the *Labartu* and the *Labassu*. Alfred Jeremias states the following in his work, *The Babylonian Conception of Heaven and Hell:*

"In a religious text occurs the passage:

High hold I the torch, put in the fire the images
Of Uttuku, of Shedu, of Rabiszu, of Ekimmu,
Of Labartu, of Labassu, of Akhkhazu."

According to Ancient Mesopotamian mythologies, the Labartu and Labassu were said to be grouped with the Akhkharu. Different than the Akhkharu, it is said that the Labartu (Spectre) and the Labassu (Phantom) alarmed their victims by appearance, not by direct attack. They affect the emotional state of their victims. Labartu is described in ancient texts as the *"sister of the storm gods."* The Mad Arab in his description of these energies makes a distinct comparison between them and Lamashtu.

*"for it is of a sickened constitution and will slay mothers at birth, like unto LAMASHTA, the Queen of Sickness and Misery."*

*Babylonian Hymns and Prayers, Volume 1,* by David W. Myhrman, lists many of the ancient exorcisms, incantations, and prayers of various deities and demons that were performed by people living in Ancient Mesopotamia. Listed among these is the *"Incantations Against The Female Demon Labartu."*

**"Labartu, daughter of Anu, called by the name of the gods, Innin, mistress, lady of the blackheaded.."**

This description is very similar to Lamashtu. One attribute of Labartu, cited in the above incantation, is Innin. Innin is often used to describe the Goddess Inanna, but it should not be interpreted as Inanna, as it has become the custom of some modern occultists and scholars. Innin can also be defined as "Great Lady" or "Lady of Heaven." The term appropriately means goddess, or goddesses. *The Monist, Volume 17,* published by Edward C. Hegeler, states the following on page 145:

**"Labartu (although = Antum i.e., the wife of Anu) is yet called the daughter of AN-NA,"**..**As the heaven is male (*father*) and the earth the female (*mother*), it so happens that Labartu could also be called a daughter of Anu."**

The supernatural forces of Earth were perceived in most cases as feminine, though they were said to derive from heavenly sources. Therefore, many goddesses were given the title *"daughter of Anu,"* or Innin. *In* is equivalent to *An,* meaning heaven, and *nin,* meaning *lady.* The word Innin was translated by later civilizations as *elohim.* Elohim means goddesses, but has often been mistranslated as *gods*, or *gods and goddesses*. *Eloh*, the feminine form of the term *el*, meaning *goddess*, and *Im* (similar to *In*, or *An*) is a masculine plural. Because of the masculine plural *im*, the word *elohim* is often mistranslated as gods and goddesses, but in view of the Chaldean tradition, which these beliefs come from, Elohim, properly means, *daughters of heaven*, or goddesses.

In ancient Mesopotamia, offerings were given to the Labartu and the Labassu while exorcisms were read. This practice is reminiscent of the times when these deities and forces were worshipped. *Nature, Volume 69*, edited by Sir Norman Lockyer, states the following on page 26:

**"the demonology of the Semitic peoples of Mesopotamia who used the cuneiform system of writing is of Sumerian origin, and there is a good reason to suspect that the greater part of Babylonian psychology and eschatology were borrowed directly from their non-Semitic predecessors in the country."**

Isaac Myer, in his work *Qabbalah*, gives us the following description of the Chaldean's magical practices, on page 453 we read:

**"The sorcery of the Chaldeans were of two kinds; one, came from the power of the gods constraining the actions of demons, which partakes the characteristics of a religion, and may be termed White Magic: the other sought to propitiate demons. The latter is witchcraft and devil worship, it is necromancy or negromancy, Black Magic. Along with the priests of the gods, witches and wizards legally flourished to an enormous extent. *They were both feared and hated.* Their great enemy was the light, the sun;"**

We can see from the sources cited above that the
Chaldeans were engaged in two rites, one of white
magick, which consisted of honoring celestial deities, and
the other being black magick, which appears to predate
the celestial workings.

The Labartu and Labassu are known in the Qliphotic
Mysteries as "occult spies," as they reveal the nature of
any given situation, or event to the Initiate. However,
their main function is to teach the Initiate how to divine
the history of an object by touch.

# GELAL AND LILIT

*"Know that GELAL and LILIT are quick to come at
Calling, and invadeth the beds of Man, robbing the
Water of Life and the Food of Life in which to quicken
the Dead, but their labors are fruitless for they do not
have the formulae. But the Priest has the formulae, and
the Food of Life and the Water of Life may be brought to
call many, for after the passage of one-tenth of a Moon
the Elements are dead.*

*And GELAL invades the bed of a Woman, and LILIT that
of a Man, and sometimes evil beings are born of these
hauntings, and as such must be slain, for the children of
GELAL are workers natural of the ANCIENT ONE,
having His Spirit; and the children of LILIT are likewise,
but are born in secret places which may not be perceived
by Man, and it is not until the time of their maturity that
such as these are given to walking in the places of Men."*

The term Gelal is Akkadian for what moderns would
describe as an incubus. Ernest Jones makes this point
very clear in the book entitled, *On The Night*. On page 119
he states:

**"..the Accadian Gelal and Kiel Galal, the Assyrian Sil
and Sileth, who are equivalent to the European Incubus
and Succubus, are demons whose special function it
was to bring about nocturnal emissions by nocturnal
embraces. According to Quedenfeldt, south of the Atlas
mountains there prevails the belief that there are old
negresses who at night suck blood from the toes of
those sleep."**

The Incubus has played a prominent role in the
demonology of all nations around the world. These

energies teach the Initiate the proper aspects of sexual alchemy. They function in a manner similar to that of the Watcher during the process of self-initiation. Relationships and marriages between an Incubus and a woman have in some cases lasted for at least thirty to forty years. In medieval times, many women, who committed themselves to the Catholic Church, did so because they were in committed relationship with demons, and could disguise these liaisons while living an ascetic lifestyle. *A History of the Inquisition of Spain, Volume 3* by Henry Charles Lea, recounts the following on page 384:

**"Liaisons of this kind would be entered into with demons, and would be maintained with the utmost fidelity on both sides for thirty to forty years; and the connection thus established was proof against all the ordinary arts of the exorciser. Alvaro Pelayo relates that in a nunnery under his direction it prevailed among the nuns, and he was utterly powerless to stop it. In fact, it was peculiarly frequent in such pious establishments."**

Another perspective concerning the incubus is found in *The Woman's Encyclopedia of Myths and Secrets,* written by Barbara G. Walker, pages 431-432 state:

**"The pagan incubus was a special priest embodying a prophetic spirit who would come in dreams or visions to those who "incubated" overnight in an earth-womb Pit of a temple... This custom of incubation was carried into Christianity. It became known as "watching" or "keeping the vigil." It was recommended in times of troublesome decision making that one should "watch and pray" in a**
**church overnight in order to court a vision of guidance. Eventually the incubus was diabolized; and no longer**

**regarded as a guiding angel. The cause for his fall from grace was tales of ancient tradition midnight sexual relationships between incubating women and priests, or incubating men and priestesses. This caused the incubi to be known as spirits of lust. The concept that sexual activity could possess a spiritual nature was completely negated.."**

Gelal acts in a manner similar to what is described concerning the Watcher in the Simon Necronomicon. For those initiated in the "Black Rites," this energy is very useful to the teachings of Left-Hand Path Tantra. The Practitioner can also use these energies, when trying to gain sexual access to a person, place, or thing.

Lilit is an Assyrian term for succubus. Many have connected this term with the Judaic legend of Lilith. However, we find conflicting reports in matters concerning this correspondence. Journal of the African Society, Volume 16, pages 85-86 state:

**"So, too, the Assyrian demons are Lilu, Lilit, Ardat Lilit,. But, as was remarked by a French writer some time ago, the Arabians, on the contrary, are said to regard Lilith, under the form Lalla, as a holy dame."**

There are many legends of the Succubi throughout the world. In India, the Mohini (succubus), are said to enter pacts with men, for up to twelve years (*Jupiter orbits around the Sun is 12 years*) wherein the Mohini will do the man's bidding, but he must satisfy her at least once a month (*in the Simon Necronomicon, the Watcher must be fed at least once a month*).

The similarities between the Incubi, Succubi, and some of the benevolent forces appearing in the Simon Necronomicon, are recorded in ancient history. *Magica*

*Sexualis* by Emile Laurent and Paul Nagour, makes the following observation on page 39:

**"The gods and goddesses of ancient time knew how to transform themselves into incubi and succubi whenever they pleased. Jupiter made himself the incubus of Alkmeme and Semele; Thetis was the succubus of Peleus, and Venus the succubus of Anchises."**

Ishtar also looked favorably upon those who sacrificed the precious gift of semen to her. This act was said to bring good fortune, health, and healing, and other benefits to the priest. In fact, the Sacred Marriage Rite ritual was based on the myth called Inanna and Dumuzi, where Dumuzi is said to have experienced fifty orgasms.

**"My beloved, the delight of my eyes, met me. We rejoiced together. He took his pleasure of me. He brought me into his house. He laid me down on the fragrant honey-bed. My sweet love, lying by my heart, Tongue-playing, one by one, My fair Dumuzi did so fifty times."**

The ancient kings of Mesopotamia had to enact a similar rite with a priestess of Ishtar. Legendary Enmerkar, King of Uruk, responding to a boast by the governor of a neighboring city claiming to be the true "beloved" of Inanna, cited that he made love to a priestess of Ishtar for approximately thirty hours.

Sexual alchemy is the foundation of the Qliphotic Mysteries. The Mad Arab makes a very peculiar statement concerning these energies:

*"But the Priest has the formulae, and the Food of Life and the Water of Life may be brought to call many, for*

*after the passage of one-tenth of a Moon the Elements
are dead."*

The term *"one-tenth of a Moon"* is a reference to the
Moon's passage from one sign of the zodiac to the next,
which occurs every two to three days. It is believed by
some Gate-Walkers that they can keep their Watcher in
the world with them, as long as they feed it every three
days. This is the origin of this custom, which would
mean that the Watcher is similar to an Incubus, or
Succubus. The reader may want to take note that the
terms *"Food of Life"* and *"Water of Life"* is mentioned in
connection with Gelal and Lilit, as these spirits feed on
such. The Magan Text gives us a similar reference
concerning Ishtar's visit to Kutha:

*"He fashioned the KURGARRU, spirit of the Earth,
He fashioned the KALATURRU, spirit of the Seas,
To the KURGARRU he gave the Food of Life
To the KALATURRU he gave the Water of Life"*

In the myth, *Of The Sleep of ISHTAR*, the KURGARRU
and the KALATURRU were given the Food of Life and
the Water of Life, which they were able to resurrect Ishtar
with. Ishtar's Watcher related to Enki that the goddess
went to the land of Cutha after the *passage of three days*.
Ancient accounts concerning Inanna's Descent, describe
the two elementals as being created from the dirt of
Enki's fingernails. This illustrates the knowledge that the
Chaldeans possessed concerning the nature of the
universe, in which there was no separation between
science and magic. The energies of the phenomenal
world were classified as spirits of different natures
among the Chaldeans. The *"spirit of the Earth"* and the
*"spirit of the Seas"* are references to bodily fluids that are
excreted during intercourse. These are good to offer to
the deities.

The Mad Arab makes mention of "evil beings" that are born from the intercourse held between these spirits and human beings. Justin Martyr once stated that 'demons are offspring of angels who yielded to the embraces of earthly women.' Famous theologian, Thomas Aquinas argued that a succubus and incubus, could bear offspring among men. There are many medieval reports of relations between spirits and human beings, even accounts where offspring were born from these unions. The Gate-Walker learns also that one of the primary reasons why they fall under the grace of the demon, when humans cannot, is due to the fact that they are offspring of these unions as well. GELAL and LILIT deal primarily with what is known as Left-Hand Path Tantra. We will discuss this topic further in our reading.

# XASTUR

*"And XASTUR is a foul demoness who slays Men in their Sleep, and devours that which she will. And of her no more may be said, for it is unlawful; but know that the worshippers of TIAMAT know her well, and that she is beloved of the Ancient Ones."*

The meaning of Xastur has escaped many Initiates of the Necronomicon Tradition. The name Xastur is composed of two Akkadian terms, *xas,* meaning *"to cut,"* and *tur,* or *dur,* meaning *"umbilical cord."* The name Xastur means to *cut the umbilical cord.* This represents the completion of the self-deification process, where the Initiate is fully transformed into a new creation. In the Qliphotic Mysteries she was revered as the 'Goddess of Independence' and revealed the sign and customs of the Initiate's divinity.

It is stated in the Urilia Text that the *"worshippers of TIAMAT know her well, and that she is the beloved of the Ancient Ones."* Xastur is an aspect of Lady Shakuguku, who is also known as the **Queen of the Cauldron.** Xastur is the right-hand of the goddess-force that is instrumental in anointing and making all the children of the divinities aware of their heritage. Xastur also represents a stage in development where the Initiate can function independently with the ability to create a spirit. This is the meaning of the Mad Arab's words that follow:

*"And know further that the legions of these Evil Ones are uncountable and stretcheth forth on all sides and into all places, though they cannot be seen, except at certain times and to certain persons. And these times are as said before, and the persons unknown, for who can know XASTUR?"*

Before we examine the mystical workings of the Urilia Text, let us first discuss the identity and meaning of Lady Shakuguku.

## LADY SHAKUGUKU

Lady SHAKUGUKU is mentioned only once in the Simon Necronomicon. She is mentioned in the workings of the Urilia Text:

*"Prepare, then the bowl of TIAMAT, the DUR of INDUR, the Lost Bowl, the Shattered Bowl of the Sages, summoning thereby the FIRIK of GID, and the Lady SHAKUGUKU, the Queen of the Cauldron."*

Lady Shakuguku is *an aspect* of the goddess Tiamat. The Sumer Aryan Dictionary by L. A. Waddell noted the following concerning the goddess on page 78:

*"saqqu-guku,* **the maid Queen of the Wine jug or bowl — a title of Tiamat, the she-serpent queen of the Deep..."**

Lady SHAKUGUKU is the messenger of Azag-Thoth. She is considered by some to be the wife of Nyarlathotep, but this is information is only known to a few Adepts. The ancient texts describe her as having white hair and eyes, silver skin, with strong African facial features. Her sacred animal is the praying mantis.

Lady SHAKUGUKU is called the Queen of the Cauldron because she represents the Initiate's ability to transfer initiation. This ability is the meaning of being an Adept in the Greater Mysteries. Sadly, the term *adept* has often been associated with an individual who has acquired a certain status in an occult organization or society.

The reader may want to note that most of the rituals and workings in the Simon Necronomicon require the practitioner to perform various *"invocations."* Invocation means to draw a spirit or force into ones' own body. Aleister Crowley stated the following in *Magick -Book 4,* page 147:

**"To "invoke" is to "call in", just as to "evoke" is to "call forth". This is the essential difference between the two branches of Magick. In invocation, the macrocosm floods the consciousness. In evocation, the magician, having become the macrocosm, creates a microcosm."**

There are a few examples in the Simon Necronomicon, where we can see how the forces that were invoked by the Initiate are employed in magickal ritual. Notice what is written in the CONJURATION OF THE FIRE GOD:

*"It is not I, but ENKI, Master of the Magicians, who summons Thee! It is not I, but MARDUK, Slayer of the Serpent, who calls Thee here now!"*

Here we see the Initiate using the force of Enki and Marduk within her/him to raise the Fire God. Understanding what invocation means is essential in the role of being an Adept. Since the Adept has successfully Walked the Gates of Initiation through invocation, the deities listed in the Simon Necronomicon, are really components of the latent powers that exist in the Practitioner. These latent forces are different psychological aspects that can be very dangerous to the novice because they are a part of the chthonic mind. These *"spirits,"* which were once *"dead but dreaming"* are now alive in the Adept's psyche. The energies are employed by the Adept voluntarily and involuntarily every time a student of the Adept is calling on the said god or goddess. For example, when the Initiate begins the process of self-initiation, the deities that they call upon exist within the chthonic mind of the Adept and travel from there to the Initiate. This interaction occurs until the Initiate has reached the Gate of Adar. The Adept is empowered each time one of his students makes the Calling to any of the deities, whether he is aware of it or not. This interaction between the Adept and the Initiate occurs not only in the Necronomicon Tradition, but all forms of mystical teachings, *since the forces that are called upon are active only in the minds of those Adepts who have resurrected the chthonic mind..* It was from this principle that the ideology of the "god-parent" was conceived. It is also the basis of the Christian Mythos, as explained by Jesus Christ in John 14:6-7:

**"Jesus said to him, "I am the way, the truth, and the life. No one comes to the Father except through Me."**

The Queen of the Cauldron is the cosmic womb. She appeared in the Gilgamesh Epics as the Priestess Shamhat. She is popularly known as the Queen of Sheba. Lady SHAKUGUKU teaches the Initiate about their true origins and spiritual family. The Adept learns that their existence is the result of human-jinn relations. The Jinn are able to "spawn" children in the human world in several ways. The most popular being the possession of one parent during the time of conception. The Simon Necronomicon describes this process in the following words:

*"BUT KNOW THAT INANNA TAKES HER OWN FOR HER OWN, AND THAT ONCE CHOSEN BY HER NO MAN MAY TAKE ANOTHER BRIDE."*

Lady SHAKUGUKU emanates the energies of love and peace. She is a shape-shifter and in the Simon Necronomicon, she is the Mad Arab. The Enochian term *Mad Arab* means, *"your God that Daughter of Light."*

This also resonates with Lovecraft's description of the Mad Arab. The Cthulhu Mythos identifies the Mad Arab as Abdul Alhazred. The term *Abdul* is Arabic for *"servant of."* However, the name "Alhazard" has often been shrouded in mystery. Alhazard is a derivative of *Al-Hazar*, meaning the Nightingale. This seems to be a reasonable definition since Arabian mystics were intrigued by the nightingale and interpreted the bird's song as a lament of a yearning lover, the soul's yearning for divine ecstasy.

Lady SHAKUGUKU appears in the text under another name-the Goddess Adueni. A Sumer Aryan Dictionary by L.A. Waddell, gives us the following definition for "Adueni" on page 6:

**"The Lady Queen –Seer Woman" and "Lady of the Magic Jar, or Bowl."**

The Goddess Adueni also finds her place in the Book of Calling with the mystical conjuration that bears her name IA ADU EN I. In other writings, Waddell likens Goddess Adueni to the Greek Goddess Athena, of which he displays an image, not of the Goddess Adueni, but of Athena to prove this. Waddell later defines her as the *"Sun-priestess of the Sumerians."*

Figure 26: The Sumerian goddess Adueni or Atueni depicted as Athene in a Greek vase painting of the 5th century BC. She is dressed as a warrior goddess of the Amazons or Valkyries. Note the snakes around her shoulders and the mass of swastikas on the robe

The Initiate will learn by her/his interactions with her, that love and peace are the greatest weapons to use in war. She is the author of the sacred text known as the *Oracle of Fire*.

# Walking In Dreams of Tao

We have discussed quite a bit of information concerning the various deities and rites that appear in the Simon Necronomicon. From our research, and quite different than popular opinion, we can easily see that the Necronomicon Tradition is real and deserves the respect and admiration as a true spiritual path for working with ancient Mesopotamian energies.

Over the past few years I have also observed some errors in judgment by those who are potential Initiates, or have an interest in the Tradition. This is mainly due to the false assumption that the Simon Necronomicon is a book of Western Ceremonial Magick. Critics of the Tradition have also taken this status in regards to the Necronomicon Tradition, which has led to erroneous speculation as to the origin of the work. If one were to investigate many of the indigenous faiths that proceeded the Abrahamic era, such as Ifa, Taoism, and etc, they will see some very strong parallels, which will discuss in the next chapter. However, for the potential Initiate, it is extremely important that they understand the meaning and purpose of the Necronomicon Tradition. This is not a work of religious faith, but it is a work of one's spiritual evolution and perfection. This is summed up very nicely by Madame Blavatsky in the *Secret Doctrine Volume 2*:

Initiates of the Necronomicon Tradition have the responsibility of acquiring immortality of themselves. This is what the work is about. It is not trying to obtain unique miraculous abilities to show off in front of other. Simon mentions this in the SN's Introduction:

"Since "the gods are forgetful", buy treading on their celestial spheres we are reminding them of their ancient obligations to us, their created ones. For, as it is said in one of man's most ancient of Covenants, the Emerald Table, "As Above, So Below". Man's power to alter the nature of his environment must develop simultaneously with his ability to master his inner environment, his own mind his psyche, soul, spirit. Perhaps, then, the lunar landing was the first collective initiation for humanity, which will bring it one step closer to a beneficial Force that resides beyond the race of the "cruel celestial spirits", past the Abyss of Knowledge. Yet, he must remember that the occult powers that accompany magickal attainment are ornamental only, indications of obstacles overcome on the Path to Perfection, and are not to be sought after in themselves, for therein lies the truth Death. Lovecraft saw this Evil, as the world passed from one War and moved menacingly towards another. Crowley prepared for it, and provided us with the formulae. The Mad Arab saw it all, in a vision, and wrote it down. He was, perhaps, one of the most advanced adepts of his time, and he certainly has something to say to us, today, in a language the Intuition understands."

The first step towards the development of spirit is to master the rituals that are set down before us in the tome. It is a training exercise in how to approach the deities that are in the tome. It also teaches us the discipline of thought and focus, as well as, the value of prayer. We are further connected to the forces behind the basic four elements that we use in ritual. The idea of trying to command spiritual entities that are thousands of years older than us is completely foolish. We can only direct the energy that we have acquired through ritual and our day-today intercourse with the stars. The Mad Arab mentions this in his Second Testimony:

*"..for the Race of Draconis was ever powerful in ancient times, when the first temples were built in MAGAN, and they drew down much strength from the stars, but now they are as Wanderers of the Wastelands, and dwell in caves and in deserts, and in all lonely places where they have set up stones."*

Through the process of Gate-Walking we reconnected to stellar energy. A relationship is established between our being and the seven stars and the stars that they meet as they travel through the zodiac, also known as the Land of the Watchers. In other rites listed in the Simon Necronomicon, we can access the Underworld above, known as Outer Space, and the Underworld energies that exist beneath the surface of the Earth. This process is mentioned by the Mad Arab in his First Testimony:

*"Know, then, that I have trod all the Zones of the Gods, and also the places of the Azonei, and have descended unto the foul places of Death and Eternal Thirst, which may be reached through the Gate of GANZIR, which was built in UR, in the days before Babylon was."*

Once the Initiate is aware of these celestial and terrestrial energies working within his very being, then, he or she, is able to manipulate these stellar forces that reside in his/her being, but to harness these energies the Initiate must acquire a soul.

The Watcher, or Jinn, is the force that is from beyond the stars. It is our primordial self and an individual part of a collective that is responsible for the creation of the universe. This is the body of Ishtar/Tiamat, which is known today as Mother Nature. The Mad Arab states:

## *"BUT KNOW THAT INANNA TAKES HER OWN FOR HER OWN, AND THAT ONCE CHOSEN BY HER NO MAN MAY TAKE ANOTHER BRIDE."*

This passage is primarily concerned with the Sacred Marriage of the macrocosm and the microcosm, or the Initiate and Ishtar / Tiamat (Mother Nature). This is the essential theme of the Greater Mysteries. W.E. Butler, in his book, *The Magician: His Training and Work*, mentions the following on pages 135-136:

**"Only the very ignorant and naïve critics of magic will believe that the occultists think of these "elements" as being the material earth, air, fire, and water. They are actually the elemental energies which lie behind express themselves through the physical plane elements. All manifestation is sacramental, the outward and visible sign being a channel of that spiritual power of which it is the expression in the phenomenal worlds....These Kings of the Elements, then are the directing Beings under whom comes the ocean of evolving life, and this evolving life is behind and working through the matter of this physical plane. Now the elemental life is not individual, as is ours. ....Although possessed of the normal powers of their plane, powers which to us appear supernormal and "miraculous," it must never be forgotten that they are below man in spiritual evolution...any attempt to drive a bargain with them, or to attempt to bribe or appease them in order that they may be induced to act on our behalf brings us on their level, and results in our becoming their slaves, not their masters."**

Butler's words are a very important message for anyone who aspires to get involved in the work. First, your intent in performing a certain rite, to obtain a job or what have you, must also be pursued in your day-to-day life just as earnestly as you are performing a ritual to obtain such things. This is a key element to any esoteric work. Otherwise any spiritual practice that we invest in becomes an obstacle. Stuart Alve Olsen in his commentaries on the Taoist text, The Jade Emperor's Mind Seal Classic, stated the following on page 69 of his translation:

**"As I grow older I too find myself attached to things that could be deemed un-Taoist and un- Buddhist. But, then I saw these same characteristics in all my teachers as well. It is human nature, and true even of cultivators, to have joy and an attachment to something outside the arduous practices…The Sixth Patriarch of Chinese Buddhism, Hui Neng, once said: "If you want to attain enlightenment, stay far away from monasteries." Why would he say that? Because more often than not, the attachment we create to an environment can become the very hindrance to what we are trying to achieve."**

The Mad Arab was of a similar opinion, as he expressed in his First Testimony:

*"These secrets I give to thee at the pain of my life, never to be revealed to the profane, or the banished, or the worshippers of the Ancient Serpent, but to keep within thine own heart, always silent upon these things."*

Where we are in life has a lot to do with where our hearts are at and this work is not a medium to escape from life, but to see the beauty in what was once dead now come back to life. Our goal is to live ritual through awareness. We are to practice ritual until we obtain memory of the text. We can then perform ritual by visualization only, followed by astral ritual. In order for us to do this, it is important for us to become "born again" or astral free.

## Interview With Dan Harms

The following is an interview between Warlock Asylum and Dan Harms, who both have shared in quite a few debates online concerning the Simon Necronomicon.

Well, this is certainly a new chapter in the Necronomicon Tradition. I am sure that many of our regular readers are more than familiar with the debates that have occurred between Dan Harms and I. It has certainly been a pleasure to get to know Dan, not only as an opponent, but as a comrade in some respects. I must say that although Dan and I have a "weird" friendship, I do respect his work in the Occult Community. We may differ on many aspects of the Necronomicon Tradition, but it is in hopes that something can be gained from our debates.

I have learned a lot from our debates than real conversation with other Gate-Walkers. It has allowed me to really dig through the canals of Ancient Mesopotamian history and really consider the origin of the layered material appearing in the Simon Necronomicon. It has also encouraged me to look more into the Lovecraft Mythos. This is something that every Gate-Walker should take the time to do.

There is something that is very intriguing about the Dan Harms Machine but it is something that cannot be calculated. Dan is sincere in his work and is cautious enough to ward off any predator who seeks to betray honesty, when it comes to presenting the Greater Mysteries. Of course, I must say that we still differ in our opinion of the Simon Necronomicon, but that is no mystery at this point! Well I had a chance to talk with

Dan the other day via email. We have been corresponding and checking out what we have read while making some suggestions to each other. I decided to Interview Dan after Venus Satanas made a comment that kind of ended a debate between Harms and myself. I will post Miss Satanas' comment after this interview, but for now let us zoom in on this conversation between Dan and I:

**Warlock Asylum:** I am sure that our regular readers are more than familiar with the name Dan Harms, as well as, many people in the Occult Community, but in your own words Dan, Can you tell us something about yourself and maybe fill us in on some of your accomplishments?

**Dan Harms:** I typically keep these short, so I'll just say I'm the author of The Cthulhu Mythos Encyclopedia and The Necronomicon Files. I also write at the blog Papers Falling from an Attic Window on grimoires, the occult, role-playing, Lovecraft, and whatever else I'm in the mood to discuss. I'm a college librarian in my "other" life.

**Warlock Asylum:** What inspired you to become a writer? What sparked your interest in H. P. Lovecraft?

**Dan Harms:** They actually happened in reverse order. I came across Lovecraft via the Call of Cthulhu role-playing game in middle school, and I was struck by the man's vision and the pantheon he created, or was attributed to him. I started to read other Mythos authors, and then I created a file on an old word processing program on the various monsters and books I was encountering. My intent was never to be a writer; I just wrote, and wrote, and had people encourage me to write, and I ended up with a book.

**Warlock Asylum:** Many people associate the name "Dan Harms" with the Necronomicon Files, as it is seen all across the internet, what was your intent and approach in writing the book?

**Dan Harms:** At the time John and I wrote the book, there wasn't any single good reference work on the topic of the various Necronomicon hoaxes that were appearing. Plus, the increased use of the Internet meant that more misinformation about the book was circulating than ever before. So we set out to document what was out there, being as thorough as possible in terms of covering texts and different perspectives. We also wanted to be entertaining, so there's some humor in there. Some people were offended by that, but it was there for a reason. There was also not much of a Gate-Walking community at the time, though we did review a few books supposed to work with the Necronomicon therein.

**Warlock Asylum:** Your essays on Lovecraft, the occult, and various other writings have sparked some controversy as to your spiritual path. Some have even accused you of being a member of the O.T.O, How do you normally go about describing your "spiritual path?"

**Dan Harms:** First, the "some" who've accused me of OTO membership is actually just you. If there's someone else, please let me know. I normally don't describe my spiritual path, for a few different reasons. One major one is that I've seen just how blinkered people can be when it comes to arguments they don't agree with. I could be anything from an atheist to a Rastafarian to – gasp! – a Gate-Walker, and people would see it as an excuse to disregard what I say. If I don't tell them what I believe, they don't have that excuse, or they have to invent some spirituality with which to attack me, which is often quite amusing and ends up making them look bad.

**Warlock Asylum:** It seems that a few practitioners of the Simon Necronomicon have become more vocal over the past couple of years; does this spark some concern on your end?

**Dan Harms:** I have actually encouraged Gate-Walkers to make their faith more public from time to time, so it'd be odd for me to be concerned about it. If people have something valid to say about their spirituality, then they can say it so the world can hear. If they have nothing valid to say, they'll reveal that. The great benefit of the Internet is that it makes it much easier to find the stupid people. So, no matter who speaks and their level of commitment, we all benefit.

**Warlock Asylum:** Over the past couple of years, Dan and I, have had quite a few debates. In your own words Dan; what insights have you gained from these debates if any?

**Dan Harms:** Overall, they have been useful, as they've meant that, from time to time, I have to reengage with the source material on Mesopotamian religion, Lovecraft, or other topics. I do wish that you'd attempt to engage with it in a similar manner, and that is a disappointment.

**Warlock Asylum:** What advice would you give Warlock Asylum, or any other practitioner of the Simon Necronomicon who chooses this tome as a spiritual path?

**Dan Harms:** Well, you asked. First, understand that what you're practicing is an amalgam of ceremonial magic, Sumerian ritual, pagan sensibilities, and pulp fiction assembled in the mid-Seventies, likely with a profit motive on the part of one or more of the main participants, and with an origin story that's changed over time. There is absolutely nothing wrong with practicing such a spiritual path and finding personal satisfaction or growth through it.

Where Gate-Walkers get into trouble is when they assume that, because the book is impressive or they're getting results, they can use the book as a source on Mesopotamian religion or Lovecraft, or decide that Simon is a holy prophet, or declare that I must be the devil, or proclaim themselves to be religiously persecuted because someone disagrees with them on the Internet. Some people will never respect Gate-Walkers because of their system, but I think they lose much of their support through trying to expound on areas where they don't have expertise or trying to blow disagreements into tales of deep personal agony. Of course, developing expertise in those areas and then talking about them deserves respect, and anyone who's lost family/friends/a home/a job because of their faith deserves sympathy.

Don't be lazy. There have been a number of times that I've asked various Gate-Walkers to read a book, or write an essay, or walk to their local library. It's amazing how these mighty wizards who can stare the Ancient Ones in the faces and undergo the most arduous initiation processes suddenly find something better to do when someone makes a suggestion that might give them greater understanding or allow them to reach more people. I don't expect them to do something just because I suggest it, but when it gets to the point where I feel I have to edit Wikipedia to reflect the practitioner's perspective, I start to wonder where these Gate-Walkers are.

Now, if those individuals are so devoted to spirituality that they don't want to engage with the outside world, that's fine. Nonetheless, that's not the case for most GateWalkers I've met. They claim that they're horribly misunderstood and looked down upon, and yet they never do anything to challenge those impressions. Either ignore your critics or engage with them by creating something of worth and value. Caring about what they say and not doing anything about it is either passive aggressive or an attempt to play the victim.

That's not to say that there isn't great potential out there – I'd cite Warlock Asylum and Ashnook as intelligent individuals who could probably turn out some impressive work that would give Gate-Walking more respectability, if they turned up matters a notch and didn't get distracted by some of the concerns I've raised above.

**Warlock Asylum:** I would like to sincerely thank Dan Harms and The Dan Harms Machine for taking the time to do this Interview. One thing that you can say about Dan, whether you like him or hate him, is that he is a living legend, and his work as a writer has been priceless to the Occult Community, even in spite of the debatablilty of his observations. I think this is a very important chapter in the Necronomicon Tradition that cannot be overlooked even by those who are not involved. I would like to close this chapter of Necronomicon History with a comment that Venus Satanas made during a debate between Dan Harms and Warlock Asylum:

**"In posting on both of your blogs and reading them for quite some time, I have seen that you are not arguing**

simply for argument's sake. That many things between you have been revealed and understood between you both. I did not mean to cause trouble, nor are your discussions with Dan any of my business, nor is it my place to judge either of you for your beliefs.

Regardless, as an observer these things fascinate me and I am always interested in learning about new and unusual methods of magic that aren't readily accepted in mainstream occult."

# Interview With Historian Denny Sargent

The following is an interview with Aion 131, which first appeared in November 2006, and was part of an Interview Series conducted by Warlock Asylum on the Simon Necronomicon Gate-Walker's Info Page.

**Warlock Asylum:** Just for our readers out there viewing the Simon Necronomicon Gate-Walker's Page, would you give us a little introduction about, who you are and some of you background in the occult world?

**Aion 131:** All one would possibly want to know about me can be found at my messy but personal website:

http://www.psychicsophia.com/aion

**There are several bios and interviews there, but for the sake of brevity here is my simple bio:**

**Aion 131**, writer, teacher and practicing Eclectic Ritualist, was first introduced to Mythology & Magick in New York where he grew up. He has since his early teens been accepted as a member of a number of initiatory groups and esoteric associations.

In 1979 he received his BA in Education and History. During this time he was one of the founding editors of Mandragore, a journal of magick and eclectic ritualism published in New York City. In 1981 he was awarded an MA in Ancient History/Cross Cultural Studies from Western Washington University where he also taught History for three years. His research has included the magickal/religious traditions of Egypt, Sumeria, Greece, Rome, China, Japan, South East Asia, India, Europe and Pacific Northwest Indians (Kwakiutl).

In the early 1980's he helped found, write and edit Aeon and Kalika, journals that were concerned with contemporary ritual practice and creative mythology. From 1980 until today, the Western Magickal Tradition, Tantrika and Taoism have formed increasingly important foci for his studies and writing. In the mundane world he has taught at several colleges and academies specializing in ESL and is currently an ESL Teacher Trainer teaching Seattle University classes.

He has written for many different Pagan and magickal magazines like Green Egg and Pangaia which carried his column Worldwide Rituals for several years. Denny taught and lived and wrote for four years in Japan. There he was also a journalist for Eye Ai Magazine, City Life News, Via Magazine, Tokyo Today, The Japan International Journal, The Japan Times Weekly, The Tokyo Weekender, Mini-World and the Asahi Evening News. Denny continues to engage in extensive traveling and on-site research in Australia, China, Indonesia, Hong Kong, Singapore, Korea, Hawaii, Mexico, Thailand, Costa Rica, Peru, Nepal, Egypt, Cambodia, America and other countries.

**WORKS PUBLISHED:**

Heal The Earth, An Environmental Textbook, Dawn Press, Japan 1991

Global Ritualism, Myth and Magick Around the World, Llewellyn Publishing, 1994
Web site:
http://www.psychicsophia.com/globalritualism.html

The Magical Garden, (with Sophia), Andrews McMeel
Publishing 2000
Website:
http://www.psychicsophia.com/magicalgarden/

The Tao of Birth Days, Tuttle Publishing 2001
Website:
http://www.psychicsophia.com/taoofbirthdays/

Your Guardian Angel & You, Redwheel / Weiser 2004
(out now)
Website:
http://www.psychicsophia.com/YourGuardianAngel/

Clean Sweep, Banishing Everything You Don't Need to
Make Room for What You Want, Redwheel /Weiser 2007
Website:
http://www.psychicsophia.com/cleansweep.html

**Editor and Publisher:**

Silver Star - A Journal of New Magick (online Journal,
2003-present)
Website: http://www.horusmaat.com/silverstar

BTW- There are a few Necronomicon-ish articles in
Silverstar more than you ever wanted to know but there
you are.

**Warlock Asylum:** Being that you were around the
Magickal Childe community, what is your opinion about
Simon and the Simon Necronomicon?

**Aion 131:** I think it is a usable system that has tenuous
historical roots, but nevertheless is quite real in many

ways. And I had and have utter respect for Simon as a writer but also as a mage. He is a very bright guy, very creative and has the rare gift of renewing and revitalizing long forgotten (or never manifested!) magickal rites and symbols so they are both usable and effective. However- I do not think that the Necronomicon itself as such ever was 'real' until manifested by Lovecraft and others like Simon. My MA is focused on ancient history and I did a lot of my research on Egypt and Mesopotamia- so what I can say, as a historian, is that Simon's work is BASED on Sumerian and other Mesopotamian magickal systems, images and incantations. It is my opinion that he was reviving a Sumerian magickal tradition within the 'schema' of the Necronomicon- and maybe he (and Herman) figured that they could make some $ as well...
:)

**Warlock Asylum:** What advice would you give to anyone who is interested in working with the Simon Necronomicon? And how do you feel about the use of the book as a magickal grimoire?

**Aion 131:** Know ALL the gods and spirits in that book. Do your homework. Don't be sarcastic, stoned, slack or silly- you will get burned. Before you do one single thing in that book, read the whole thing, get some books on Sumerian & Mesopotamian mythology and read them etc. Then ask yourself- why do I want to mess with THIS system? What about Norse, Tantric, Qabala, Egyptian, Celtic....etc- systems? Most people seem drawn to the Necronomicon due to some sort of Goth 'demonic' Lovecraftian fixation for those people Id suggest a role-playing game like Call of Cthulhu etc. Magick of any sort is fire- know what you are doing or don't do it- or at least don't cry about it when hell breaks lose. So, IF you are going to do this system I'd suggest having a CLEAR idea why and what you want out of it, a clear plan on how you will do it and a commitment to REALLY doing it correctly. In short, don't fuck around. Like any good program, it is GIGO. Also- I'd develop my general meditation, ritual and banishing skills – you should have a strong and magickally developed Will and a deep knowledge of magickal Love. One should have already developed in another magickal system before jumping into the Necronomicon, IMHO. BTW- I had a magickal friend in NYC who died horribly in the 1980s- the last thing he was doing was this system- he had the sigils all over his room- utterly disorganized and chaotic- gave me the creeps a month later he was dead. Not for the novice. Not for the dabbler. Not for the drugged or imbalanced. Not for the weak-willed or silly.

**Warlock Asylum:** Have you ever experimented of used any sections of the Simon Necronomicon? If so, what were some of your experiences?

**Aion 131:** NO. It is not for me, the mythology doesn't interest me except from an academic point of view and (see my answer above) I would not mess with 'part' of this system in any way. That would be halfassed. I am very much an eclectic ritualist (I wrote a book on it! Global Ritualism) but this is not an 'open source' mythic system- it is magickal and not devotional- One should not dabble to try out this system. DO IT or do NOT do it – don't dabble. Read the book first!!!

**Warlock Asylum:** Are there any points of interest that you feel need clarification since the controversy of the Simon Necronomicon has grown over the years?

**Aion 131:** LOL!!!! Look, reality is quite flexible- quantum & string theory clearly tell us that the observer affects/creates the outcome- do whatever you like- don't even try to argue historical reality of this booknot going to happen- but practical reality? It is a system that I know works- take that at face value. What is there to argue about? Are these entities 'real'- yes, I have met many of them in dreams. Is that 'real'??? Up to you. Keep in mind- the Simon I knew was VERY funny and VERY witty and VERY sharp- way more together than most of the fuzzy occult types I met at the Warlock Shop in the 70s (and I was then a fuzzy-headed occultist myself) Think about it.

**Warlock Asylum**: What message would you like to leave with everyone hear at the Simon Necronomicon Gate-Walker's Info Page?

**Aion 131:** That there are three basic steps to ALL Magickal Paths:

1- Using a system to understand and become proficient at magick: mental, astral, spiritual, ritual, meditation training etc.

2- Knowledge and Conversation with One's Holy Guardian Angel- the Guardian Spirit

3- Crossing the Abyss

It doesn't matter what system it is these are your steps to awareness via magick- if Simon's system helps you do any of these (Im very doubtful about it helping with #2) Go for it!

My #1 suggestion? That everyone achieves a clear connection with your Guardian Angel (Spirit, Self etc) before doing Simon's Necronomicon system. That said- if you are dead set (!) on using his Necronomicin, then do so intelligently and with a clear plan- this is how the book is set use-step-by-step. The whole layer-by-layer pattern is important- don't skit around and don't be half-assed! Think of Crowley's definition of magick:

The Method of science-The aim of religion!

Made in United States
North Haven, CT
12 June 2024

53564423R00217